MARJORY HARPER is Professor of History at the U
Associate Professor at the University of the Higł
History. In her teaching, research and publications she specialises in nineteenth
and twentieth-century migration history, particularly from Scotland, and
has recently introduced a strong element of oral testimony into her writing.
She has published five monographs and four edited collections, along with
over seventy articles in scholarly and popular journals and newspapers, and
is regularly involved in international conferences and media consultancies.
Her study of Scottish emigration in the nineteenth century, *Adventurers and
Exiles*, won the Saltire Society Scottish History Book of the Year Prize in 2004.
With Professor Stephen Constantine, she co-authored *Migration and Empire*
(2010), a Companion volume in the Oxford History of the British Empire. She
is currently working on a commissioned monograph on Scottish emigration
to New Zealand, as well as a multi-disciplinary research project on migration
and mental health in Canada in historical and contemporary contexts. She and
her husband live in rural Aberdeenshire.

Scotland No More?

The Scots Who Left Scotland in the Twentieth Century

MARJORY HARPER

Luath Press Limited

EDINBURGH

www.luath.co.uk

First published 2012

ISBN: 978 1908373 35 9

The paper used in this book is recyclable. It is made from low chlorine pulps
produced in a low energy, low emissions manner from renewable forests.

The author's right to be identified as author of this book under the Copyright,
Designs and Patents Act 1988 has been asserted.

Printed in the UK by Bell & Bain Ltd., Glasgow

Typeset in 10.5 point Sabon

To Andrew

Contents

Acknowledgements

One of my greatest pleasures in preparing this book has been the support and advice I have received from colleagues and friends, old and new, in many corners of the world. Closest to home, the conversion of research notes to deliverable text was hugely facilitated by the award of a half-session of study leave from my employer, and I wish to record my gratitude to the Research Committee of the School of Divinity, History and Philosophy at the University of Aberdeen for enabling the project to be brought to timely completion. Funding from the School Research Committee and from the Carnegie Trust for the Universities of Scotland covered the cost of illustrations. A British Academy ACU Grant for International Collaboration enabled me to include information from Canadian archives on the mental health of migrants. Fellow historians at Aberdeen, and at the University of the Highlands and Islands, have encouraged and challenged me along the way, as have students, at all levels, in both institutions. I am particularly grateful to Jim Hunter, not only for the insights gleaned from his seminal writings, but for (re)convincing me of the importance of engaging with one's readership.

Throughout Scotland and beyond, I have benefited from the expertise and assistance of librarians, archivists and academics. As always, the staff of the inter-library-loans department at the University of Aberdeen provided sterling service; Alison Steed gave much-appreciated help in locating elusive statistics; Angus Johnson at Shetland Archives regularly sent me gold nuggets from the Northern Isles; and Jane Brown at the National Records of Scotland alerted me to vital but neglected materials stored in the bowels of Thomas Thomson House. Archivists and librarians in Halifax, Ottawa, Toronto, Vancouver, Dunedin, Christchurch and Wellington went the second mile in enabling me to make maximum use of research visits to Canada and New Zealand. Among academic colleagues at home and overseas, I have valued the advice and friendship of Marilyn Barber, Alison Brown, Ewen Cameron, Stephen Constantine, Andrew Dilley, Jill Harland, Karly Kehoe, Angela McCarthy, Margaret Maciver, Rosalind McClean, John MacKenzie, Andrew Mackillop, Eric Richards, Ebby Ritchie, Steve Schwinghamer, Margaret Connell Szasz, the late Ferenc Szasz, Andrew Thompson, Annie Tindley, Mike Vance and Nancy Wachowich. I am particularly grateful to the Reverend Michael Lind for granting me permission to use his late father's Canadian letters, to Angus and Anne Pelham Burn for their hospitality and to Calum and Rory Macdonald of Runrig to quote, without charge, from 'Rocket to the Moon'. Jennie Renton's editorial skills made the final stage a pleasure rather than a chore.

It has been a particular privilege to correspond and meet with many first- and second-generation migrants, and I am grateful to all the individuals who gave up their time to be interviewed, or to write or email. In England members of the Scottish diaspora to Corby have been keen supporters of the project from the start. Throughout Scotland, as well as in England, New Zealand and Canada, I have been warmed by the hospitality, friendship and enthusiasm of men and women with a range of fascinating, and sometimes poignant, experiences of migration. Many of their stories appear in the final chapter of this book. Dunedin holds particularly happy memories, thanks to a host of wonderful interviewees and new friends.

My particular thanks go to my husband, Andrew Shere, not least for frequent technical assistance, and for his willingness to incorporate archives and site visits in obscure locations into vacation itineraries.

While this book has been shaped by academic sources, its agenda is not in essence an academic one. It is an attempt to render the fruits of archival research accessible by integrating documentation relating to high-level policies and strategies with the lived experiences of real migrants, analysing the significance of demographic upheaval through the experiences of those who – in various ways – formed part of the jigsaw of Scotland's 20th-century diaspora.

Wandering Scots

IN 1967, AS CANADA celebrated its centennial, Dr Roddy Campbell from South Uist took up the post of GP in the small town of Nakusp, deep in the interior of British Columbia. Little did he know when he arrived there that the mountainous, forested heart of the province was already home to several Gaelic-speaking compatriots from the western isles, not least those who laboured in the lead and zinc smelter at Trail, 113 miles to the south, or crewed the ferries that plied the arterial Arrow and Kootenay Lakes, to the west and south-east. At first glance, Roddy's experience had little in common with that of Annie Matheson from Coll, who 15 years earlier had left her home, at the other end of the Long Island, to settle across the US border, 1,500 miles to the east of British Columbia. But amid the skyscrapers of cosmopolitan Detroit, Annie too found herself surrounded and supported by the language, culture and community networks of her native island of Lewis. Meanwhile, on the other side of the world, while linguistic identity may have been less explicit, Scottish emigrants continued to imprint national and regional ethnic stamps on a variety of workplace environments. In Australia, foreman stonemason and jazz piper Tom MacKay, along with his two brothers and several other tradesmen from Aberdeenshire, cut the granite that was used to face the piers and pylons of Sydney's iconic Harbour Bridge in the 1920s, while in the post-war era, Marie Jarvis from Hawick was one of a stream of Scots from border textile towns who transferred their skills to the woollen mills of New Zealand.

These random snapshots – which could be replicated *ad infinitum* – testify anecdotally to the persistence and diversity of Scottish emigration in modern times. The wanderlust that had been part of the Scots' DNA since the forging of the nation generated heated debate in the late 18th century, and continued to attract public and political notice as the human haemorrhage escalated to a total of two million in the century following the defeat of Napoleon in 1815. Between the death of Queen Victoria and the outbreak of the First World War, the promotion and practice of emigration moved into a particularly high gear. From 1901 to 1914, 64 per cent more people left the British Isles than had been the case in the previous 14 years, but from Scotland the increase was a striking 139 per cent. Moreover, Canada, which had played second fiddle to the United States in all but four years from 1848 to 1906, accounted for 42 per cent of Scottish emigrants between 1901 and 1914, compared with only 10.5 per cent in the previous 14 years.[1]

Trends set by the Victorians and Edwardians continued into the post-war period and beyond. Statistical precision is impossible, because of incomplete and ambiguous data, frequent changes in classification criteria, and the absorption of separate Scottish returns into UK figures, but by the end of the 20th century a further two million or so Scots had packed their bags and gone overseas.[2] Far from being destroyed or even diluted by the cataclysmic events of 1914–18, emigration resumed with renewed fervour in the 1920s, when nearly 500,000 Scots left for non-European destinations. It was a decade when the stampede exceeded the natural increase of population, producing an unprecedented inter-censal decline. It has been estimated that Scottish departures in the 1920s equalled the total of those who left Belgium, Holland, Norway, Sweden, Denmark, Switzerland and Finland combined in those years, and that by 1931 between a quarter and a fifth of all Scots were not living in their native country.[3] Their choice of destinations in the 1920s and '30s also followed the immediate pre-war pattern, with Canada accounting for 36.2 per cent between 1919 and 1938. An unknown number of those, of course, subsequently crossed the porous border to the United States, which accounted officially for 32.7 per cent, but illegally for many more who successfully evaded the quota restrictions. North America was followed by Australia and New Zealand (17.8 per cent) and South Africa (3.9 per cent).

Ninety-one per cent of Scots who emigrated between the wars did so in the 1920s. When – as a consequence of the Depression – the movement was dramatically reversed in the following decade, it was from the main host countries that the influx was greatest: between 1931 and 1938 a total of 62,308 Scots arrived from North America and Australasia, just over 44 per cent of them from Canada, 39.5 per cent from the USA and 16.4 per cent from the antipodes.[4] Enthusiasm for the traditional destinations was rekindled when emigration began to gather momentum again in the 1950s and 1960s, with up to 40,000 Scots leaving in some years. A significant fall-off from 1966 was triggered by the combined impact of immigration controls overseas and a downturn in the world economy, with Canada in particular exercising greater selectivity. Although the rate of natural increase dropped at the same time, it generally exceeded net migration until 1974, when the Scottish population reached a peak of 5.24 million, falling thereafter to 5.05 million in 2002, its lowest level since just after the Second World War. By then the emphasis on the old Commonwealth was giving way to a much more explicitly global outlook. At the same time, Scotland, which had enticed very few of Britain's New Commonwealth immigrants in the post-war era, began to attract Eastern Europeans, a trend that helped to stabilise the population base and increased significantly after the expansion of the European Union in 2004.[5]

A long-standing tradition of comings and goings meant that 20th-century emigrants, like their predecessors, rarely bolted the door securely behind them when they left. It was not only that links were maintained through visits or that returners brought back to Scotland infusions of new cultures along with the capital they repatriated and the intercontinental networks they nurtured. Many of those who put down permanent roots overseas transplanted elements of their ethnic and cultural lineage to those new soils, sowing the seeds of a worldwide diaspora that currently embraces over 25 million people who claim Scottish ancestry. 'They carry with them their language, their opinions, their popular songs, and hereditary merriment', Samuel Johnson observed in 1773 of departing shiploads of Highlanders, who, he concluded, 'change nothing but the place of their abode'. If Johnson and Boswell had revisited Scotland and its diaspora more than two centuries after they had watched the people of southern Skye whirl each other around in 'The Dance Called America', they would have found that while the 'brisk reel' had been replaced by Runrig's eponymous folk rock lament for the clearances, and the spectrum of destinations had become global, the sentiments themselves were timeless.

But there was – and is – no single narrative of diaspora. Dr Johnson himself had recognised that not all emigrants came from the same mould. Solitary individuals, he pointed out, were generally less likely than prepackaged groups of colonists to imprint their identity on host societies, and many emigrants wanted to look forward rather than back, embracing the opportunities of a new land and putting the past firmly behind them. By the 20th century individualism reigned, particularly after 1945, and emigrants ploughed their own furrow – not so much in literal terms by then, as in business, the professions and blue-collar work. While they were happy to develop or tap into family, community and ethnic networks that might help them relocate, find a job or develop a social life, the function of those relationships was cosmetic rather than crucial, and a Scottish identity was usually an optional extra that could be picked up or discarded as circumstances dictated. It was an attitude captured in the words of a late 20th-century song by the Canadian folk-rock band Spirit of the West:

> We soon found our own kind,
> Formed clubs and social nights,
> And we practised on each other
> Just to keep our accents right.
> For there's more tartan here
> than in all the motherland.
> We came 5,000 miles
> To the gathering of the clans.
> There's none more Scots
> than the Scots abroad,
> There's a place in our hearts
> For the old sod.[6]

By the time the sun finally set on the long Victorian age, Scots were well aware not only of their diasporic heritage and the relentless ongoing exodus, but that the interpretation of those phenomena was disputed territory. For decades they had been bombarded from all sides, both with quantitative evidence of emigration, and with a concoction of encouragements, warnings and practical advice packaged in books, newspapers, letters, illustrated lectures and much, much more. Emigration, depending on what you read or who you heard, was either the opportunity of a lifetime or the last, despairing, and sometimes enforced response to poverty, unemployment and misery. And if – to paraphrase David Fitzpatrick's comment on the Irish – growing up in Scotland often meant preparing to leave it, those preparatory steps were shaped, assisted or impeded by a host of interested organisations and individuals with their own particular agendas.

Controversies and paradoxes were also woven firmly into the 20th-century tapestry of Scottish emigration, not least because of the persistently negative images of economic exile that still dominate and at times distort public perceptions of the diaspora. Some of these tensions emerge *en passant* in the pages that follow, before coming under the full glare of the spotlight in Chapter 5. The overall narrative is rooted in a half century of fluctuating movement that followed the end of the First World War, when Scots – despite the increasingly global reach of their diaspora – were still attracted mainly to traditional areas of settlement in North America and the Antipodes. The demise of preferential Commonwealth legislation in 1972, followed by Britain's accession to the EEC in 1973, confirmed the realignment of Britain's economic and political interests, at the same time as immigration was replacing emigration at the centre of national demographic debates.

At the heart of this book is a desire to explore the causes and consequences of the Scottish exodus by giving free rein to the pens and voices of those who experienced it in different ways and successive generations. By training the searchlight on a mixture of long-standing preoccupations and new departures we can compare the profile of participants, sponsors, opponents and administrators with that of their 19th-century predecessors. And through chronological and thematic lenses we can view some of the carrots and sticks that shaped their decisions, as well as highs and lows in the experiences of men, women and children whose hopes were fulfilled, disappointed or reconfigured in a variety of locations.

Never has the time been more opportune to tell this hidden tale and to investigate some of the many faces of the modern Scottish diaspora. As the new century moves through its teenaged years, we are bombarded from all quarters with evidence of popular, scholarly, and political interest in the comings and goings of the peoples of the British Isles, a sustained curiosity that shows no sign of waning. The public's passion with genealogy generates and feeds on media interest. Emigration and immigration are part and parcel of television programmes such as *Who Do You Think You Are?* and Radio Scotland's *Digging Up Your Roots*. Genealogical websites abound, and National Museums Scotland's 20th-century gallery includes migration as one of its four major themes.

In the political realm, there have been concerns about both the loss and accession of population. In December 2006 the BBC reported that almost a tenth of the UK population lived permanently overseas, with one survey suggesting that one in three Britons was actively considering emigrating.[7] The Scottish debate was particularly acute, since the country's population had been falling faster than anywhere in Europe and was expected to drop below five million by 2009. Haunted by the spectre of a declining and ageing workforce, in 2004 the Scottish Executive launched the 'Fresh Talent Initiative', a five-year campaign to attract 8,000 immigrants a year to Scotland made in response to the claim of the then First Minister, Labour's Jack McConnell, that population loss was the 'single biggest challenge facing Scotland in the 21st century'.[8]

The population had, however, begun to rise after 2002, and by the time the Fresh Talent Initiative – part of which was targeted on expatriate Scots – was terminated in 2008, it had attracted almost 8,500 successful applications.[9] Yet McConnell's prediction was simply a reiteration of age-old fears about demographic decline that have echoed down the corridors of Scottish history. Emigration is a subject that has engaged the attention of policy-makers since time immemorial, and much ink has been expended in debating its merits and defects. Past and present are closely interwoven in a web of recurring political dilemmas. The former First Minister's comments resonated closely with the Westminster government's antagonism to the depletion of the Scottish population in the late 1700s, and throughout the 19th century politicians wrestled with conflicting arguments surrounding the shovelling out of paupers and misfits and the debilitating haemorrhage of the youthful, enterprising heart of the nation. As we shall see in Chapter 5, these issues were to be revisited frequently throughout the 20th century. In the new millennium, as the Scottish National Party flexes increasingly powerful muscles, it remains to be seen what effect political developments, particularly the possibility of independence, will have on the perception and presentation of a cultural nationalism that has always been evident across the diaspora.

Despite its significance to Scotland's socio-economic, cultural and political fabric, remarkably little systematic attention has been paid – at least in print – to the country's 20th-century emigration history. Earlier eras have been reasonably well documented, although the first seeds of scholarly interest, sown by Gordon Donaldson in the 1960s, seemed initially to fall on barren ground.[10] It was not until the 1980s that an ever-swelling stream of publications – ranging from broad-brush overviews to detailed regional studies – began to delve into the domestic environment that produced the emigrants, and to track their experiences in the locations where they settled or sojourned.[11] It was a trend that both reflected and fed public interest in the subject, and it shows no sign of waning, whether from a scholarly or popular perspective, or indeed the commercial dimension that generated the Year of Homecoming in 2009 and a repeat performance in 2014, the 700th anniversary year of the battle of Bannockburn. But much of the story still remains to be told, and it is the aim of this book to weave some new threads into the complex, multi-dimensional but patchy tapestry of the Scottish diaspora.

CHAPTER I

The Road to England

THE SCOTS HAVE ALWAYS TRAVELLED southwards as well as outwards. 'The noblest prospect which a Scotsman ever sees,' Samuel Johnson famously declared in 1763, 'is the high road that leads him to England.'[1] By no means all departing Scots crossed oceans and continents, or even international frontiers, in their search for adventure or advancement. The road to England, which they had tramped steadily for centuries before 1900, continued to entice them south throughout the 20th century, and in larger numbers than to any single overseas destination. A diverse collection of politicians and professionals, skilled tradesmen and casual labourers, they settled and sojourned throughout the country, but with a few notable – and sometimes persistent – clusters.

Meaningful quantification of the Scottish presence in England became possible from 1911, when the census began to record the birth counties of Scots who lived on the other side of the border. Forensic scrutiny of their regional settlement patterns has only become possible since the expiry of the 100-year closure of the full census, and is still in its infancy, but even before 2011 it was possible to distil information about the collective and individual impact of these cross-border migrants from provincial newspapers and institutional records. For the most part, Scots were uncontroversial incomers whose presence – unlike that of their Irish and New Commonwealth counterparts – was simply taken for granted, and whose origins were demonstrated mainly in their accents. Occasionally, however, we are confronted with splenetic eruptions of Scotophobia provoked by perceptions of a tartan takeover of English politics, business, jobs and the media.

It would be not only tedious, but impossible, to consider exhaustively every avenue of English life penetrated by Scottish incomers and influences. We might more usefully focus on a selection of employments and activities in which Scots have made their most memorable mark south of the Tweed and Solway. While some hitched their wagon to existing occupational and social networks established by their compatriots generations, or even centuries, earlier, others forged new career paths in unfamiliar or specially created locations, perhaps most visibly in the Northamptonshire steel town of Corby. For a wide variety of ambitious, optimistic or desperate migrants, London remained the dominant magnet, a cosmopolitan market-place where Scots, like many others, hit the heights, plumbed the depths or – in the majority of cases – found an anonymous niche.

Underpinning the outflow was the negative perception among many Scots that their homeland had only a past, not a future. Coupled with dis-illusionment was a confidence that the road to England was paved with opportunities for work, wealth and an enhanced lifestyle in a country with which they were already familiar. While fluctuating economic circumstances affected the balance of attraction and repulsion, in general the existence of a broader industrial base in south-east England and the Midlands offered bet-ter openings to skilled and semi-skilled workers than Scotland or northern England. Socially and culturally, as well as in economic terms, migration also operated within a context of ever-increasing, multi-layered and seam-less contacts and communications that were generally easier to forge and maintain than overseas networks.

Counting Scots: Regional Settlement Patterns

Scottish migration to England and Wales has for long been the Cinderella of the UK's demographic historiography. No doubt this is due partly to the challenge of counting an unregulated, unenumerated army of southward-bound Scots of whose relocation until the 20th century 'we lack entirely any kind of chronological account'.[2] The neglect of quantification is also a consequence of a public perception that such mobility did not really con-stitute a definitive migration. Despite a wave of post-union Scotophobia, such 'non-othering' was reinforced after 1707, when Scotland was con-stitutionally harnessed to its southern neighbour and played a prominent part in the collaborative promotion of British imperialism. The more obvi-ous distinguishing characteristics of England's overseas immigrants also pushed the Scots into greater anonymity, at least in the public record.[3]

But cross-border mobility was a fact of life, which from time to time did attract comment. Even in the 15th century there were allegedly up to 11,000 Scots in England, mainly in Northumberland and London.[4] Numbers swelled after the parliamentary union, and continued to increase slowly but steadily over the next two centuries as industrial development generated a range of employment opportunities. The 1851 census recorded 130,087 Scots-born residents of England and Wales.

A century later, the figure had risen to 653,626, and by 1991 to 766,973. Scotland's remarkable outflow during the 1920s was directed more towards England than overseas; the two decades after 1931 saw a 58 per cent increase in the numbers of Scots-born resident in England and Wales; and between 1951 and 1981, 45 per cent of departing Scots headed south of the border.[5] But while actual numbers climbed, Scots-born constituted less than one per cent of the total population of England and Wales up to and including the 1931 census. Their presence, which had been fairly constant until the turn of the century, showed 'an appreciable diminution':[6] from 974 per 100,000 in 1901 to 892 per 100,000 in 1911, falling slightly further to 880 per 100,000 in 1921. In the post-war decades, Scots-born comprised between 1.3 per cent and 1.7 per cent of the English and Welsh population.[7]

The Scots tended to cluster in identifiable regions. Their centuries-long preference for the border counties and the south-east was maintained, reinforced in Northumberland and Durham by opportunities in shipbuilding, and in the home counties by the persistent magnetism of London. In 1911 nearly three quarters of the 321,825 Scots in England were located in the northern counties and in London and its hinterland: Northumberland, Durham and Cumberland accounted for over 62,000, Lancashire and Yorkshire for almost 79,000 and London, together with Middlesex, Surrey, Kent and urban parts of Essex for a further 90,000. They came mainly from the counties of Lanark, Edinburgh and Aberdeen. Twenty years later 'the severity of the industrial depression in the north as compared with that in the south' had brought about a 13 per cent inter-censal decrease in the Scots-born resident in Northumberland, Durham, Cumberland and Westmorland, but a 26 per cent increase in those enumerated in London and its five surrounding counties. Unlike the Irish, they did not gravitate to Wales, but – as we shall see in the case of Corby – they were propelled into new areas by prospects of better work and wages.

Maintaining Trends and Traditions

There was both continuity and innovation in southbound migration. The patronage that had propelled ambitious Scots over the border after 1707 gave way in the 19th century to a more meritocratic approach, as the products of the five Scottish universities – and many more besides –

flocked to England to take up positions in medicine, publishing, business and industry. Peripatetic tradesmen came to work in construction or in extractive industries like coal mining or slate quarrying, while others found permanent employment in shipbuilding.

Significant numbers of Scots found their way to East Anglia from time to time. A handful of Ayrshire dairy farmers, taking advantage of the financial plight of the area's wheat barons during the late 19th-century depression, moved to Essex before the First World War, and turned former arable land into dairy farms. But most of East Anglia's Scots were fishermen and ancillary workers, who migrated annually, following the herring shoals as they moved, clockwise, from the Hebrides in June, through Shetland and the Moray coast in July and August, and on across the border, sometimes via South Shields and Scarborough, to finish the season in Yarmouth and Lowestoft. At the peak of the industry's prosperity, in 1913, those two ports alone landed and processed almost 900 million herring, worth £1 million, in a 14-week period from September until the beginning of December.[8] Within a decade, however, when the vital Russian and German markets collapsed in the face of the Bolshevik Revolution of 1917 and the German monetary crisis of 1923, the golden age of the pre-war era became a fast-fading memory, as curers went bankrupt, wages fell and the migration of boats, fishermen and shore workers began to tail off. Yet even in the face of these difficulties, the Scots maintained a constant – and sometimes controversial – presence in East Anglia throughout the 1930s and 1940s. It was only in the 1960s that a century of fishing migration finally came to an end.

The female gutters and packers who processed the herring in shore stations have attracted much more attention than either the fishermen or the contingents of Scottish coopers who also followed the fishing. In 1913 around 6,000 girls – mainly from Shetland, Wick, Nairn and the Buchan and Fife ports, but also from the Western Isles – flooded into Yarmouth and Lowestoft. By 1935 the annual influx had shrunk to 2,600 and by 1962 to less than a dozen, but their legacy remains in visual, verbal and written testimony.[9] Most embarked on their itinerant careers between the ages of 15 and 18, learning knife-wielding dexterity from their mothers and older sisters as they followed the boats on which their fathers, husbands and brothers fished for herring. Employed by curing firms whose representatives came to Scotland in spring to engage them for the ensuing season, the girls formed themselves into crews of three: two gutters plus one packer who was usually responsible for negotiating the contract and ensuring that the remuneration was right at the end of the term. Many partnerships

Scots girls at Yarmouth, 1912
(Image by Alfred Yallop courtesy of Norfolk County Council Library and Information Service)

persisted for years, usually until they were severed by marriage, although some spinsters continued to follow the fishing until they were in their sixties or even older. Shetlander Christina Jackman, who ultimately settled in Yarmouth after marrying a local man in 1948, recalled that many of the Hebridean migrants from Harris were 'owld maids' who worked their crofts in the winter and 'ida summertime dey cam ta da fishing'.[10]

The cost of transporting the women and their 'kists' to and from the fishing ports was borne by the curers. Some of the workforce came to Yarmouth after working in Ireland or the Isle of Man, but most travelled from Aberdeen, often immediately after coming down on the boat from Lerwick. On 10 October 1936 the *Yarmouth Independent* noted the arrival at the town's Beach station of the first fisher-girls' express of the autumn. The LNER train, comprising eight passenger coaches and three baggage vans, had travelled through the night with 250 girls, all of whom were allegedly 'glad once more to be back in Yarmouth'.[11] Seven weeks later, the scene was reversed, as five trains left the same station, taking around 1,000 girls back to Aberdeen, Kyle of Lochalsh and the Hebrides. Motor coaches transported a contingent of 60 girls back to Peterhead, and, as the curing yards closed, over 150 drifters also began the return journey to their home ports in Scotland.[12]

Scots women packing herring into barrels, Yarmouth, 1930s
(Image by George Swain courtesy of Norfolk County Council Library and Information Service)

In the 1930s it was still common for special carriages to be reserved for the Scottish gutters and coopers, but by the 1950s it was only necessary to reserve seats, not entire coaches. Despite slow and sometimes filthy trains, Annie Watt (from Peterhead) and Christina Jackman both remembered the 15-hour journey as a pleasurable experience, during which the travellers rarely slept, but spent the time playing records on a portable gramophone, singing and dancing – often with porters on station platforms – and brewing tea. The safety aspect of the girls' habit of cooking their meals on primus stoves in the train corridor in the 1950s was recalled with horror by Newham Timm, station master at Yarmouth Vauxhall, who also described having 'to be careful who you put together' in order to avoid quarrels.[13]

Tensions, not surprisingly, also surfaced both in the harsh environment of the gutting yards and in the cramped lodgings, where the girls were often crowded six to a room and three to a bed. Landladies lifted the carpets that they had laid for summer visitors, protected their walls with brown paper or oil cloth, imposed a 10 pm curfew and discouraged visitors. Washing facilities were minimal, just a ewer and basin in each room, and it was impossible to eradicate the smell of fish from hair and clothing for Saturday night dancing and Sunday churchgoing. At the yards the women gutted, salted, graded and packed the herring in barrels between layers of salt, working flat out for up to 15 hours after a catch was landed, often having to break the ice on top of the barrels at the beginning of the day. In 1914 the average weekly wage was 25 shillings, but by 1924 it had dropped to 20 shillings, and to 15 shillings by 1936. The team also shared a shilling for every barrel filled, and at the end of the season 'barrel money' was paid for every one they had topped up.

Remuneration was a common bone of contention, and the 'herring quines' gained a reputation for militancy and strategically planned collective action. Strikes were common, particularly in the 1930s. In late October 1936, at the height of the season, the East Anglian curing yards were paralysed by a three-day stoppage against wage reductions that may have been planned in Lerwick several weeks earlier, but had been delayed by a light fishing. Led by Maria Gatt from Rosehearty, the strikers – 3,000 in Yarmouth and 1,000 in Lowestoft – demanded the restoration of the barrel filling payment from tenpence to a shilling per barrel, along with an extra half crown (two shillings and sixpence) in their weekly wage packet. According to a *Yarmouth Mercury* reporter, 'A great crowd of cheering girls, growing like a snowball with almost every step they took, swept round the loyal yards and called upon the workers to give in.' Those who refused were pelted with herring, an attack which in some yards 'developed into a miniature fusillade'. The curers' response was to bolt the gates of their premises and – in one case – to unleash a hosepipe attack. As a tide of 'yelling girls, some of them not out of their teens' surged through the streets of the fishing quarter, 'searching for blacklegs', the police, including one mounted officer, were summoned to deal with an acrimonious confrontation at a yard near the gas works. After an hour-long stand-off, six non-striking gutters were taken home in a police vehicle, one of them claiming that the experience had been 'worse than the war in Spain' and another bewailing that she had been physically attacked by her 'own kind'.[14]

By the next day (Saturday) 800 boats were tied up in the harbour, and the quaysides were swarming with both chanting gutters, who 'wiled (sic) away the time by knitting', and with 10,000 idle fishermen. Although the girls claimed that most of them supported their action, such solidarity was probably confined to the Scots: the *Yarmouth Mercury* claimed that local fishermen resented their enforced holiday, and was 'pretty sure that not all the Scotties liked it'.[15] By Sunday it appeared that their holiday was over, when in the morning local church announcements, delivered in both English and Gaelic, declared that agreement had been reached on the first demand. The following morning, however, the strike was reactivated by a handful of girls who continued to push for the weekly wage to be raised from 15s 6d to 17s. It finally came to an end later that day, after the curers warned girls who did not resume work that they would have to return to Scotland at their own expense.

During the strike, negotiations had been hampered by the girls' lack of trade union representation, and in its aftermath, a number of them joined the Transport and General Workers' Union, whose local representative had mediated in the dispute. From the curers' perspective, the dispute had been instigated by a handful of girls who 'had not been brought up to face the hard working conditions of the fishing yards', and there was irritation that gutters who had broken their pre-season contracts were going home from East Anglia with earnings of £10 or £15.[16] But while the girls had achieved partial success in their demands, it was, at least for Christina Jackman, a pyrrhic victory, since her landlady took the opportunity to increase the rent by a shilling a week. The strikers' power of protest was limited, since they could not afford to wreck the industry on which they depended.[17] Yet strikes continued, with a day-long stoppage of work by over 100 Scottish stevedores in Yarmouth before the end of the 1936 season, and further downing of knives by the gutters in 1946, 1949 and 1953.[18]

More surprising than tensions and militancy, however, is the evident camaraderie and merriment of the girls in the midst of arduous, backbreaking toil. 'We aa got on together,' recalled Christina Jackman, 'because we just lived in a world a wir ane'.[19] They mixed only with each other, rather than with the local women, who tended to work in canning factories, or the Irish men who worked alongside them in the gutting yards. Most eagerly anticipated was early December, for it was then, in Yarmouth, that they received their pay for a season that had often begun in the Western Isles six months earlier. As well as signifying their independence, those wages enabled the girls to return to their families in Scotland with money and gifts to brighten the gloom of a northern winter. The brief taste of freedom also compensated for the primitive working conditions and poor sanitation which predisposed them to ulcerated hands and kidney complaints. Some girls met their future husbands during their annual sojourn in East Anglia. Social activities frowned upon in moralistic, introspective Scottish fishing communities were cheap and plentiful: Annie Watt recalled paying fourpence (2p) for 'grand shows' at the Yarmouth Hippodrome, and Christina Jackman enjoyed the forbidden pleasure of going occasionally to the pub.[20]

Yet the fisherfolk carried their religious principles, as well as their gramophones and knitting needles, across the border, and dancing often went hand-in-hand with hymn-singing. At times their sabbatarianism segregated them from the host society. In 1931 and 1936, the women downed

St Monan's herring gutters being given a lift home to their lodgings in Yarmouth, c. 1920
(Image courtesy of the Scottish Fisheries Museum)

tools, not for higher wages, but in protest at the introduction of Sunday fishing, and in the 1950s the Scottish boats, in contrast to the English ones, still remained in port on Sundays. Conformity was no doubt encouraged by the presence of mission stations operated by the Scottish Presbyterian churches to which many of the fisherfolk belonged, but these institutions cared for the girls' bodies, as well as their souls. Like the Red Cross, the churches and para-church organisations ran first-aid stations that treated their cuts and sprains, and canteens which fed several hundred workers each day, including lorry drivers and coopers, as well as gutters and packers. Recreational facilities eased the tedium of the workplace and offered 'pleasant surroundings' where scattered families could meet, as 'fathers and brothers came from their boats, and girls from their lodgings'.[21] The mission superintendents also prepared lists of suitable lodgings before the girls arrived, visited those who were ill, and organised services in both English and Gaelic.

At times the support agencies were confronted with deep distress. In many ways the 1936 season was a good one, with fish worth £500,000 brought to Yarmouth, and a Banff boat, the *Boy Andrew,* winning the Prunier trophy for the biggest single catch of fresh herrings landed. But the season was marred by the loss of 18 fishermen – nine Scots and nine local men – in two fishing tragedies. A severe storm in late November resulted in the loss of the Peterhead motor drifter, *Olive Branch,* and its crew of nine, six of whom were from a single family. Three of the wives were living or working in Yarmouth while their husbands fished, and one of them, the skipper's wife, lost not only her husband, but also three of her five sons.[22] The same storm almost claimed boats from Banff and Glasgow, while two weeks later a local boat went down off Calais with the loss of nine of its ten-strong crew.

The Scots who followed the fishing to East Anglia came and went with the seasons. Further up the east coast, in the shipyards and coalfields of Northumberland and Durham, we can identify a much older, deeper rooted migratory tradition of Scottish businessmen, tradesmen and labourers, who by the 20th century were building on cross-border links and networks that had existed, in some cases, since the middle ages. In the shipping industry's Victorian heyday, Scottish entrepreneurs expanded their interests to the Tyne, recruiting workers who were attracted by their employers' provision of housing and an infrastructure of Scottish churches, schools and institutes. By the 1870s the community of Hebburn in County Durham boasted a 'Scottish colony' of 300 houses, built by local shipyard owner Andrew Leslie, who also subsidised the school and church. Many of the householders and their hordes of lodgers came from Aberdeen, where Leslie, a Shetland crofter's son, had served his apprenticeship.[23] At the turn of the century, when Newcastle's leading Anglo-Scots mounted an abortive campaign to raise a kilted Scottish corps to serve in the Boer War, it was claimed that the 900 men who had signed up as volunteers were 'all of Scotch nationality or of Scotch parentage'.[24]

Meanwhile, on the opposite coast, Scots came to Barrow-in-Furness to mingle with incomers from many other parts of the British Isles and beyond in the shipyards, engineering works, furnaces and jute factories of a rapidly growing industrial centre. In 1871–72 the Scottish influence was visibly imprinted on the local landscape with the construction of the 'Scotch Flats', a squalid three- and four-storey tenement courtyard block erected by Dundee firm Smith and Caird to house about 260 families who worked in the flax, jute and steel industries.[25] To dip into the Barrow census returns for certain wards of the parish is to uncover a significant body of Scots – in 1881, for example, almost 19 per cent of the 4,200 residents of Walney; 31 per cent of a sample of 100 residents of Hawcote; and 10 per cent of a sample of 200 residents of Hindpool were Scots-born; 20th-century census summaries continued to remark on the 'conspicuous' Scottish presence in Barrow.[26]

Even in the chillier economic climate of the first half of the 20th century,

Scots workers continued to be drawn to Tyneside and West Cumbria by a combination of family and community networks and the perceived similarity of the industrial landscape to that of their homeland. The Clydeside shipyards which haemorrhaged many surplus workers overseas after the First World War spilled others southwards, and it was only after 1945 that the traffic dropped significantly in tandem with the terminal decline of both shipbuilding and mining. The early years of the century saw more Scots flock to Barrow to work in rearmament projects at the Naval Construction Works that had been purchased by Vickers of Sheffield in 1896. Many of the skilled artisans lived in Vickerstown, the works village erected on Walney Island, where tenancy of a property depended on the recommendation of a foreman. Despite Vickers' attempt at paternalistic control of its workforce, an influx of 'committed Socialists' from Scotland energised the trade union movement in the shipyard and helped to reshape local politics, so that by the end of the First World War the Labour Party had won all three seats on Walney and Barrow council.[27] By 1922, however, 44 per cent of Barrow's insured male population was unemployed, provoking 'thousands of people' – Scots no doubt included – 'to try their luck in America or Canada, Australia or South Africa'.[28] In the following decade, as the shipyard's order books filled up again, the Vickerstown houses were steadily sold off to sitting tenants, while elsewhere in the town another visible symbol of the Scottish presence – Scotch Flats – was declared unfit for human habitation and later demolished.

A Monument of Weeping or a Delectable Land? The Corby Venture

Not all cross-border migration followed patterns established in the 19th century or earlier. During the Depression, the Ministry of Labour's notorious industrial transference scheme removed surplus workers from unemployment blackspots to more prosperous areas of the country, often generating huge resentment in both the sending and receiving communities. Central Scotland was an obvious recruitment zone, and in May 1936 the *Bellshill Speaker* reported that 100 youths from the distressed areas of Scotland were to be given an all-expenses-paid holiday at the YMCA camp at Skegness, before being sent to jobs in the Midlands. Recruits would be selected from applications received at labour exchanges and were required, with the consent of their parents, to accept the situations offered to them at the end of the holiday. While at Skegness, the report continued, 'each

Corby, late 1930s, first housing estate constructed for the steel workers
(© William Cowie)

Corby, late 1940s, construction of prefabricated housing by Corby Urban District Council
(© William Cowie)

boy will be consulted as to the type of work desired, and an attempt will be made to find the most suitable situation among those available, which are in engineering, factories, offices, warehouses, aeroplane manufacture, and hotels. In all the situations there is provision for promotion'.[29] Two weeks later, the same newspaper reported that the Ministry of Labour was sending south a number of families whose sons had previously been transferred to jobs in England, where they had then secured work for their parents, usually in the same firm.[30]

The most enduring industrial transference venture of the inter-war period was not, however, the brainchild of the Ministry of Labour, but a consequence of consolidation within the privately owned steel industry. The centres of supply and demand were, respectively, Mossend in the heart of industrial Lanarkshire and the village of Corby in Northamptonshire. 'Forged in steel',[31] Corby's birth as a distinctive outpost of Scotland in the English Midlands came about as a consequence of the British steel industry's rationalisation of production in response to international competition. In 1928 the firm of Stewarts and Lloyds, which since 1910 and 1911 had operated two small blast furnaces in the town, began to investigate the feasibility of integrating the firm's ironstone works with its Glasgow-based tube-making operation. The directors gave the green light once the necessary financial support of £3 million had been secured in November 1932. Proximity to the orefields and railway network dictated that Corby would be the site of the new enterprise, which was to specialise in the production of welded tubes. The existing workforce of 600 would be increased to almost 2,600, the new recruits to comprise men made redundant from small units owned by the company in Staffordshire and North Lincolnshire, as well as, primarily, from its Clydesdale Works at Mossend. The Universal Plate Mill at Mossend employed about 900 men, only 180 of whom were retained locally when the plant closed.[32]

Scotland, along with Ireland, also supplied many of the construction workers and tradesmen who during 1934 and 1935 transformed Corby from a village of 1,800 into an industrial settlement of 10,000. A major part of that transformation involved the initial provision of around 1,000 homes for the new workforce. When the local authority declined to take any responsibility for house-building, Stewarts and Lloyds purchased East Carlton Park and Hall, about four miles from Corby, where they constructed a bachelor hostel as well as 80 superior homes for executive staff and their families. Residents of this 'miniature garden city' were promised elegant dwellings in a variety of architectural styles, 'with steep gables and elm-boarded porches, hipped roofs and white stucco walls, Mansard pantiled roofs, and outlines of Georgian symmetry'. They were also to have access to a swimming pool, tennis courts, billiard and reading rooms, football and cricket pitches, as well as garages 'in which will be kept the cars that… will take them backwards and forwards to their work at Corby'.[33]

Much more extensive was the simultaneous development of workmen's housing close to the steel plant in Corby. Indoor recreational facilities were to be provided in a Works' Club, and outdoor sport at cricket and football grounds, a bowling green, tennis courts and a short-hole golf course. The houses themselves were designed to meet the needs of men employed on dirty jobs, the downstairs bathroom being so arranged that, 'on returning home grimy and greasy from his day's work, [he] can step into his bath almost as soon as he is over his doorstep. Thus, without leaving dirty footmarks in the hall or on the stair carpet, he can remove all traces of his day's activities before sitting down to tea'.[34]

Almost half a century later, Brian Saunders, a native of Corby, emphasised in an interview that 'by most people's standards Stewarts and Lloyds houses in Corby were – are – of very, very high quality. There isn't any doubt about that.'[35] To many of the inter-war migrants – as well as those who arrived later – they were in a completely different league from the dwellings they had left, being bigger and 'much better than anything we could have hoped for back in Scotland'.[36] On the other hand, a discordant note was struck by architectural journalist G.M. Boumphrey, in a BBC radio broadcast in March 1935 which berated town planners for the 'missed opportunities' that he feared would turn Corby into a ghetto rather than a garden suburb. The unwise segregation of management and workers was, he alleged, compounded by inadequate attention to aesthetic and practical aspects of both types of housing. Windows were allegedly too small and low-set, and staircases too narrow, while different architectural styles and building materials created a 'restless, muddled effect'. Company housing was both too near the plant yet inaccessible to it because the railway line bisected the site, creating an impenetrable barrier between the labour force and its place of work. The Corby developments, Boumphrey predicted, resurrected the spectre of uncontrolled building that had blighted town planning more than a century earlier, when many industrial towns had been turned into 'evil, unhealthy, inefficient muddles'.[37]

These doom-laden prophecies kindled an immediate response of mixed 'commendation and consternation'. The Rector of Corby, A. Brooke Westcott, agreed with all the criticisms but went even further, declaring that for him, Corby was 'not so much a place of "missed opportunity" as a monument of weeping'. Members of the town planning committee, on the other hand, claimed Boumphrey had spoken from a position of complete ignorance, an assertion reinforced by Laurence Gotch, architect for the housing development. Boumphrey had, claimed Gotch, come to Corby 'with all the destructive effort of a mechanical digger but with much less productive result', and the new houses, whose rents were set at between 8 and 10 shillings a week, represented untold but affordable luxury to the incoming Glaswegians.[38]

The local press, too, in both Northamptonshire and Lanarkshire, reported favourably on the construction of homes, the transfer of workers and the development of the steel works on which everything else hinged. In February 1935 the *Kettering Leader* anticipated that before the end of the year Corby would have absorbed 700 men laid off by the Universal Plate Mill at Mossend, and in September it noted that more than two houses were being completed every day in 'the most modern town in the Midlands'.[39] A month later, the *Bellshill Speaker* published the alluring – if over-optimistic – predictions of A.A. Dick JP, President of the Bellshill Brotherhood. Predicting that Corby would provide an inspiration for future town planning, and praising the beauty of its new domestic architecture, he anticipated that the innovative developments would produce a town of 'beauty and substance' which would 'outstrip our own in every desirable feature'. 'Altogether,' he concluded, 'the immigrants to Corby have struck a delectable land.'[40]

Delectability was diminished by the initial absence of services. A particularly critical part of the new infrastructure was the provision of schools for the families that were an integral part of the migration. In 1934 it was predicted that the Scottish influx would generate an extra 900 schoolchildren, necessitating the construction of a new elementary school. Secondary-school children travelled to Kettering, which also absorbed schoolleavers into its clothing and footwear factories.[41] Marion Tester, a native of Corby (born in 1919), recalled that 'every week at the railway station a fresh boy or girl would board our train to Kettering to the High or Grammar School, full of life and vitality. We were invited to their homes and learnt for the first time about haggis, dumpling, Hallowe'en and 'first footing'. She also remembered the 'crowds of strange children, mostly in kilts', who passed her house every Monday morning on their way to enrol at the Corby village school, 'which soon had 800 instead of the 250 for whom it was originally built'.[42] By the time 12-year-old Euclid Tipaldi (a Scot of Italian descent) arrived in Corby from Galashiels just before the war, he was able to go to the new Samuel Lloyd school, where his particular friends were the 'Lanarkshire Scots whose accents were somewhat harsher than my Lowland burr'. The Scottish accents were even more alien to Bill Carlyle, who came to Corby from nearby Cottingham in 1946 and was enrolled in the Rowlett School, which had been opened 12 years earlier.[43]

Such was Corby's fame, that even by 1935 job applications were allegedly being received from Orkney and the Outer Hebrides, as well as the Central Belt. So claimed Ian Carmichael, labour officer at Stewarts and Lloyds, in an address to the Kettering and District Caledonian Society. Carmichael, who had previously supervised the Welfare Department at Mossend, went on to praise the particular attributes of the Lanarkshire migrants, 'an industrial people accustomed to wrest a living from blazing furnaces and from the bowels of the earth'. Leaving behind a region with an unemployment rate of up to 90 per cent, some were starting work for the first time at the age of 20, and for the sake of a wage and a future were prepared to tolerate and overcome the inconveniences of relocating to a town with undeveloped transport, medical, educational and recreational facilities.[44] From January 1934, the Bellshill Speaker maintained a running commentary on departures as batches of men began to be transferred south and fleets of furniture vans gathered at the railway goods yard to transport their household effects.[45] By 1938, when local government was transferred from Northamptonshire County Council and Kettering Rural Council to a new urban district authority, over 2,000 houses had been built and October of that year also saw the opening of the Corby Monotechnic Institute for Engineering, built by Stewarts & Lloyds for the training of student apprentices throughout Northamptonshire.

The pioneers included Harry Johnstone, who had never left Scotland until he was offered a job in Corby in December 1933. Given only two days to settle his affairs in Glasgow, he arrived in Northamptonshire to find a 'small village' which was soon completely transformed by the construction of 2,000 company houses. Within a fortnight he secured a home, where he was joined by his wife and child, and began a 25-year career in the steel works. In the early years he frequently worked a 12-hour day, but, as he recalled at the age of 96, although 'you had no power, absolutely no power' and 'nobody to fight your battles', the threat of unemployment meant that no one grumbled.[46] John Hay, who also worked 12-hour days, was less positive about his early experiences. Anticipating redundancy from the Phoenix Tube Works in Rutherglen, he secured a job in the half-built despatch office at Corby, and in January 1935 Stewarts & Lloyds paid his train fare south. Lodging initially with the Irvines, a family of recent migrants from Lanarkshire, he recalled that 'everyday life for me in those early days was dull and depressing'. But while he was bored and would have returned to Glasgow if prospects had been any better there, he admitted that his situation was 'infinitely better' than that of men who had walked, cycled or hitch-hiked to Corby, sleeping under hedges, in barns or in hostels.[47]

Among the younger generation of incomers from Lanarkshire, William Gibson Cockin and Nessie Phillips – who both arrived in 1934 – described Corby in those early days as a village in a sea of mud. William's mother immediately kitted him out with gumboots at one of the few local stores, because 'there was no roads made up [and] you were up to your calves in mud'.[48] Nessie Phillips likewise recalled 'a sort of pioneering township', where the dominant Lanarkshire influx was mixed with new arrivals from Birmingham, Ireland, Poland and Latvia. It consisted of 'a rash of quickly thrown up raw houses, un-made up roads and mud, mud, mud', as well as a dearth of shops and a flea-pit of a cinema.[49] Negative comparisons with 'some of the lovely cinemas in Glasgow' (the European city with the most picture-houses per head of population) also featured in the memories of Ethel Marshall, a 1935 arrival who later served as Chairman of Corby Urban District Council and a JP.[50]

For some migrants, the lack of facilities mattered much less than the severing of lifelong ties, but the pain of parting was assuaged by frequent reunions. The *Bellshill Speaker* documented the regular arrival of trainloads of 'our emigrant sons and daughters from Corby' – 200 for Easter 1935, for instance, followed a month later by a contingent of 230 travelling in the opposite direction on a cheap 19s 6d return fare. At least one of the northbound visitors regretted that he was not on a one-way ticket, remarking cynically that 'Corby is a grand place when you are coming home on the train'.[51]

Homesickness apart, the steel worker's life was far from easy. The risk of injury or worse was ever present. By December 1935 the St John's Ambulance Brigade in Corby was dealing with an average of two accidents a week, and the ambulance men were sleeping 'almost with one eye open'.[52] The *Bellshill Speaker* regularly reported fatalities among migrants, including Bartholomew Gallagher (aged 23), a well-known Lanarkshire junior footballer and electrician's labourer. His death generated several column inches in the newspaper, which reported how, having been unemployed for some time after being laid off from the Clydesdale Works, he had first cycled to Corby in an unsuccessful attempt to find work. Back in Glasgow, he was recalled to Corby in August 1934, only to be killed nine months later when runaway wagons on an overhead railway threw him 50 feet from a ladder to the ground.[53]

Corby's experience of Scottish migration was not confined to the 1930s. The steelworks played a vital part in the war effort, and five years after the end of hostilities Corby was designated a new town. The Development Corporation's objective of increasing the population from 18,000 to 40,000 by 1963 was achieved, mainly by a further – and more disparate – influx from Scotland, supplemented by displaced persons from Europe. The new Scots were attracted by a combination of established social networks, housing and work, until the consolidation policy of the nationalised British Steel Corporation in the 1970s ultimately led to the closure of the plant, the loss of 11,000 jobs and an unemployment rate of over 30 per cent in the early 1980s.[54]

Alice Stewart came to Corby just after the war. Her husband had been there since the 1930s, and his job had been kept for him while he was on active service. The newly married Alice – who spent her honeymoon with her husband's aunt and uncle – immediately 'liked the atmosphere and wanted to stay' and although the couple later retired to Wemyss Bay they returned to Corby after only nine months.[55] Gertie Morrison was less enthusiastic about leaving Aberdeen with her husband and four children, 'but there was no work and we decided in 1957 to come to Corby' where 'the future was good'. Although she initially wondered if she had done the right thing, her dislike of the 'dull, dirty, brick houses' that replaced Aberdeen's 'lovely granite' was mitigated by the four-bedroom house and large garden which awaited the family.[56]

Gertie was not alone in highlighting the significance of accommodation. It was the preoccupation of many of the post-war migrants, as well as the pioneers of the 1930s, and their mixed experiences also mirrored those of their predecessors. The shortage of municipal housing in Scotland for a long time after the war – and the shared lavatory facilities in cramped tenement blocks – were significant catalysts in the second wave of migration. Glaswegian John Douglas suffered many sleepless nights before deciding in 1955 that he could not condemn his family to ten more years in a sunless, vermin-infested two-roomed tenement in Scotstoun while he waited for a council house. That was the 'deciding factor' in the 'traumatic and painful' relocation to Corby, where within six weeks the family moved into 'a brand new house with lounge, kitchen, two bedrooms, bathroom... front and back garden'.[57] In similar vein, trawlerman John Cowling was lodging with his family in his mother's house in Aberdeen in 1962, when, as he recalled, 'I saw an advertisement in the dole office saying "Come to Corby the town of steel". It meant a house and a job. Why not?, I thought. Aberdeen Council couldn't house us for years.' Not that his initial accommodation in Northamptonshire was much better: after being allocated a bunk and a locker in a four-bedded dormitory in a Nissen hut at Brigstock Labour Camp for £3 2s 6d a week, he moved his family south to a rented attic in Corby where they 'stuck it out until we eventually got our own house'.[58]

Scots in London

Corby's Scots were visible because their initial migration was clearly focused and well publicised in specific donor and host areas; because the pioneers maintained Scottish networks that facilitated an ongoing influx; and because the area of settlement lacked strong competing traditions of incoming migration. It is perhaps more remarkable that Scots have maintained a high profile in London, which for centuries has been a magnet and a melting pot for immigrants from all over the British Isles and the world at large.

Following an upsurge in arrivals in the late 19th century, there were about 100,000 Scots-born in Greater London around the time of the First World War.[59] During the 20th century their numbers remained remarkably stable, and according to the 2001 census, London's seven million residents included 110,000 (1.57 per cent) who had been born in Scotland.[60] Four years earlier, their visibility within the most powerful institution in the UK – the Westminster Parliament – had been demonstrated by the election of a Labour government dominated by Scots. As well as 47 English constituencies with Scots-born MPs, eight Cabinet seats were occupied by Scots, including the most powerful offices of Prime Minister, Chancellor of the Exchequer and Foreign Secretary.[61] Tony Blair may have followed the example of his 18th-century predecessors in anglicising his accent and disguising his roots, but Gordon Brown was relentlessly caricatured by the media as the austere and ambitious son of the Scottish presbyterian manse.

The London media might well have turned the spotlight on itself, for at the end of the 20th century Scots still maintained their long-established influence in Broadcasting House and a (dispersed) Fleet Street. John Reith, like Gordon Brown, was a son of the manse. Born in Stonehaven and educated at Glasgow Academy and at Gresham's School in Norfolk, he served an engineering apprenticeship before going to London in 1914, driven by the 'same urge as countless others have felt, and without any sound reason'.[62] After war service, spent partly supervising armament contracts in the United States, he returned to London, and then to Glasgow. When in 1922 he answered an advertisement for a General Manager for the new British Broadcasting Corporation, he put his faith in the efficacy of Scottish networking, retrieving his application from the post to add a reference to his Aberdonian ancestry in the hope that the chairman of the committee, Sir William Noble, might know his family.[63]

In the same decade, the journalist and travel writer H.V. Morton referred to English journalism being 'red with the hair of Aberdonians' whose brains were 'like iced encyclopaedias' and whose caution and accuracy were worth their weight in gold to newspaper proprietors anxious to minimise the risk of libel actions.[64] John Junor, a notorious philanderer whose journalistic pen spouted constant vitriol, was a product of the other side of Scotland, inner-city Glasgow. While he never wished to return north, he was, according to his daughter, 'proud of his Scottish origins' and the classlessness bestowed by his roots and accent.[65] For 32 years from 1948 Junor edited the *Sunday Express,* initially under the eagle eye of Lord Beaverbrook (Max Aitken), the Scots-Canadian who, says David Stenhouse, was almost single-handedly responsible for the Scottish domination of Fleet Street in the 20th century. Beaverbrook's *Scottish Daily Express* was edited by Scots for more than half a century, while the *Daily Express* had three Scottish editors in the 1970s.[66]

Just as Highlanders have traditionally served in the Glasgow police force, so Scots in general have carved out a significant niche in the Metropolitan Police. An analysis of the service records of 23,000 men who joined the force as constables between 1889 and 1909 reveals that 893 were Scots-born, with 'an amazingly high proportion' – almost 12 per cent – coming from Aberdeenshire. Some had transferred from the Scottish police service, while others had come from civilian careers on both sides of the border.[67] Word-of-mouth recommendations and Freemasonry networks were reinforced by the opening of a recruitment office in Glasgow in the 1960s, and until the 1980s the 'Met' explicitly targeted Scottish recruits.

Doug Cameron, then a journalist with the *Financial Times,* offered an unashamedly materialistic rationale for Scottish migration in an article in the *New Statesman* in 2002, before the credit crunch:

> Whatever our ambivalence towards London, the simple truth is that everybody goes there... The city's sheer scale allows us to enjoy our surprising yearning for anonymity. London's Scots by and large eschew the communities favoured by other imports, save gatherings in the William Wallace by Baker Street Station or the Caledonian Club near Hyde Park. No Irish-themed or Brazilian samba bars for us. We blend

in nicely to the throng, so we think, while maintaining our snooty sense of Not Being English...

Commerce is the final binding attraction of the city for the Scots here, who cannot bring themselves to admit that they may love what few would dare to call their adopted home. We are here because we are paid to be here, many kid themselves, a southbound economic clearance from barren employment opportunities at home. This carefully ignores a housing boom in Edinburgh fuelled by bankers and fund managers returning home misty-eyed after a lucrative stint in the City. With more pounds in our pockets, the rise and rise of the discount airlines has only cemented the capital's affections in our hearts, with its convenient connections to Luton and Stansted.[68]

At the other end of the spectrum, London has, since time immemorial, lured countless individuals from disturbed, dysfunctional and dislocated backgrounds. Their attitudes, David Stenhouse suggests in *On the Make*, were not necessarily very different from those of their high-achieving compatriots in the capital, for 'they all share a fundamental belief that Scotland somehow isn't *enough;* that the range of opportunities it offers is too narrow, or too proscribed, and that the only way in which they can achieve their full potential is by leaving'.[69] But most of them lacked finance and contacts, with the result that they simply transferred their problems – often in an intensified form – to London. Whereas their Irish counterparts had traditionally used ethnic networks to secure accommodation and employment, the absence of a visible, viable Scottish community in London deprived them of an important support mechanism on which migrants have relied through the ages.

In the late 20th century the prominence of desperate and destitute Scots on London's streets generated a dedicated remedial initiative to tackle homelessness within that constituency. The UK 's main charity for the young homeless, Centrepoint, began in 1969 in the crypt of a church in Soho, helping young people who came mainly from unemployment blackspots in the north of England, followed by Scotland.[70] For almost a century from its foundation in 1887, the Caledonian Christian Club had provided support and hostel accommodation for newly arrived Scots in London, and after it closed in 1976 its mantle was taken over by a new charity, the Church of Scotland London Advisory Service (COSLAS). During the 1980s, its emphasis was on providing subsidised hostel accommodation for economic migrants to London, at a time when unemployment in Scotland was twice the UK average. The shift to helping the vulnerable and destitute came in 1990, following a steady increase in the number of homeless Scots, who by then constituted an estimated 10–14 per cent of London's homeless population.

Since then, the Borderline Project, created by COSLAS, run by London's two Church of Scotland congregations and dedicated specifically to Scots, has advised, housed, and sometimes repatriated, homeless and vulnerable Scots in the capital. In its first decade it dealt with over 3,500 individuals, soon expanding its services from the young to cater for all age groups.[71]

Two interview-based surveys by Borderline – one with 70 clients in 1990 and another with 41 clients in 2000 – identified recurring patterns in the migrants' motives and experiences. Most came from broken homes or relationships and several had been in care or prison; 85 per cent were male, few had any qualifications, most were unemployed when they left Scotland, and several had health problems, drug or alcohol addiction. Nearly three quarters of the sample in 2000 came from Glasgow or other towns in the west of Scotland, echoing the 'disproportionately high number' who had come from Strathclyde a decade earlier.[72] Very few had made financial preparations, and 31 per cent of those in the 1990 survey had arrived with less than one pound in their pocket.[73] Although driven south by expulsive factors – notably the recurring anthem that Scotland was 'depressing', 'dreary' and had nothing for them, they were also attracted by the belief that London really did offer better opportunities for work and wages.[74]

Idealistic expectations of betterment were seldom realised and many migrants quickly became caught in a vicious circle of homelessness and unemployment. Some were sucked into the negative networks of an underworld that they had tried to leave behind, with one interviewee from Borderline's 2000 survey, who had left Glasgow for a 'fresh start' in London, finding that 'it only took me three days to meet people who'd been in prison with me in Scotland'.[75] Just over a quarter of interviewees from the earlier sample warned others against following their example, and a desire to return to Scotland was evident in both surveys, although migrants were often inhibited by a reluctance to admit failure or a persistent belief that their life chances were better in London. Borderline's planned resettlement programme has been developed, in conjunction with agencies in Scotland, to address the needs of those who wish to return but think it is unrealistic.

Some interviewees who had no desire to return north were influenced by the expectation of employment, others by the anonymity of metropolitan life, or a perception that attitudes were better than in Scotland. One 20-year-old compared the response to homelessness in London and Glasgow. 'Down here in London, you're just another human being in a hostel who doesn't want to be there, but at the end of the day you're trying to screw your head on. They see that you'll get a job, move out to another hostel then onto a flat. In Glasgow, the council would prefer you stay in hostels than in a house.' A heroin addict from the same sample claimed he was less likely to be barred from hostels in London, while another man felt he had escaped the stigma that clung to him in his home area. 'I'm still labelled up the road, 'Mike the Junkie', down here I'm not labelled, I can start afresh'.[76] Borderline's unique 'understanding of Scottish life and culture' was also appreciated by several homeless Scots, who compared it favourably with agencies which took no account of their clients' origins. 'We're getting treated as if we're from London, but we're not, we're from Scotland. London is much bigger than Scotland. Scottish people are used to Scottish things. Down here it's all new to us.'[77]

Being Scottish in England

The homeless Scots' appreciation of Borderline's Scottish focus reminds us of the complex, multi-dimensional nature of the migrant experience. Migration was not simply a hard-headed economic phenomenon or – for a minority – an attempt to escape a dysfunctional background. Like migrants the world over, many transplanted Scots from across the social spectrum valued their culture more keenly once they had been uprooted, and although they may not have prioritised – or sometimes even recognised – the ethnic markers that they planted in southern soil, it was generally through the celebration or reinvention of their national traditions that they maintained a visible distinctiveness within English society.

An important, though diminishing, part of that distinctiveness was their religious identity. While maintaining the faith – or the institutional religion – of their fathers was certainly less important to 20th-century Scots than to their Victorian predecessors, churches offered migrants not only spiritual benefits but also access to a range of useful social networks and recreational facilities. Many Scots gravitated to the Presbyterian Church of England or other nonconformist denominations. The 19th-century minute books of Cumbria's Congregational and Evangelical Union churches are full of references to the arrival and departure of Scottish migrants, while in Barrow, the Disjunction Certificate Book of St Andrew's Presbyterian Church, Walney, records that between 1931 and 1956, 12 of the 28 members who 'lifted their lines' (resigned their membership) were going – perhaps returning – to Scotland, mainly to Glasgow and its hinterland, but also to Edinburgh, Alness and Conon Bridge.[78]

Localities that attracted substantial clusters of Scottish migrants warranted special attention from the churches. The seasonal ebb and flow of evangelistic work among itinerant fisherfolk in East Anglia was joined from the 1930s by a more permanent presence in Corby, from where, in January 1934, the rector, A.B. Westcott, wrote to the minister of Bellshill to assure him that local Anglicans were 'anxious to do anything we can to soften the uprooting of your people'.[79] Meanwhile, Stewarts & Lloyds were not unmindful of their employees' spiritual needs, providing financial support for Presbyterian church extension.[80] 'The religious scramble for Corby' was how the Reverend L.A. Wide, the minister of Kettering Congregational Church, perceived the upsurge of church extension activity by Presbyterians, Congregationalists, Methodists and Catholics alike in 1934. Nine months earlier, Wide had stirred up a minor hornet's nest by his invitation to the Scottish Presbyterians to hold a service in his church. Some members of the recently formed Caledonian Society – and especially its chaplain – took offence because they had not been consulted and because the chaplain had not been asked to conduct the service. Before the end of the year, in an atmosphere of competition rather than collaboration, the Church of Scotland announced that it planned to build its own sanctuary and hall. Until that could be accomplished, services were conducted in a wooden hut by the Reverend Campbell Macleroy, who spent almost a year in the charge before returning to Scotland in June 1935.[81] A year later, when Scots on both sides of the border were urged to contribute to the new church building, the Corby congregation had 400 members, an increase which Macleroy's successor, A.D. Macdonald, attributed to the transferred steelworkers' desire to make 'a fresh start in their religious life'.[82]

At the opening of the new church hall in December 1935, the Moderator of the Church of Scotland, Dr Marshall Lang, urged his compatriots in Corby to 'retain their national characteristics amid a strange people'.[83] Many migrants did indeed develop a social life that was centred on the church – though not necessarily the Church of Scotland, for Catholics also migrated in significant numbers, and before the construction of a Catholic church and the creation of a new parish, mass was held in a Shanks and McEwan hut at the steelworks.[84]

The first Communion in St Andrew's Church of Scotland in Corby was celebrated using vessels loaned by Crown Court Church in London. Following the union of the Church of Scotland and the United Free Church in 1929, the three former English presbyteries had been combined into one Presbytery of England, and Crown Court – whose 17th-century roots made it the oldest Scottish Presbyterian church in London – developed a particular link with its young counterpart in Corby.

At one time there were at least 30 Scottish Presbyterian congregations in London. In recent decades, however, activity has revolved around the two city-centre establishments whose missions had spawned the other churches: Crown Court, located in Covent Garden since 1719, and St Columba's in Pont Street, Knightsbridge, formed in 1883 by the minister and most of the congregation of Crown Court. The breakaway was a consequence of geographical convenience rather than doctrinal dispute, and St Columba's gave financial aid to the older church until by the 1950s, with over 900 members, it was able to become self-supporting. Its minister from 1917 to 1962, Joseph Moffett, put Crown Court back on the map by promoting quarterly Gaelic services and an annual service for the Scottish Clans Association of London, as well as serving as Scottish chaplain to a number of Scottish institutions in London. Although the high turnover of worshippers was reflected in Moffett's comment that it was 'like preaching to a procession', his successors compensated for the lack of continuity by developing initiatives such as the kirking of Scottish peers and MPs at the beginning of each parliament.[85]

St Columba's Church, Pont Street, Knightsbridge, London (© Jim Blackwood)

In 1902 the new minister of St Columba's had nailed his colours firmly to the ethnic mast. In his first sermon, Archibald Fleming unambiguously declared that his church should be a centre of Scottish spiritual and cultural life, where anxious parents could take comfort from the knowledge that their migrant offspring could avail themselves of 'the friendship and warmth of a Scottish welcome' in a church whose form of worship would rekindle 'the tender and sacred associations of the home and the religion of their youth'. The ever-increasing Scottish population of London was, he reminded his listeners, 'equal to that of a great city. And our chief business is with them. We are not a Presbyterian Mission to Englishmen… We are neither Nonconformists nor Dissenters… We are exiled Scots, desiring to worship still under the banner of that grand old Church of our fathers, whose form of worship we love and whose traditions we are proud to inherit'.[86]

Fleming fostered St Columba's Scottish identity through a long-running parish magazine, affiliations with secular societies and an annual Scottish Festival service in November. During the First World War the church gave hospitality to over 20,000 Scottish soldiers each year as they passed through London on leave. Gaelic speakers were welcomed in their own language and inebriated servicemen were rescued from local pubs before they could be found and arrested by the military police. A hostel for Scotswomen who took up business and professional posts in London was sponsored by the church from 1920 to the 1970s, after which it was remodelled as a hostel for 35 homeless young Scots men. At the other end of the age spectrum, a substantial gift from a church member in the 1950s funded Lyle Park, a sheltered housing complex in Putney, which is administered by a St Columba's committee.[87]

As these examples demonstrate, there was a close association between ethnically based spiritual, charitable and social activities, an inter-relationship that was also displayed in the considerable overlap in the membership of Scottish churches, Burns' clubs, St Andrew's and Caledonian societies and Masonic lodges. In London, the most persistent relationship has probably been that between the Scottish churches and the Royal Scottish Corporation, a charity which traces its roots back to the union of the crowns, and which has helped more than a million Scots during the last four centuries. The Corporation's remit is to relieve hardship among those living within a 35-mile radius of Charing Cross who are Scots-born, of Scottish parentage, or widows of Scots-born spouses. During the inter-war period it was kept busy supplying temporary financial relief, food and clothing to destitute Scots who had come to London in the vain hope of finding work, as well as supporting several hundred pensioners. In 2002 it was worth £31.3 million, and its beneficiaries include students, the disabled, the elderly and the homeless, funding for the latter being channelled through Borderline.[88]

The Royal Scottish Corporation's Fetter Lane premises hosted the gatherings of numerous Scottish societies until the building was sold in 1972. By then it shared that role with the Caledonian Club, which had been founded in 1891 as an exclusive dining club 'where Scotsmen of good social position will find the traditions of their country encouraged and upheld'.[89] Also at the top of the league table, in terms of exclusiveness, influence and greater longevity, were the Highland Society of London and the Caledonian Society of London. The Highland Society, founded in 1788 and including men such as Sir John Sinclair and Henry Dundas among its early presidents, was an elite, men-only social club whose objective was to foster interest in Highland society and culture. The Caledonian Society, on the other hand, was founded in 1837 'to promote good fellowship and brotherhood' among Scots as a whole. Members had to swear allegiance to both the Royal Scottish Corporation and the Royal Caledonian Asylum, a school for the children of Scottish soldiers. The Caledonian Society therefore had philanthropic as well as social objectives, and in the 1890s – when it was providing most of the administrators for the Royal Scottish Corporation – it was described as 'the playground of the workers in the London-Scottish charities'.[90] Initially non-Scots were allowed to join its ranks, but by 1890 membership was confined to Scots and capped at 100. Seventy years later it was still a men-only, Scots-only club, whose members had to be 'prepared to contribute in cash and in kind, prepared to attend all meetings to the exclusion of all other social engagements; and... a credit to Scotland'.[91]

Scots probably had a more enthusiastic and wide-ranging commitment to associational culture than any other ethnic group in London. At the beginning of the 20th century the capital boasted 28 Scottish clubs with a total membership of between 4,000 and 5,000. Regulations – at least in the early years – usually required members to be of Scottish birth, or, more specifically, to be natives of the particular area to which the club was dedicated. By the beginning of the 20th century, the exchange of news and views among the diverse territorial, sporting, literary, debating, musical and charitable associations was being fostered by an ethnic newspaper, the *London Scotsman*. In its first incarnation, in 1888, it quickly withered, but it was relaunched in 1897 with less nostalgic sentimentality in content and a firmer financial foundation, thanks to the support of a number of the Scottish associations whose activities it publicised. A year later, it outlined a plan to offer better support to new migrants by creating a federation of all London's Scottish societies, which would operate an employment bureau, a register of lodgings, reading and recreation rooms and a debating society.[92]

Scottish associational culture was found in its most concentrated form in London, but it was not confined to the capital. An internet search for Scottish societies across England which produced 24 hits in March 2012 by no means represents the full picture, but equally, we should not forget that many migrants despised or ignored the sentimentality and celebratory ethnicity embodied in Scottish clubs. The list does, however, give a snapshot of geographically scattered clusters of Scots and their descendants, whose celebration of Scotland most commonly manifested itself in weekly Scottish country dancing classes and annual Burns' suppers.[93] Most Scottish organisations in England for which information could be found were established in the first half of the 20th century, though the Caledonian Society of Sheffield was created in 1822 by migrant doctors and steel workers. A Caledonian Association was established in Barrow-in-Furness in 1877, the town's St Andrew's Society a year later, and the Chesterfield and District Caledonian Association in 1886. While some organisations restricted membership to the Scots-born, their spouses and their children, others were open to all who enjoyed Scottish music, dancing, literature and sport. Over 270 people attended the inaugural meeting of the mid-Sussex Caledonian Society in Cuckfield in January 1926, when the local minister – and driving force behind the Society – justified its existence on the grounds that 'it was of the utmost importance' to the prosperity of Scotland, the United Kingdom and the empire 'that they of the North should continue to remind themselves of their history' and 'their ancestors' noble struggle for liberty'.[94] A number of societies came into being after enthusiasts canvassed support in the press and circulated fellow Scots in the area. Two societies which came into existence in that way were the Wolverhampton and District Caledonian Society and the Scottish Society of Jersey, each of which had 400 members in 1950 and 1978 respectively.

Northumbrian Scots celebrated their ethnicity through a variety of interlocking organisations. The Burns Clubs of Sunderland and Darlington were constituted in 1897 and 1906 respectively, though both ceased to exist in the late 20th century.[95] Heated debates about membership criteria pepper the pages of their minute books. Exclusive requirements that members be 'Scotchmen' were modified over the years to include, first, those of Scottish descent, and then admirers of Burns, whatever their nationality, although restrictions on female members continued.[96] Literary events were coupled with a commitment to offer financial assistance to destitute Scots nominated by members, but involvement with political issues such as home rule was generally avoided. The membership was mainly professional, unlike pipe bands, which tended to draw on a skilled working-class constituency and often relied on making money through public engagements.

Further down the east coast, however, where the Burns Club of Hull was allegedly 'composed mostly of English people', demand for a 'genuine Scottish Society', led to the creation of a separate organisation in 1910.[97]

Entry to the Scots' Society of St Andrew was initially restricted to Scotsmen or the sons of a Scottish parent, before women were admitted in 1917, members' spouses in 1974 and individuals of Scottish descent in 1979. Surviving minutes, correspondence and magazines, covering more than seven decades, reveal a relatively affluent membership, which grew from 92 at the Society's birth to 463 in the 1950s. Like its counterparts elsewhere, financial donations were made to other Scottish societies and charities, as well as to needy individuals, some of whom were repatriated from Hull to Scotland. In 1912 Hull's migrant female fish workers were invited to the Society's first 'Grand Scottish Concert' in the City Hall, while other social activities included annual excursions to Scotland in the 1920s and 1930s and joint events with other local ethnic clubs. The standard gatherings on 25 January and 30 November were not neglected, although by the 1980s the perceived lack of collaboration among the 20 Scottish societies across Yorkshire and Humberside led to complaints of 'insularity'.[98]

As well as establishing their own distinctive organisations and selling Lanarkshire newspapers in the heart of England, the Scots of Corby joined local institutions such as the Kettering Insurance Cooperative Society and the Women's Cooperative Guild.[99] Like the herring workers in East Anglia, they also established a reputation for workplace militancy. In the 1930s, the steelworks' management acknowledged that the transfer of the first wave of workers was not accomplished 'without a certain amount of difficulty'. This they attributed to the 'exorbitant claims' made by Glaswegian workers and their union representatives, who arrived with a 'fixed idea that their wage rates and earnings should be higher than in their former employment'.[100] Forty years later, another generation of Scottish migrants was prominent in the campaign to save the ailing steelworks, marching to London in a small-scale re-enactment of the Jarrow crusade.[101]

As in Northumbria, ethnic solidarity also operated at an elite level in Northamptonshire. In January 1934, the Burns' Supper of the recently formed Kettering and District Caledonian Society attracted 150 diners.[102] Word of the Society's existence soon led to many destitute new arrivals from Scotland making their way straight to the President's door to solicit relief from their more affluent countrymen. But unlike their counterparts in London, north-east England and many overseas locations, it was not a philanthropic organisation, and the pleas fell on deaf ears. Dr John Allison, the President, complained that some of the men 'had been so rude that the maids had been afraid to go to the door' and in March, the Society agreed that all such cases should be referred to the Public Assistance Institution rather than relieved from its own limited coffers.[103]

A year later, Ian Carmichael, the steel company's labour officer, spoke to the Caledonian Society about the long-term implications of the migration for both sides. The English, he predicted, who had a 'happier outlook and more of the *joie de vivre*', would teach the serious-minded, argumentative and inquiring Scots 'how to live', and he came to the somewhat questionable conclusion that 'the combination of the two elements should give a quality and distinction to the whole community'.[104] Carmichael also predicted that Corby's Scottish identity would be lost within three generations. In the early years it was undoubtedly dominant. When local girl Rita Bennington was promised a kilt as a child, she wanted one like her Scottish friends, as 'this made me feel I then belonged to Corby'. Another local girl was Paula Bolton, born in Corby in 1957 to parents who had migrated from Manchester. Having belonged to one of the only English families in a street of Scots, 'I got a shock when I went to York to study and found out that there was another England with no Scotch pies or Aberdeen bread in the shops'.[105]

For some Scots, however, 'Little Scotland' was no substitute for the real thing. A handful of serial migrants moved back and forth between Scotland and Northamptonshire, while others holidayed in Scotland every year. Although Ann Dean was less than two years old when her family moved from Kirkfieldbank in Lanarkshire to Corby in 1951, she and her sisters maintained the tradition, established by their parents, of making an annual pilgrimage to their home village, and despite a lifetime in Northamptonshire, she remained insistent that she was 'definitely Scottish... I'm seeped (sic) in England, but I don't feel I'd rest here'.[106]

By the early 21st century, as Ian Carmichael had anticipated, Corby's Scottish identity could no longer be taken for granted. When the town's Highland Gathering (first held in 1969) was jeopardised by council cutbacks in 2002, appeals for corporate sponsorship were harnessed to a sense of outrage that Scottish traditions were under attack. 'Corby is a Scottish town,' declared Mark Pengelly, a Labour councillor with a Cornish name. 'What we also want to do in future years is celebrate the other cultures. But people came from Glasgow, Aberdeen and other places to build Corby and we have to celebrate the Scottish things that go on.'[107] A local radio programme in 2005 provided further evidence that Corby's Scottishness was fading in the face of a broader-based influx and the English accents of third-generation Scots. Graham Martindale was born in Corby in 1944 to a father and mother who had been brought up in Peebles and Lanarkshire respectively. Interviewed about attitudes to language, he argued that while it was 'still a very Scottish town' with a clear residual west of Scotland dialect, memories of the birth and development of 'Little Scotland' were heading for extinction. 'When I was a boy, I mean, every person, we could say 90 per cent, were definitely Scottish, but not any more', he reflected, predicting that future generations would learn about Corby's Scottish heritage only from books, rather than from personal testimony.[108]

Integration and Antagonism

Associational culture helped many expatriate Scots to develop multiple or hybrid identities, maintaining their distinctiveness while simultaneously integrating into their new localities through the formation of overlapping professional, political, social and religious networks. But while most migrants slipped effortlessly into the rhythms of English life and work, Anglo-Scottish relations were not entirely harmonious. From time to time, the Scot-bashing that had characterised the mid-18th century re-emerged in outbursts of resentment or ridicule. Scots migrants tended to react to such criticism and to the cultural gulf between north and south by cultivating an overt pride and communal complacency in 'Not Being English'.[109]

English hostility was demonstrated in recurring depictions of migrant Scots as a plundering army that was hell-bent on taking English jobs, filling its sporrans with English wealth and infiltrating English society at all levels. Other stereotypes portrayed them as hypocritically pious misers, pedantic bureaucrats, militant agitators, violent drunkards or potential traitors who demanded English favours at the same time as they threatened to break the bond of union. A high self-regard, coupled with a clannish mutual support network that was described in 1844 as a tendency to 'herd lovingly together',[110] allegedly helped them to fulfil their ambitions, and generated cries of cronyism.

We have already caught occasional glimpses of anti-Scottish sentiment in the reaction to the fishworkers' strike in East Anglia in 1936, the resentment stirred up by the industrial transference scheme, the controversy surrounding the development of Corby, and the lampooning of Scottish politicians at Westminster. Corby, despite the optimistic predictions of men like A.A. Dick and Ian Carmichael, was far from being an idyllic Caledonian island in the middle of Northamptonshire. Factory workers in nearby Kettering resented the higher wages paid to skilled steel men in the 1930s, and there was general disquiet at the area being 'flooded with Irishmen and Scotsmen', who, it was alleged, drank heavily, disturbed the peace and obstructed the police.[111] On at least one occasion the Rector of Corby ap-

pealed from his pulpit for a greater generosity of spirit to replace the preva-
lent 'suspicion and jealousy' and the 'murmurings against the newcomers'.[112] Destitution and hunger played a part in the crimes of some of those
who found themselves in court, particularly in the pioneering years,[113] but
the Scots never really shook off their reputation for rowdiness, pugilism
and sectarianism, and in the late 1970s they became easy scapegoats for the
social disintegration that accompanied the collapse of the local economy.

Scottish offence at perceived slights sometimes surfaced in newspaper
correspondence. Issues of dress could ignite indignation and when the
Tyneside Scottish Brigade was raised in 1914 (albeit with only a minority
of Scots in its ranks) the War Office's refusal to sanction the wearing of
the kilt provoked a flurry of indignant letters to the local press. 'Only a
Scotsman knows the feeling of national pride awakened by the sight of the
kilt', wrote a 'Tyneside Scot', who was also convinced that 'the adoption
of so distinguishing a dress would bring in a better class of recruit'. His
outrage was echoed by 'A Dumfries lad', who doubted that 'men in mere
trousers' could match the 'brilliant exploits of Scotia's sons in national
garb'.[114] Scots also tended to be more critical of their countrymen who had
taken the road to England than of those who had gone further afield, an
ambivalence that went back to the 17th century.

It was in London that anti-Scottish sentiment was most overtly and
scathingly articulated. The opening salvo was fired in 1902, when the poet
and humorist T.W.H. Crosland intoned against clannish Scots who he
claimed were taking over the literary, journalistic and political establishment of London. England, he declared, was 'a Scot-ridden country' with
a 'rooted dislike' of the 'bumptiousness and uncouthness' of those of its
northern neighbours who had migrated south. 'Out of Scotchmen you can
get nothing businesslike and nothing dignified', he maintained. 'Their ambitions are illimitable, but their powers of execution not worth counting'.[115]

It got worse. The closing chapter of the book contained a scathing
summary of Scots' character defects.

> The Scot, in fact, never soars above mediocrity; he never has an
> inspiration or a happy thought; he cannot rise to occasions, and while
> he is most punctual in his addiction to duty and most assiduous and
> steadfast as a labourer, his work is never perfectly done, and too
> frequently it is scamped and carried out without regard to finish or
> excellence. Of pride or delight in labour the Scotchman knows nothing.
> He works in order that he may get money and serve his own personal
> advancement.
>
> I believe that throughout England there is a very strong anti-Scotch
> feeling. I have found it difficult to meet an Englishman who, if you

questioned him straightly, would not admit that he has a rooted dislike for Scotchmen. That dislike the Scotchman has himself aroused. His bumptiousness and uncouthness, his lack of manners, his lack of principle, and his want of decent feeling, have brought and will continue to bring their own reward.[116]

The final sting in the tail was delivered in the last of ten recommendations offered by Crosland to young Scots who wished to succeed in England. After reminding them to remember they were foreigners, speak the King's English, avoid dourness and moralising, refrain from extolling the virtues of thrift and forget the Battle of Bannockburn, he concluded – in capital letters, for extra emphasis: 'IF WITHOUT SERIOUS INCONVENIENCE TO YOURSELF YOU CAN MANAGE TO REMAIN AT HOME, PLEASE DO'.[117]

Crosland was a minor literary figure who was responding to his publisher's request to write a bestseller and his own need to make some money. His tongue was probably firmly in his cheek, and he soon penned two counterblasts: *The Unspeakable Crosland,* which was published anonymously, and *The Egregious English,* which he published under the pseudonym of Angus McNeill.[118] His Scotophobia was provoked partly by a parliament where all three major parties were led by Scots: the Liberal League by Lord Rosebery, the Liberal Party by Henry Campbell-Bannerman, and the Tory Party by Arthur Balfour. It was a record that would be replayed with greater vitriol almost a century later, in claims that New Labour's electoral victory in 1997 had infested Westminster's corridors of power with Scottish accents and influences. When H.R. Boyne, political correspondent of the *Daily Telegraph,* had addressed the Royal Corporation of London in 1961, he spoke warmly of the number of Scots in the government, and urged his hosts to encourage young Scots to become involved in politics. There was, he said, 'no better or quicker way of advancing Scotland's interests than getting the best of her men and women, irrespective of party, to represent her in Parliament'.[119]

Perhaps Boyne's advice was heeded more enthusiastically than he or his newspaper might have wished, as by the 1990s, the high profile of Scottish politicians in the Mother of Parliaments had sparked off a swelling wave of media criticism, especially in the right-wing press. In the words of Edward Heathcote-Amery, the 'tiny incestuous world' of the Scottish elite, who 'belong to the same clubs, drink in the same bars, compete for the same jobs, and run off with each other's wives' had come to London.[120]

The confrontational approach was also maintained by journalists such as the BBC's Jeremy Paxman, who referred to a 'Scottish Raj' of politicians and broadcasters and the *Daily Mail's* Geoffrey Wheatcroft, who described Scottish politicians as 'unusually corrupt, drunken, and worthless'.[121] Simon Heffer, Wheatcroft's fellow columnist at the *Mail*, also suggested that the Scots had brought to Westminster a 'culture of corruption and low moral standards' and bewailed the large sums of money that were sent north 'to keep the Scots in the style to which they have become accustomed'.[122] In 2005 Boris Johnson – then a member of the shadow cabinet – claimed that Scotland was 'full of rotten boroughs' and argued that Gordon Brown should not become prime minister 'mainly because he is a Scot and government by a Scot is not conceivable in the present constitutional context'.[123] From a very different point on the political spectrum, Ken Livingstone, whom Johnston unseated as mayor of London in 2008, introduced an element of Scotophobia into his 1999 election campaign when he said that it was wrong 'that Londoners should pay through their taxes to support a level of services in Scotland that the Scottish Chancellor then refuses Londoners the right to have themselves'.[124]

Scottish devolution was the issue that lit the fuse, creating confusion about identity south of the border that soon developed into a new and aggressive sense of English nationalism. In 1917 Ian Hay had complained that English modesty and reserve had allowed 'aggressively patriotic' Scots (among others) to claim the credit for imperial achievements, bringing about a situation in which the armed forces, judiciary and government were dominated 'by Scotsmen of the most ruthless type'.[125] Eighty years later, criticism focused on the increased political power of the Scots who maintained a persistently high profile at Westminster even after they had their own parliament. Although Scottish MPs had held English seats since the 18th century, their arrival in the House of Commons in unprecedented numbers in 1997 was contrasted with the lack of English MPs representing Scottish constituencies. This situation raised the temperature of debate about the inequities of the Barnett formula (a mechanism for adjusting public expenditure on the basis of population levels which gives Scotland a bigger *per capita* allocation than England)[126] and, more particularly, the West Lothian Question, which was first raised in 1977 by Tam Dalyell, MP for that constituency. It was wrong, Dalyell argued, that in the event of devolution, Scottish MPs at Westminster would be able to vote on matters affecting England, but not on such matters affecting their own constituencies, since those issues would have been devolved to a Scottish parliament. Since devolution, the argument has shifted to the unfairness of Scottish MPs continuing to vote on English matters while Westminster politicians cannot influence Scottish affairs which have been devolved to the parliament in Edinburgh.

Comparative Perspectives

Cross-border traffic did not travel on a one-way street, even though it flowed most heavily and consistently down the southward lane. Quite apart from homebound Scots-born, the 1911 census enumerated 165,102 natives of England and Wales resident in Scotland, mainly in the Lothians and the counties of Lanark, Renfrew, Ayr, Fife, Angus and Aberdeen. By 1931 the percentage figure was the same (3.5) but the actual number had risen slightly. By 1971 there were 279,340 English- and Welsh-born in Scotland (5.3 per cent of the population), by 1991 354,268 (7 per cent) and by 2001 425,571 (8.4 per cent). In the 1990s 48,000 migrants came to Scotland from the rest of the UK and 29,000 from overseas.[127]

From fishing to steel-making, the occupations that took Scots to England sometimes brought a smattering of their English counterparts north, many of them in a managerial capacity, while conscription, especially 1939–45, increased contact on both sides of the border. Southern influences therefore filtered into Scotland with English migrants, sojourners and service personnel as well as with returning Scots. The 1921 religious revival, which had a particularly powerful impact on Aberdeenshire, began in Yarmouth during the autumn fishing season and was brought back to Scotland with the returning boats.[128] Half a century later, the offshore industry that turned Aberdeen into the oil capital of Europe brought not only ten-gallon hats and Texan accents, but also an influx from south of the border, that reached well beyond the north-east corner.

On the whole the English were invisible migrants who blended seamlessly into Scottish society. But sometimes the seams came apart. Scottish xenophobia has been targeted most infamously on Irish immigrants, especially in the 1920s, but, as we shall see in Chapter 5, the splenetic net was sometimes cast more widely.[129] By the early 1990s Anglophobia was rooted in a potent mix of political, economic and cultural resentment. The Conservative government presided over a country which had not voted for it, incomers were blamed for inflated house prices, a few high profile jobs went to 'confident southerners', and one Free Presbyterian minister in Skye intoned against English 'hedonists' who ignored the Sabbath and filled the island's airwaves with 'their lah-de-dah voices'.[130] Movements such as Settler Watch in the north-east and Scottish Watch in the south-west achieved brief notoriety through their efforts to portray English migrants as culturally insensitive colonisers who should be encouraged to pack their bags and go.[131]

For much of the 20th century, English and Irish migrants to Scotland took central roles on the ethnic stage, with walk-on parts being played by Lithuanian miners, Newfoundland and British Honduran lumberjacks, Polish servicemen, Asian and Italian shopkeepers and a miscellany of overseas students. Only a handful of the New Commonwealth immigrants who flocked to Britain after 1945 came to Scotland, which they perceived as an area of high unemployment and low opportunity. Even in 2001 – by which time the immigrant profile was being reshaped by asylum seekers, along with economic migrants from the expanded European Union – 25 per cent of overseas migrants entering Scotland were Scots-born returners, including 40 per cent of those who arrived from Australia.[132] As we now turn our spotlight on the overseas diaspora, these statistics remind us that the migratory process is – as it always was – a dynamic, multi-faceted and multi-directional phenomenon that defies static or simplistic definition.

CHAPTER 2

Legacies of War and New Dawns

FROM WINDSWEPT OUTER HEBRIDEAN promontories to manicured munici-pal gardens, memorials across the length and breadth of Scotland bear silent witness to the carnage of the First World War. At the same time, their inscriptions are a visible reminder of the remarkable number of young Scots who returned from Canada, New Zealand, Australia and South Af-rica to serve – and die – in imperial regiments. With the passing of these returners there also passed the golden age of emigration, the long 19th century of demographic upheaval that had seen 22 million people from the British Isles – including two million Scots – carve out new lives in the brave new worlds of the Americas and the Antipodes, before their confidence collapsed in the face of global conflict.

The Great War, every schoolchild learns, shook Britain's economic and political foundations and ushered in new social and cultural identities. Less acknowledged is the watershed it created in the history of emigra-tion, from the perspective of both participants and promoters. There was a clear change of gear, as uncertainty about the future replaced assurance in the durability of empire, and the scaled-down exodus of the 1920s was characterised by a mixture of war-weary disillusionment and the hope of a new dawn under kinder foreign skies. The government's unprecedented commitment to the sponsorship of emigration through the Empire Settle-ment Act was a rearguard attempt to strengthen the faltering imperial re-lationship, but one which failed to meet expectations on all sides, and by 1930 the icy blast of international depression had brought the movement to a virtual standstill.

In Scotland, the change of gear took the form of an unprecedented demographic crisis that saw the population decline by 0.8 per cent in the 1920s, despite a natural increase of 7.2 per cent. Almost 83 per cent of the 447,000 departures were for overseas destinations, peaking in 1923 as 88,584 passengers embarked, many of them rushing to beat the imposition of stricter American quotas. Throughout the decade, two-thirds of British emigrants came from Scotland, where the net loss was 80 per 1,000,

53

Canadian Pavilion at the British Empire Exhibition, Wembley, 1924–25
(Library and Archives Canada, C-145707)

compared with 5 per 1,000 from England and Wales.

Echoing trends within the British Isles as a whole, Canada was the most popular of the four main overseas destinations recorded in the statistics, featuring prominently in the Wembley Exhibition of 1924–5. It accounted for almost 39 per cent of Scotland's 417,905 emigrants to those locations, closely followed by the United States, with almost 38 per cent, while Australia and New Zealand took 15 per cent and South Africa 3 per cent. In the 1930s the pattern was reversed, when 33,595 Scottish emigrants were eclipsed by an influx of 76,869 between 1931 and 1938. Canada once again led the way, with over 30 per cent of the inward movement, followed by the United States (28 per cent) and the Antipodes (10.8 per cent). Only in South Africa did the balance remain unchanged, although the margin was very small, with 930 more emigrants than immigrants.[1]

Catalysts and Mechanisms

We shall see in Chapter 5 that these demographic convulsions did not pass unnoticed or uncontested. If empire settlement was embraced in Whitehall and in certain political and press circles, there was also a wide spectrum of political and public opinion that lamented the loss of brain and sinew.

Meanwhile, the real people embedded in the statistics and debates were rarely concerned with the politics and philosophies that underlay emigration. Individuals and families sought, as they had always done, to escape hardship and pursue opportunity, capitalising on specific assistance schemes or job offers if they complemented their personal circumstances. In the 1920s emigrants' decisions were also infused with the legacy of total war: the despair engendered by fractured lives, decimated communities and widespread unemployment, alongside the hope inspired by the prospect of new starts and reconfigured identities.

Nowhere were those sentiments more dramatically displayed than in the Outer Hebrides. On the evening of 31 December 1918, the 900-ton steam yacht *Iolaire*, owned by a Clyde shipping magnate but commandeered by the government for war duties, left Kyle of Lochalsh with 284 crew and passengers, most of them servicemen on the last leg of their journey home to Lewis and Harris. At 1.55am on New Year's Day, the wooden boat foundered on the Beasts of Holm, a reef of rocks just outside Stornoway. Within sight of the port's lights and only 50 yards from shore, 205 men drowned, including 175 natives of Lewis.[2] The poignancy of their deaths, on top of the 1,000 islanders who had perished in the war, plunged the Hebrides into deep gloom, as well as into a demographic crisis which was compounded by a remarkable resurgence of emigration in the early 1920s.

That haemorrhage was all the more striking because it seemed to contradict the long-standing and implacable Hebridean opposition to emigration. The memories and folklore of a century of clearance and enforced expatriation were reinforced by a more recent history of land raiding, which flared up again in 1922–23, as war veterans lost patience with the failure of Lloyd George's promise to provide 'homes fit for heroes', and simply took possession of the crofts they claimed. It seemed unlikely that such barren soil would produce a crop of voluntary – and apparently enthusiastic – emigrants. That it did was a measure of both the desperation and the widening horizons of those involved.

Economic conditions in the Outer Hebrides and adjacent mainland after the war showed an alarming similarity to the famine years of the 1840s. Agriculture was in turmoil, with low livestock prices after wartime protection was removed. Fuel was also in short supply, and fishing was in deep crisis as a result of poor catches and the loss of the German and Russian markets for herring. In 1923 penniless deckhands had difficulty paying their fares back to Lewis after the east coast fishing season, at the same time as the once-prosperous line fishing around the island was 'completely ruined by the depredations of trawlers'.[3] Potato blight and a wet summer which prevented the harvesting of hay and peats, led to the establishment of local distress committees before the year was over, to relieve a situation in which many children were allegedly 'starving for want of food', while some unemployed Lewismen found temporary work on the job creation scheme of the island's owner, Lord Leverhulme, building a road between Tolsta and Ness.[4]

The revival of emigration was partly the familiar, negative response of an embattled and embittered people to the perennial problems of living on the margins. But the emigrants of the 1920s were also influenced, to a much greater extent than their predecessors, by a conviction that acceptable, even exciting, opportunities were on offer overseas. After the war, a number of external factors coalesced to present emigration as a stepping stone to advancement, rather than a punishment. Ex-servicemen who had experienced life beyond the Hebrides were able to compare their subsistence struggles with living standards in other parts of Britain and the empire. That awareness was reinforced among other islanders by contacts with a growing number of tourists and by the window opened on the world by the wireless. Paradoxically, as crofters and cottars began to achieve the tenurial security and redistribution of land so long denied them, they became more and more aware of the insurmountable physical limitations and health hazards of their environment. Tuberculosis had reached almost epidemic proportions in the Hebrides, where its record was worse than in some of the most overcrowded Glasgow slums. Emigration seemed to offer better physical, as well as economic, guarantees, at the same time as crofting legislation and state pensions promised a measure of security to elderly parents, releasing their children to seek better opportunities elsewhere, free from the enervating spectres of guilt and financial responsibility.

More important still were the specific incentives to emigrate contained in glowing letters, persuasive propaganda and attractive job advertisements. Charismatic agents were commonly the key to translating a vague restlessness into decisive action, but not all were professional recruiters peddling imperial colonisation schemes. Most notably on the sheep farms of the Falkland Islands and Patagonia, where there had been a strong Highland presence since the mid-19th century, recruitment was maintained through private commercial incentives and word-of-mouth encouragement by homecoming sojourners and amateur propagandists. Particularly active among the latter was Donald MacCallum, a Church of Scotland minister in Lewis, who persuaded over 100 shepherds from the island to go to Patagonia to work on the large *estancias* whose interests he represented for almost half a century before and after the war.[5]

Much larger numbers of emigrants were attracted by the recruitment campaigns of professional agents representing imperial destinations. From May 1922 they were able to gild their encouragement with the offer of sponsorship under the Empire Settlement Act, although the *Stornoway Gazette* claimed that debt-shy Highlanders shunned the scheme for fear it had hidden financial strings attached.[6] On the other hand, empire settlement funding offered a viable option – often the only option – for many impoverished crofters and cottars, and since it applied to the whole country, Highlanders now had no reason to feel stigmatised because they were being singled out for patronising charity.

The novelty of an illustrated lecture always attracted a crowd and agents found it worthwhile to make regular recruitment trips to the Highlands. William Stillman, chief clerk at the Australian Government's Migration and Settlement Office in London, made the long journey to Lewis on at least four occasions in 1923 and 1924, liaising with the Stornoway booking agent (and local poor law inspector), Murdo Maclean, to persuade several 'splendid families' to go to Western Australia under a funded group settlement scheme, and a contingent of young single men and women to emigrate to Victoria.[7] Angus Macdonald from North Uist recalled in 1987 how he had been lured to New South Wales almost 60 years earlier by a combination of the Australia House agent's visit to Lochmaddy, the advance of his £33 fare, and the encouragement of his father, who had spent time in Australia and believed that it was 'an up and coming country... the place of the future'.[8] Gilbert Halcrow saw Australia in a similar light. After demobilisation from the Royal Navy in 1919 he had embarked on a successful fruit-farming career in Glenorie, New South Wales, where within less than four years he had quadrupled the value of his property. As honorary secretary of the Orkney and Shetland Society of Australia, he wholeheartedly endorsed its objective of 'promoting the settlement of his countrymen on the land in Australia'. His avid recruitment (which had brought 16 people to his property at Glenrorie) encompassed his own family: by 1924 he had nominated two brothers, a sister-in-law, sister, mother and an acquaintance to join him from locations in Scotland and New York.[9]

For many Highlanders, however, Australia was an intermittent sideshow compared to Canada, where the special relationship that had characterised the 19th-century exodus persisted into the 1920s. After Confederation, the Canadian immigration authorities, keen to maintain and increase the transatlantic traffic, invested more time and effort than any other destination in promoting the dominion, and sending visiting lecturers throughout the country, including to the remotest corners of the Highlands. Operating initially out of Glasgow, the location of Canada's first Scottish emigration office, they were subsequently based in Aberdeen where a second office was opened in 1907 to cope with the increasing demand from the north, and in 1923 the ongoing expansion of the Highland work persuaded the Canadian government to open a third regional office in Inverness. Travelling agents reflected and stimulated enthusiasm for Canada. In 1911, the Gaelic-speaking Ontarian Hugh McKerracher was given a rapturous welcome when he took his horse-drawn exhibition wagon to Carloway in Lewis. Basing himself at the school, where extra seating had to be brought in to accommodate the crowd, he delivered an illustrated lecture, speaking first in Gaelic and then in English, 'forcefully and eloquently describing [Canada] as an unrivalled field for emigration, a country of vast extent and inexhaustible resources and of great potentialities for the future'.[10] By 1923 the Aberdeen agent, D.J. Murphy, had upgraded to a motor car and local chauffeur for his lecture tour of Skye in the hostile month of January. Contending with gales, mists and mountainous roads', and (at Uig) 'one of those abominations called Inns', his nine lectures all drew large audiences, including 147 at Colbost, and many of his hearers 'had ancestors who had helped to develop Canada'.[11] Murphy's policy of using Hebridean schools as temporary office accommodation also made him painfully aware of the region's endemic poverty, and at the end of the year his office sent three large boxes of clothing, along with a consignment of confectionary and books, to all the locations he had recently visited. 'I think,' he wrote to his boss in London, 'propaganda of this kind will reach further and be longer remembered than almost any other method I can think of,' and it had been undertaken, he stressed, at 'no expense to the Government'.[12]

Many of the 595 emigrants who on 15 and 21 April took their leave of the Hebrides from the decks of the Canadian Pacific liners *Marloch* and *Metagama* were simultaneously fleeing poverty and seeking the opportunities held out by agents. Survivors of the *Iolaire* sought to lay the ghosts of their drowned shipmates by putting the broad Atlantic between them and their daily encounters with the widows, children and parents of those who had not survived. Since steam had eclipsed sail in the 1860s, emigrant vessels had not been seen at Hebridean quaysides, and passengers from all over Scotland had to make their way south to Glasgow or Liverpool. The Canadian Pacific Company's decision to call in at the Long Island was a recognition both of the financial strain that an initial journey to the Clyde would impose on the islanders, and a response to the remarkable demand for passages from the Western Isles.

The *Metagama* leaves Stornoway, April 1923
(Glenbow Alberta Archives NZ 3315)

The mixed sentiments of the emigrants are encapsulated in the poetry of An t-Urr. Iain MacLeòid (Rev. John MacLeod, 1918–95). A native of Arnol, whose father drowned on the *Iolaire*, he later spent 13 years (1947–60) in Ontario and Alberta as a Presbyterian minister, while also collecting two postgraduate degrees from the universities of Montreal and Calgary. He was already familiar with Canada, an aunt having returned thence to Arnol to take care of Iain and his brother after their mother's death, while his brother Norman went on to spend his adult life in Canada. The following extract from 'Bàs Baile' ('The Death of a Township)' turns a poignant spotlight on the legacies of war and depression.

> Mo ghràdh-sa-òigridh ar là
> 'nam fiasaig dhùint' bho chluais gu cluais.
> Mun d'ràinig na balaich againn aois fiasaig
> no aois smaoineachaidh
> dh'éigh iad Cogadh
> is chaidh am marbhadh anns an Fhraing.
> Bha 'm murt ud laghail.
> A' chuid dhiubh a thàrr ás,

fhuair an fhairge iad a' tilleadh dhachaigh
agus dh'fhàg i na cuirp air an tràigh
's b'e marbh-phaisg fhuar an fheamainn.

A'chuid a thill leòinte 's beò,
cha robh gam feitheamh ach geallaidhean briste –
bàtaichean is lìn a' breothadh,
iasg gu leòr sa chuan gun comas thoirt ás.
Bhuain iad mòine, chuir iad buntàta
is chaidh le crodh gu àirigh
is dh'fhàs cnàmhan briste làidir.

Cur seachad oidhche gheamhraidh
chaidh na balaich chun an taigh-sgoile
a dh'fhaicinn dealbhan mu Chanada
le 'magic lantern'. Dé 'n cron a bh' ann?
Is chunnaic iad crodh am feur gu'n cluasan,
caileag bhòidheach 's a h-uchd air geat
le fiamh a' ghàir' is sràbh 'na bial,
is chaid iad chachaigh 'g ràdh, Tha sinne falbh.
Thuirt a' chlann-nighean, Thà is sinne.

How I love the modern youngsters
enclosed in beards from ear to ear.
Before our lads reached beard-growing age
or were old enough to think
War was declared
and they were killed in France.
That murder was lawful.

Those of them who survived,
the sea got them on their way home
and left the bodies on the beach
and the seaweed was a cold shroud.

Those who returned wounded and alive,
nothing awaited them but broken promises –
boats and nets rotting,
fish aplenty in the sea without the means to take it out.
They cut peats, planted potatoes

and went with cattle to shieling
and broken bones grew strong.

By way of passing a winter's night
the lads went to the schoolhouse
to see pictures about Canada
with a 'magic lantern'. What was the harm?
And they saw cows up to their ears in grass,
a lovely girl leaning on a gate
smiling with a straw in her mouth,
and they went home saying, We're off.
The girls said, So are we.[13]

The *Marloch*'s passengers, mostly family groups, were recruited by Andrew MacDonell, a one-time Benedictine priest and alumnus of Fort Augustus Abbey, who in 1912 had begun to cultivate a new career as an emigration agent for Canada, bringing British orphans to a training farm on Vancouver Island. After distinguished war service, during which he won the Military Cross, he returned to Canada, where he expanded his recruitment work from war orphans to ex-servicemen. In 1921 he came home to select 150 Highland veterans under Canada's Soldier Settlement Scheme, and in 1922 he formed the Scottish Immigrant Aid Society in order to take advantage of funding under the Empire Settlement Act. Donald MacIntyre, the priest at Castlebay in Barra, was appointed as Assistant Managing Director of his charity, and in autumn 1922 MacIntyre led a four-man delegation to the prairies to identify a site for a proposed Hebridean colony. Once the decision had been made to locate the settlement at Red Deer, near Edmonton in northern Alberta, MacIntyre returned to the Hebrides to orchestrate recruitment, while MacDonell remained in Canada to supervise nomination and settlement. When the *Marloch* slipped anchor off Lochboisdale on 15 April, the first-class passengers included MacIntyre and two fellow priests, who offered 'encouragement and guidance' to the 280 emigrants from Barra, South Uist and Benbecula, as they turned their backs on what one newspaper described as their 'bleak island homes' and 'bare, drab existence' in anticipation of new lives as prairie pioneers.[14]

Although Andrew MacDonell always insisted that his vision was non-sectarian, his objective was clearly to create a Catholic colony in Canada. During his recruitment trip in summer 1921 he had targeted the traditional belt of Catholicism in the Highlands, running westwards from Tomintoul, through Stratherrick and Glengarry, to Glenfinnan and Knoydart, and out

to the southern tip of the Long Island. His campaign was endorsed by the
Canadian government's Aberdeen-based agent, D.J. Murphy, who was a
fellow Catholic, and – at least initially – by the Catholic hierarchy in both
Scotland and Alberta. Directors of the Scottish Immigrant Aid Society included Lord Lovat, another influential co-religionist and keen supporter
of empire settlement, whose vast Highland estates included MacDonell's
early stamping ground around Fort Augustus, and J.S. Dennis, Chief Commissioner of the Canadian Pacific Railway's Department of Colonisation
and Development. Within a year of the *Marloch*'s first visit to Lochboisdale, she was back at the quayside to collect a further 198 islanders who
had been persuaded to emigrate by a combination of ongoing hardships,
encouragement from some of the 1923 pioneers, and the assurances of
MacDonell and his associates. The net was then cast more widely, and
when at the end of July the *Marburn* sailed from Glasgow with an even
larger contingent of Hebrideans, the Scottish Immigrant Aid Society's recruits also numbered 250 impoverished Catholics from northern Ireland,
and a handful from Scotland's Central Belt. Those urban Catholics may
have been pushed into leaving by sectarian strife, as well as by the poverty
and ambition that motivated their Highland counterparts.

Six days after the *Marloch* left Lochboisdale with its first consignment
of Hebridean Catholic families for Alberta, the *Metagama* left Stornoway
with 315 Presbyterians from the northern Hebrides, most of them young,
single men and women, all but 55 of whom came from Lewis. The *Press
and Journal*'s allegation that the quayside scenes were 'gloomy and artificial' compared to the farewelling of the *Marloch,* was out of step with the
sentiments of the *Glasgow Herald* and the *Highland News*. The *Herald*'s
reporter described the young passengers as 'pulsating with hope, perfervid
in enthusiasms… setting out with confidence to conquer worlds' while for
the *Highland News,* the sailing was 'not a tragic happening, but… the first
glimmer of the dawn of better things'.[15]

The *Metagama*'s Hebridean contingent had been recruited by William
Noxon, Ontario's Agent-General, with the offer of a 75 per cent passage
loan and a year's farm work in southern Ontario. Successful labourers
would then be offered farms on uncolonised soldier settlement blocks
further north, near Sudbury. In canvassing the islanders, Noxon worked in
tandem with another provincial agent, Major Goodliff, who gave several
lectures in and around Stornoway in the early weeks of 1923 and then
sailed with the emigrants on the *Metagama*. The agents had been ordered
to intensify their efforts among farmers in the hope of counteracting the
anticipated disappearance of many of Ontario's rural workers to better-

WE'RE SAILING WEST. WE'RE SAILING WEST.
TO PRAIRIE LANDS SUNKISSED AND BLEST—
THE CROFTER'S TRAIL TO HAPPINESS.

Scottish emigrants to Canada, 1920s
(CP Archives, NS8454)

paid jobs in American car factories across the Great Lakes. The scheme also had the blessing of the Scottish Office and Board of Agriculture for Scotland, which hoped that it would prevent a fresh epidemic of land raids by diverting impatient applicants for domestic land settlement into an overseas alternative.[16]

Many of the *Metagama*'s passengers were also encouraged by relatives in Canada, and the 1923 emigrants in turn sent remittances to siblings who had been left at home. During 1924, the Ontario agents successfully consolidated and extended recruitment, with 290 passengers leaving from Stornoway in April, and a further 270 in May.[17] The Highland mainland was also enthusiastically canvassed throughout the 1920s, thanks not least to Anne Macdonald, the Canadian government's Inverness-based agent for nine years. From time to time she complained about obstacles to her work, partly in the shape of the maverick Andrew MacDonell, whose alleged mismanagement of his colonisation schemes was, she claimed, damaging Canada's reputation among potential emigrants. She also lambasted her own employers for parsimony and lack of vision, particularly in the provision of women's literature.

During one lecture tour in Caithness, having driven and walked nine miles across an inaccessible moor near Bilbster to interview a family of would-be emigrants, she had plied the crofter with pamphlets, but had been unable to give his anxious wife anything more than verbal reassurance. Such neglect, she complained, 'is apt to convey the impression that the women's side is not treated with great importance'.[18]

Anne Macdonald herself came under fire from within the ranks of the Canadian agency hierarchy and some booking agents, on the grounds that since she was neither a man nor a Canadian resident, she lacked credibility and was likely to lose valuable business.[19] Throughout the 1920s, recruiters representing a variety of countries and companies competed with each other across the whole of Scotland, wooing not only prospective emigrants, but also the booking agents, whose priority was to maximise their commissions, rather than to promote any particular destination. The farming and fishing crisis that affected the Hebrides so acutely was also causing dislocation in the rural and coastal Lowlands, and agents expended most of their efforts in relentlessly canvassing the rural communities that they hoped would supply eligible candidates for the land schemes conceived under the Empire Settlement Act, or for the Canadian railway companies' vast prairie territories.

Depopulation of the Scottish countryside was nothing new in the 1920s. Victorian commentators had frequently beaten their breasts about the way in which commercialised agricultural practices – in particular the consolidation of farms and swingeing rent increases – had driven a steady stream of stalwart farmers and labourers into urban centres, across the border to England, or overseas. By the 1920s the key catalyst was recession, as farmers, many of whom had recently become owner-occupiers, were exposed to the full blast of foreign competition following the removal of wartime controls. Living and working conditions for farm servants, much criticised in the 19th century, also remained a sore point, and a higher proportion of the farm labour force allegedly emigrated in 1924–26 than from any other occupation.[20]

The farming community was kept abreast of overseas opportunities and the wider debate through advertisements and editorials in the general and agricultural press. The socialist *Scottish Farm Servant,* the monthly mouthpiece of the Scottish Farm Servants' Union, was particularly critical of misleading promises made to a downcast and downtrodden workforce, while the Scottish National Farmers Union complained about the way in which agents spirited away the best labourers, often by making unsolicited visits to farms. But their magazine, the *Scottish Farmer*, was more upbeat in encouraging its own constituency to consider overseas openings, particularly in Canada, while provincial newspapers regularly advertised land settlement ventures across the dominions.

These were mostly collaborative schemes funded under the Empire Settlement Act. There were very few openings in South Africa, which was set apart from the other dominions by its elitist immigration policy and insistence that the settlers should possess substantial assets. It attracted under one per cent of subsidised settlers. New Zealand accounted for almost 11 per cent, mainly domestics and rural labourers, but was inhibited by economic problems and workplace militancy. The spotlight therefore fell on Australia and Canada, which respectively absorbed 43 per cent and 46 per cent of sponsored settlers. While New South Wales and Victoria hoped to recruit affluent ex-officers for their 6,000 and 2,000 families schemes, Western Australia was willing to accept people without capital or experience, who – after training – would compete for 6,000 dairy farms across the state. Scotland was a receptive constituency: an internal memorandum in 1926 reported that a recent visit to the north by Australia's Deputy Director of Migration had elicited 'very large numbers' of applications from individuals seeking assisted passages.[21]

Canada's flagship programme was the 3,000 Families Scheme, introduced in 1925 to colonise lands that the government had originally purchased for soldier settlement, but which had been abandoned or never taken up. Families with £25 for immediate use could receive advances of up to £300 each from the British government to buy stock and equipment, while Canada supplied the farms. By the time the scheme ended in 1929 it had brought in 3,346 families (more than 18,600 individuals), while New Brunswick's 500 Families Scheme simultaneously attempted to direct migrants' attention to the forgotten Maritime provinces.[22] Recruits were attracted both by specific marketing of these ventures and by the general diet of illustrated winter lectures which since the 1890s had been attracting audiences of between 800 and 1,200 people. Agents preferred tried-and-trusted lantern slides to the new medium of moving film for various reasons: they were cheaper; they did not have to be shown only in specially fireproofed, licensed halls; they allegedly attracted a more desirable, serious clientele than the frivolous audiences who frequented picture houses; and, most importantly, they allowed the agents to inject their own commentaries and recommendations into the visual displays.[23] By the 1920s the Department of the Interior's large slide library included images of industrial development and urban life, but arable and livestock farming continued to dominate the collections. By the late 1920s, however, as lantern slides gave way to film, the land grant ventures came to an end in a climate of mounting settler debt, more restrictive immigration policies and increasing difficulties in retaining families on the land.

Emigrant farmers in the 1920s were propelled along a well-worn trail by the same sentiments of hope and frustration that had characterised their predecessors. Fishermen, however, had always been particularly sporadic and reluctant emigrants, who went overseas as a last resort – during the first major downturn in the herring industry in the 1880s, more patchily just before the war, and in unprecedented numbers in the 1920s. Caught in a vicious circle of poverty and unemployment, and unable to replace obsolete boats and gear, many fled overseas, especially from the Buchan and Moray Firth coasts, where some communities lost up to a third of their inhabitants. Annie Noble, who met her Fraserburgh-born husband in Illinois and for nine years was part of an extensive Scottish network around Chicago, recalled the 'massive evacuation to America' from her home village of Inverallochy after the First World War, as well as the reverse flow in the 1930s.[24] Of those who settled permanently around the Great Lakes, some were rumoured to have been involved in smuggling the 'midnight herring' across Lake Erie during Prohibition.[25]

The overwhelming majority of Scottish emigrants between the wars came not from crofting, farming or fishing constituencies, but from the urban Lowlands. It was hardly surprising that activity should be greatest in an area that for more than a century had been a magnet to an ever increasing proportion of Scots. Well before 1918 Scotland had become one of the most highly urbanised countries in Europe, with four-fifths of the population crowded into the industrial heartland of the Central Belt. By the 1920s this was also the area where the winds of economic depression, social alienation and political tension blew most keenly, as Scotland reaped the legacy of its disproportionate dependence on heavy industry and squalid housing. In an echo of the post-Napoleonic era a century earlier, the artificial wartime boom had masked huge cracks in an economy that collapsed after 1918. The coal, steel and shipbuilding industries went into terminal retreat under the challenges of technical obsolescence, foreign competition and unfavourable exchange rates. The result was widespread and persistent unemployment, averaging 20 per cent of the insured labour force throughout the 1920s and 1930s, and escalating to an astounding 75.8 per cent of jobless shipbuilders in 1932.[26]

Scotland's problems were more than just a northern manifestation of a wider British crisis. Unemployment figures were 50 per cent higher than south of the border, employment was growing at only half the national rate, and production fell by 12 per cent between 1907 and

1930, compared to a 20 per cent growth rate in England. Remoteness from markets, expensive local rates and the legacy of Red Clydeside inhibited investment, and entrepreneurs lacked the vision and flexibility to diversify into the manufacture of cars, aircraft and consumer goods. Social deprivation was also particularly acute, most visibly in the housing sector, where overcrowding, and the related problem of high infant mortality, persisted throughout the 20th century. Resentment at huge inequalities in the distribution of wealth led to political and industrial unrest, along with a collective loss of self-confidence, an obsession with national identity and a feeling that the nation was in 'terminal decline'.[27] As the journalist George MalcolmThomson observed gloomily, 'the hands of the clock have begun to move backwards'.[28]

Against such a backdrop, emigration might well have been seen as an escape route from the inequalities, deprivation and dole queues of an economic wasteland. Jim Comerford's move to Australia in 1921 was, his son recalled in 1987, precipitated by his political militancy and alleged victimisation during the miners' lock-out of that year:

> He was a member of the Independent Labour Party and during the lockout he was in the local pub selling the Independent Labour Party's paper, The *Glasgow Forward*. The mine manager was there and the old man bursted up to him. He had a good premise. He said, 'Would you like to buy the *Forward*, Dave? And as he told it to me the manager spun round and said, 'You bastard, you'll never work here again.' And he didn't. That's what he was victimised for. And so we came out here.[29]

Bitterness was not the only ingredient in Jim Comerford's apparently hasty decision, for he had previously worked in the United States and Nova Scotia and, like many of his countrymen, was very comfortable with playing the emigration card. Scotland, even within the urban Central Belt, was also a land of contrasts, and many of the skilled artisans who in the 1920s cast their lot in North America or the Antipodes were pursuing opportunity more than fleeing poverty. They were arguably galvanised, not paralysed, by their country's economic plight, since overseas relocation was not an option for the impoverished and unconnected. People like Marion Watt had to make the best of a bad job at home. Struggling to raise her family in a single room in Aberdeen, Marion pinpointed the problem when she recalled that her frequently unemployed husband 'did think about going abroad, but you'd still need money for that, and you'd have needed someone out there to give ye a job'.[30]

Families like the Watts, with no money, no farming credentials and no skills, were of little interest to dominion government emigration agents, who sought either full-paying recruits or those eligible for assistance under imperial land settlement schemes, Occasionally, they also head-hunted contract workers for particular jobs. In 1924 John Gilmore, a native of Kemnay in Aberdeenshire and an experienced quarry manager, was appointed to run the quarrying operations at Moruya, New South Wales, where the Middlesborough civil engineering firm of Dorman & Long was preparing to extract granite for the construction of Sydney Harbour Bridge. Other Scots were also recruited to the management team, then in 1926 Dorman & Long liaised with William Stillman and the booking agents, Mackay Brothers, to recruit two contingents of Aberdeenshire masons on five-year, passage-paid contracts. Many of these recruits took their families with them, unlike the Italians who were also recruited to Moruya, but whose families were probably excluded because of the White Australia policy.[31]

Most men and women whose urban backgrounds and artisan occupations disqualified them from imperial sponsorship looked towards the United States which, despite the Quota Acts of 1921 and 1924, still opened its 'golden door' to large numbers of emigrants from the British Isles. When John Will's father took his family from Cupar to Los Angeles, his decision was influenced, the son recalled, by a combination of 'lousy economic conditions' and a desire to give his five children a better start in life. A seasoned sojourner, who had spent five years in South Africa in the 1890s, he was attracted by glowing descriptions of California, 'the orange groves, the climate, land of opportunity, and all the things you hear about'. In 1924 he gave up the unequal struggle to keep his coach-building business solvent, auctioned the shop, equipment and family home, and – sponsored by his wife's cousin – relocated his family in the golden state.[32]

The dominance of the United States in a year when almost all advertising focused on Canada is confirmed by the Board of Trade statistics, and also by the Scottish Emigration Database, a snapshot of passenger manifests from all transatlantic liners that left Scotland in the first four months of 1923.[33] Of the 18,518 passengers who embarked on the lower Clyde – all but 125 of them emigrants – 61 per cent were bound for the United States and 36 per cent for Canada. These urban emigrants were predominantly young males, more than half of whom were either single or travelling without dependents. Their occupations demonstrate unambiguously the link between heavy industry and emigration, especially the outpouring of skilled tradesmen from the counties of Lanark, Renfrew and Dunbarton to the towns and cities of the eastern states. Many of them came from shipbuilding enclaves such as Govan, Partick and Clydebank, with some evidence of recruitment hotspots in specific streets – Langlands Road in Govan, for example. The shipbuilders in particular took with them a wide range of specialist occupations, and they do not represent a roll call of the destitute, for despite having to pay the full fare, by no means all opted for the cheapest steerage passage.

On the other side of the Atlantic, Ellis Island was the first experience of the new world for 25 million passengers – including around 600,000 Scots – who passed through the famous immigration station in New York harbour on their way into the United States.[34] The Ellis Island database demonstrates that some Scottish tradesmen were able find accommodation and employment by plugging into transatlantic networks of kinship and community. On 27 January 1923 four riveters from Clydebank – William Farrell, Joseph Reid, George Richardson and John O'Neill – embarked for New York on the *Columbia*. Farrell was a 24-year-old bachelor going to join his cousin, James Wotherspoon, in Bethlehem, Pennsylvania. His father, also William Farrell, had joined Wotherspoon the previous year, leaving behind his wife and family at 70 Crown Avenue, Clydebank, but by August 1924, when Catherine Farrell arrived with her five remaining children, her husband had secured independent living quarters for the family in Bethlehem. Joseph Reid also left his wife Catherine behind with her parents in Blackford when he emigrated from Clydebank to join a friend, Archibald Bowman, in Philadelphia. Bowman was the brother-in-law of Reid's colleague, George Richardson, who was accompanied by his wife, Lydia (Bowman's sister). Joseph Reid was reunited with his wife and four-year-old son, Joseph, in New York before the end of the year, but John O'Neill's wife Mary remained in Clydebank when her husband and 15-year-old daughter, Catherine, a factory worker, emigrated to Philadelphia to join an older sister.[35]

Catherine O'Neill was one of a growing number of female factory workers, particularly from the textile sector, who opted for emigration rather than a life at the loom. Many of them came from Dundee, where the collapse of jute manufacturing created an acute crisis in that single-industry city. More modern employments were represented in a scattering of shop assistants and typists, but by far the biggest occupational category among single women emigrants was still domestic service, along with related, more specialised areas such as cooking or housekeeping.[36] That traditional sector was supported by imperial funding for the training and relocation of domestic servants, and was promoted both by paid female recruiters and by the booking agents whose interest was in the bonus payments attached to every ticket sold to a domestic servant. Eighty per cent of British women who took advantage of subsidised passages under the Empire Settlement Act went to Canada, followed by Australia and then New Zealand, but many more paid their own way, particularly to the United States, preferring independence and freedom of choice to the perceived drudgery and social constraints of domestic service.

While recognising that memories can be distorted or filtered by time, distance and inclination, the interviews conducted under the Ellis Island Oral History Project are still an invaluable source.[37] From the recorded conversations with female Scots who disembarked at the island in the 1920s we can capture something of the impulses and expectations that lay behind their decisions. All but one came from the Central Belt – mainly from Glasgow – and most emigrated as children, either accompanying their parents or following on later, usually with their mothers. One seven-year-old orphan, however – Margaret Cook from Chirnside in Berwickshire – crossed the Atlantic alone in 1920, after her mother had died in the 1919 influenza epidemic. She joined her aunt and uncle in a part of Maine where Scottish settlers, including some from Berwickshire, had built 'a tremendous number of paper mills'. Her experience of Scottish enclaves was echoed by three other interviewees: Helen Hansen in the steel town of Gary, Indiana; Maisie Pedersen in Brooklyn; and Anne Quinn in the textile centre of Carnie, New Jersey, where large numbers of mill workers had been recruited from the parent firm in Paisley.[38]

In most cases the stimulus – along with the necessary sponsorship and financial guarantees – came from family or friends who were already in America, in an ongoing process of chain migration. Maisie Pedersen from Greenock was 18 when she followed an ex-schoolfriend to New York, and she was joined in turn by two of her sisters. Four years later, 10-year-old Anne Quinn's emigration from Paisley, along with her parents and youngest brother, was sponsored by her eldest brother, who had been in the United States for six years with the rest of the family. Her uncle, a judge in Kansas City, had also used his influence to gain entry for them since Anne's father had been partially disabled by a stroke in 1922 and the authorities on both sides of the Atlantic were initially reluctant to sanction his emigration.

Virtually all interviewees recalled that they, or their parents, had been captivated by the American dream. Agnes Schilling from Motherwell was attracted by news of a neighbour's daughters who were earning good money in factory work, but she had to surmount 'lots of red tape' and parental opposition before being allowed to emigrate in 1922, aged only 15, to a country where she knew no one. 'My whole idea was to get to the

United States', she recalled, 'and that I could work when I got here and help to bring my family eventually, each one would come over, because there were many people migrating'.[39] As she had predicted, she was soon joined in New Jersey by her brother, followed by a sister, three other family members within a year, and finally by her parents.

Equally enthusiastic was Mary Dunn, who emigrated from Stirling in pursuit of better prospects than were likely to come the way of an 18-year-old milliner's message girl,[40] while for Anne Quinn's mother, coming to America was the fulfillment of a long-held ambition to settle in the 'land of opportunity'. Margaret Kirk from Glasgow waited two years for a visa and had to recruit a sponsor before securing a passage to New York in 1923 at the age of 22. Thwarted by lack of money in her ambition to study medicine, her recollections highlighted the contrasting images of Scotland as a moribund economic wilderness and America as the vibrant land of progress and opportunity.

> There was loads of work while the war was on. Shipyards were booming. As soon as the war was finished, everybody was getting laid off. There was depression in the country, and everybody wanted to come to America. Everybody was putting in to get to America, to go to Canada, anywhere, so that that was when everybody came to America, 1918. The men came over to America first, and then they brought their families over, you see, so that it was – that's why so many people came from Scotland, because of the depression. There was nothing, there was no work, so they were gasping for a job. And America sent out signals that everything was wonderful here, so they came to America, and that's why they all came.[41]

It was the disturbing impact of sectarianism, as well the quest for economic betterment, which took 15-year-old Marge Glasgow from Motherwell to New Jersey in 1922.

> There was such fighting between the Catholics and Protestants. I used to feel sorry for the priest coming around on sick calls on his bicycle and being disrupted and having things done to it. My religion was so strong that I think that's why I wasn't so in love with Scotland. Also when we had a May procession, my mother would dress us up in a pretty white dress and a veil, and these people would stop and pull our veil off and molest us along the way. Scotland is a beautiful place, and I've been back many times, many times. But it wasn't nice living.[42]

Marge was also determined that she would make enough money to bring the rest of her family to the USA, and although her parents at first refused to allow her to go to a country where she had no relatives, she eventually won them over.

The Migrant Experience: Bouquets and Brickbats, Priorities and Identities

It was only when Marge Glasgow reached her sponsors' home that she discovered she was too young to work legally. Undaunted, she found a place as a live-in child carer in Newark. Within a year, as she had hoped, she was reunited with her family when, one by one, she was joined by her brother, sisters and parents, whom she met off the boat at Ellis Island. In due course, after a spell in domestic service, Marge went into business and went on to own two successful dress boutiques.

While some Scots, like Marge Glasgow, found their pot of gold at the end of an overseas rainbow, the hopes and expectations of others were sadly disappointed. The evidence has to be handled carefully with an eye to self-selection and hidden agendas. Most emigrants were anonymously and unremarkably absorbed into their new environments: those who penned glowing accounts were sometimes responding to pressure from sponsors, while disgruntled individuals with an axe to grind were more likely than satisfied settlers to broadcast their opinions in the press. Most of those who put themselves forward for interview for the Ellis Island archive were, not surprisingly, positive, although Margaret Cook was mistreated by her aunt and uncle in Maine, and Mary Dunn's encounter with hostile officials on the island initially undermined the image of America as a welcoming land of opportunity.

The emigration of single women was particularly controversial in some of the dominions, incurring criticism from parents, immigration authorities, employers and the girls themselves. Booking agents were frequently berated, particularly by their Canadian paymasters, for irresponsible recruitment that burdened the host country with an untrained, 'nondescript crowd', as

'Canada wants women for household work'
(Library and Archives Canada, C-56944)

well as lax administration that risked the welfare and safety of those they despatched.[43] Delays in processing applications no doubt undermined the reputation of family placement schemes, as the Canadian government's Aberdeen agent complained, but a bigger deterrent was probably the hardship, loneliness and exploitation periodically described in letters to the *Scottish Farmer*, particularly from disappointed female migrants.[44]

In the Antipodes too, the sharpest criticism usually came from emigrants and employers who felt they had been misled or defrauded. Although 'Bell Heather', whose letter was published in the *Scottish Farmer* in 1920, relished her new life in Auckland, and was glad to have escaped 'the dull depressing days of the Scottish winter', she deplored the practice of enticing inexperienced girls to New Zealand farms which were nothing more than uncomfortable wood shacks served by virtually non-existent transport facilities.[45] And in 1928 Jane Hughes, an emigrant from Windygates, Fife – who six months earlier had taken up a post in Freeling, South Australia – gave her notice and asked the state immigration authorities for a transfer to a less lonely location 'where there are other maids kept' and where she could work as a housemaid or take care of children.[46] From a more public perspective, the British Migrants' Association of Australia petitioned the House of Commons in 1932 to protest against the 'extravagant, misleading, and in many cases indubitably false' government migration agreement under which they had been recruited. Requesting immediate repatriation, they maintained that they had been

> reduced to misery, semi-starvation and despair. Suicides are frequent. Some have lost their reason. Young women have sold their virtue, and many of our young men are herded together in camps of unemployed in conditions barely better than the conditions of convicts in British prisons.[47]

The dissatisfied employer's perspective was clearly demonstrated in the case of Elizabeth Wray from Ibrox, who in 1925 was recruited by a CPR agent, Esther Mackie, for a cook's post in Barrie, Ontario. She immediately proved to be an unteachable liability rather than an asset. After only a week her exasperated employer wrote to the matron of the Women's Hostel in Toronto, asking her to relocate 35-year-old Elizabeth as a dish-washer or kitchen maid in an institution or hotel, since 'in a private house she is impossible'. In 25 years of employing and training British domestics, Justine Calderwood had never encountered a woman 'as uncouth or hopelessly ignorant'. Her cooking abilities were limited to tea and porridge, only once in her life had she seen a cooked chicken, and pastry making was completely beyond her ken. When Mrs Calderwood asked her how she came to be offered the position, Elizabeth replied, 'When your letter was read I said "but I can't cook" and the lady said, "Oh! If you can do anything at all, you will do for Canada"'.[48]

By the late 1920s the Canadian immigration authorities were accusing the Ministry of Labour of a similar carelessness in its approach to the selection and training of emigrants sponsored under the Empire Settlement Act. Initially, there had been cautious optimism that artisans could be turned into competent colonial farmers, and some positive feedback – albeit from a biased source – seemed to bear this out. In 1929 the Canadian Immigration Department published a pamphlet featuring prize essays written by successful settlers under the 3,000 Families Scheme. One was written by William Wilson, formerly a railway carter in Portsoy, Banffshire, who was attracted by an advertisement in a shipping agent's window. Fluctuating between intermittent work and the dole, and struggling to feed and clothe his wife and seven children, he took up the offer of a farm at Delburne, Alberta, and was in no doubt that he had made the right decision. 'I have had experience of city life', he wrote, 'but there's nothing to beat this life, so City dwellers, if you want to know what a real happy life is come to the prairie'.[49]

Another winning entry was penned by 15-year-old Cissie Stevenson, who reminded emigrants of the importance of preliminary training, thrift and integrity, as well as a willingness to accept whatever work was offered. Her father, a miner, had taken his family from Harthill, Lanarkshire to British Columbia after his savings evaporated during the General Strike. While her mother ran the farm near Armstrong, the others were all working locally for wages, with her father and brother having spent two months harvesting in Alberta.

Emigrants from rural backgrounds were most likely to meet the requirements of sponsored land settlement schemes. Australia was commended by a handful of *Leosachs* as a place of plentiful employment and good prospects. One of 99 islanders who in 1923 enrolled in a Western Australian group settlement scheme, John Maciver wrote to the Stornoway shipping agent, Murdo Maclean, of the warm welcome his party had received in the largely Scottish Peel settlement. And from the same place, another islander wrote to her father-in-law that despite the uncertainty of success, she 'would not go home now for anything' from a 'lovely' place where 'the trees are green all the year round'.[50]

From New Brunswick, a handful of recruits to the 500 Families Scheme wrote warmly of the care shown to them by Land Settlement Board officials. Further west, their commendation was echoed by Mary Campbell

The first contingent of British harvesters for the Canadian prairies, 1923
(CP Archives, A-12293)

from Caithness, who in 1928 emigrated to Olds, Alberta with her husband and two children under the 3,000 Families Scheme. Welcomed by Scottish neighbours, the Anglican Church and a range of voluntary organisations, she was also grateful to local LSB officials in Calgary for remembering to send the family Christmas gifts as well as pamphlets of practical advice. A year into her new life, she was hopeful about the family's prospects in a community into which they had been accepted, but was realistic enough to acknowledge that prior farming experience was no guarantee of success in an unfamiliar environment. As she wrote, 'we know that we have much more learning and living to do before we can truly say that yes, it has been worthwhile'.[51]

Canada may have concentrated its recruitment efforts on the farming community, but those with professional skills were also attracted across the Atlantic. James Young Lind from Elderslie went to Toronto in 1928 in pursuit of better opportunities and remuneration as a trainee architect. Shortly after arriving, he wrote home reassuringly from his lodgings at the city's Central YMCA.

> I am getting on here very well, in fact I think I have struck one of these lucky streaks that you read of but never realise, although I can't very well save money just now, as I have to buy my experience so to speak, I think I am 'well set' as the Americans say So there is no need to worry The people here are not very much different from the people at home, there is one good difference there are no loafers, and every one hustles much quicker, so do I than at home.[52]

Lind's 'hustling' took the form of working longer than his stipulated hours and taking two classes at a local college. He anticipated that by the spring he would have 'a pretty good chance' of promotion to a chief draughtsman, earning about £15 a week. By December he had a new job, working on the replacement for Trinity College School, which had burned down, and on the pathology building at the University of Toronto. He was well satisfied with his circumstances – 'I am finding the work here much more interesting than at home, as I get much better work to do' – and even declared that Toronto's winter weather 'would turn auld Scotland green with envy'. In March he changed employment once more, and in April he moved on again, each time for better-paid positions.[53]

But James Lind may have overdone the contrast between his homeland and Canada. 'Jessie [his sister] was telling me that you said I was to stop running down Scotland', he wrote to his mother in January 1929. He went on to defend himself.

> I don't think I have said much against it except perhaps about Scottish Architects comic ideas about salaries. Would you rather have me at home working for £8 a month or in Canada at a minimum £8 a week with more coming along? That's one thing that's all wrong anyway. They would hold up their hands in horror if one asked them for £5 a week and I don't consider that a living wage considering the training. I should not come home for less than £7 a month and and (sic) I've the same chances of getting that as a lamb has of life in a blizzard.[54]

When Lind, along with a friend, moved away from the 'semi-public life' at the YMCA and into a rented apartment in Wellesley Street, he showed every sign of settling in Canada. As well as being cheaper (£3 15s a month plus electricity), the apartment had a large electric stove with five heating rings, 'an electric refrigerator for keeping groceries, and two washing tubs... constant hot water and janitor service'.[55] Yet by the summer he was back – permanently – in Scotland, and although his letters gave little hint of his impending return – rather the opposite – it was probably triggered by a combination of his father's illness and a parental business offer that he could not refuse. By 19 June 1929 Lind's father, a quarrymaster and contractor, was in the throes of establishing a new Company, William Lind and Co., Ltd. When it was incorporated on 28 June, two of the three principal shareholders and directors were William Lind and his son.[56]

James Young Lind was not therefore a victim of the reversal of fortune and expectations suffered by many – not least in the building trade – after the Wall Street Crash. The Depression saw many migrants scuttling back to Scotland,[57] and probably many more trapped in penury and unemployment, without the means to return. But reverse migration was not simply a product of economic downturn, nor was it characterised only by disappointment or destitution. Even during the 19th century, about a third of Scotland's migrants had come back to their native land, and as transport technology improved and globalisation began to feature in the lexicon, constant mobility became increasingly integral to the definition of migration. For many, the decision to return was built into the relocation venture right from the start, and demonstrated success in playing the international labour market. Others came back temporarily, to assuage homesickness, or as tourists, by no means all of whom were drawn from the top end of the income bracket, even in the 1930s.

From time to time 'tartan tourism' hit the headlines in *The Scotsman*. Almost biennially, between 1924 and 1938, the Order of Scottish Clans in the United States chartered Anchor liners such as the *Transylvania, Caledonia* and *California* to ship Scottish artisans back to their homeland for a holiday. Founded on St Andrew's Day 1878, one of the Order's objectives was 'to cultivate fond recollections of Scotland' among its membership, which by the mid-1920s numbered 24,000.[58] The first transatlantic trip, in August 1924, saw 1,000 visitors disembark at Glasgow, where they were formally welcomed by the presidents of *An Comunn Gàidhealach* and the Lewis and Harris Society, the minister of St Columba's Gaelic Church in Glasgow, the city's provost, magistrates and town council, and Sir Harry Lauder, who had been a schoolmate of Duncan MacInnes, Chief of the Order of Scottish Clans. In acknowledging the lavish and unexpected civic welcome, MacInnes – a Berwickshire man whose high-profile day job was chief accountant for New York City – said that the tourists 'were looking forward to making their trip not an exception but a habit'.[59] That wish was fulfilled, as over the next 14 years, MacInnes headed up six subsequent trips, most of which brought parties of between 1,000 and 2,400 exiles or second-generation Scots on tours of their native land which extended from a fortnight to several weeks. By the early 1930s icy economic winds had curtailed the number of transatlantic tourists (only 500 disembarked in 1934) and reshaped the industrial landscape of Clydeside. *The Scotsman*

correspondent's report on the arrival of the *Caledonia* in July 1932 identified a wide spectrum of sentiments and images.

> There were men and women whose accents had scarcely changed from
> the time they left Scotland, and some who, although they had just gone
> out eight or ten years ago, had come back with an American accent
> which, it seemed to British ears, could be cut with a knife. The children,
> of course, self-confident and bursting with life, were as American in
> their speech as any talking picture, but their national feelings were
> doubtless summed up sincerely by the 13-year-old boy who, standing
> beside me yesterday forenoon, turned from contemplating the hills and
> the fields and the river, and said to his mother – 'Gosh, ma! I'm proud
> to be Scahtch'...
>   From time to time as the liner steamed up river pleasure steamers went
> by, packed full, going down. The home-coming people cheered wildly
> and the passengers in the pleasure steamers cheered back. Elsewhere,
> at street ends and along the river banks, onlookers stood singly or in
> groups or crowds, and looked on, with handkerchiefs fluttering... There
> was, I fancy, one passenger who must have felt thankful, as he looked
> at the empty shipyards and mouldy slipways, that he gave up working
> in a shipyard in Scotland some years ago, and went to America, where
> he now found life rather more prosperous, I gathered, as a bar tender
> in a club, dispensing alcoholic drinks with an entirely open mind on the
> question, if not always in an entirely open manner.[60]

In 1936 – a year in which there was no documented excursion under
the auspices of the Order of Scottish Clans – a contingent of 82 Scottish
Australians got in on the act, when, after arriving in London, they travelled
north for a month's tour of their homeland.[61]

The best documented settlement stories of the 1920s belong to the
Hebrideans who embarked so publicly on the *Marloch* and the *Metagama*
in April 1923. Both schemes were plagued by controversy, as crofters
discovered they had jumped out of the frying pan of Highland depression
into the fire of Canadian hostility. When the ships left the Outer Hebrides,
Scottish editors were divided as to whether the stampede reflected a counsel
of despair or a more enlightened attitude in the crofting community. When
they disembarked, the Canadian press, which had predicted the arrival of a
'race of giants', was at first disappointed to find the new arrivals were quite
ordinary. Before long the *Metagama*'s emigrants were vilified for taking up
non-agricultural employment, defecting to the United States, and allegedly
breaking a strike in a Toronto brewery. Some confirmed that they had
crossed the Great Lakes in search of more lucrative work, particularly in
the car factories of Detroit, while others preferred the water to the land,
and found employment on the Lakes. Some had clearly made premeditated

use of the Canadian assisted passage scheme as an illegal back door into the United States, but others claimed they had been driven off the land, and in some cases across the border, by low or even non-existent wages, poor living conditions and unremitting work in Canada.

As economic conditions worsened, casual employment and frequent changes of workplace became more and more common. Disillusioned by the number of recruits who 'broke their agreements almost immediately on landing', William Noxon shifted his recruitment efforts from footloose individuals to family groups, and the Ontario authorities sometimes hounded emigrants' parents in Lewis in an attempt to track down defaulters.[62] But not all emigrants reneged on their debts, and most of those still alive in the 1980s had positive recollections when interviewed by the journalist, Jim Wilkie.[63] Summer fishing or freighting work on the Lakes might be interspersed with winter employment in American factories, and several Lewismen also worked on construction projects at Niagara Falls. Many used their island connections to find work and accommodation, while a network of ethnic clubs and Gaelic churches in centres like Toronto, Buffalo, Cleveland and New York ensured that most of them married fellow-islanders.

Further west, in the town of Clandonald, Alberta, the inscription on the cemetery gates implores visitors to 'remember us'. That the Hebrideans who colonised Clandonald are indeed remembered is, unfortunately, a consequence of the difficulties that dogged their settlement, difficulties which began with the sailing of the *Marloch* from Lochboisdale in 1923 and which were played out in the press, the Canadian Immigration Department's correspondence, and the unhappy memories of a dwindling band of colonists and their children. To this day, Andrew MacDonell's antics arouse strong feelings on both sides of the Atlantic. Opinion is divided over whether the erstwhile priest presided over a 'notable piece of work in Canadian land settlement' or an ill-conceived, egocentric and mismanaged fiasco.[64] At the height of his activity, between 1923 and 1928, 1,315 colonists, most of them Highlanders, crossed the Atlantic under his auspices, while he also dabbled – albeit fruitlessly – in juvenile and female colonisation projects. Although his agency activity was to earn him the MBE in 1955, the Canadian press and immigration authorities were often scathing about an agent who was something of a loose cannon, whose penchant for specially created ethnic colonies ran counter to the general policy of empire settlement between the wars, and whose recruits struggled to subsist in a climate that was both environmentally and economically hostile.

Problems began to emerge even before MacDonell's first recruits set foot on Canadian soil. He was badly served by his Scottish representatives, who held out misleading assurances of prosperity to a much bigger and more impoverished party of recruits than had been agreed. Several settlers rejected the farms allocated to them, on the grounds of excessive down-payments and distance from the railway, and while MacDonell negotiated with the authorities for alternatives, over 200 disgruntled colonists remained cooped up at an inadequate reception centre in Red Deer, easy prey for real estate fraudsters, as well as epidemics of measles and chicken pox. They were joined by a handful of families who had refused to take up emergency accommodation and farm work across the prairie provinces, and within less than two months the 'deplorable plight' of the Hebrideans had attracted the condemnation of the Member of Parliament for Red Deer, as well as a number of Scottish Labour MPs at Westminster.[65] Some Canadian commentators blamed the difficulties on the settlers rather than the sponsors, claiming that they were 'a clannish people of peculiar psychology', who had expected instantaneous success to be handed to them on a plate.[66]

The sorry tale of exaggerated promises, careless selection and over-commitment was repeated the following year, when MacDonell returned to Scotland to recruit a second contingent of colonists. According to Harold Roy, a Soldier Settlement Board field officer in Alberta, the emigrants – many of whom were 'men of dotage' – had been falsely promised houses, employment and farms.[67] His sentiments were corroborated in the complaints of disillusioned colonists, some of whom pleaded, unsuccessfully, to be sent home. Turning a deaf ear to their distress, and to the disquiet of the Canadian immigration authorities, MacDonell pressed on in 1926 to his most ambitious project, the creation of a Hebridean colony 160 miles east of Edmonton. Christened Clandonald, it was located on an inhospitable tract of land purchased on mortgage from the CPR, whose tracks bisected the community. Once again, rhetoric and reality failed to coincide, as settlers shivered in poorly insulated cottages, suffered the resentment of neighbouring farmers whose cattle pasture had been absorbed into the new colony, and struggled with the onset of the Depression. Very few passage costs were ever recovered, very little rent was ever paid, and in 1939 the colonists were still more than $50,000 in debt.

Some of Andrew MacDonell's problems were clearly of his own making. His headstrong determination to expand his activity beyond manageable bounds undermined his credibility and the welfare of his colonists. His confidence in unworkable ethnic settlements ignored the lessons of history, and the ghosts of earlier Hebridean colonies on the prairies. The denominational exclusiveness of his ventures belied his claim that they were non-sectarian, and his fear that the colonists would be subverted by Communist infiltrators verged on paranoia. But he was also a victim of circumstances. As well as having to contend with political enemies on both sides of the Atlantic, his recruits were still finding their feet when the Depression put an end to any hope of debt repayment and plunged some families into destitution. Even the critical Canadian Immigration Department admitted in 1938 that the Clandonald venture had been bedeviled by economic circumstances over which the colonists had little control.

The jury is still out on whether Andrew MacDonell was a willing or unwitting collaborator in Lady Emily Gordon Cathcart's disingenuous campaign to exile Catholic crofters from her southern Hebridean estates to Canada. Ever since the brutal evictions perpetrated by Colonel John Gordon on the former Clanranald lands in the mid-19th century, anti-emigration sentiment had been deeply woven into the fabric of life in Barra, South Uist and Benbecula. Antagonism had been rekindled in 1883 when Lady Cathcart – Gordon's daughter-in-law – orchestrated a further transatlantic exodus at a time when the land war was raging. Prominent among her critics at that time were the islands' Catholic clergy, who resented her vitriolic anti-Catholicism and victimisation of Catholic tenants. MacDonell's advocacy of emigration 40 years later, chiming with Lady Cathcart's ongoing support for selective emigration, therefore struck a raw nerve, and although criticism has rarely been voiced candidly, he was – and is – clearly regarded as a quisling by the Catholic hierarchy and by many islanders in Scotland and Canada.

As we shall see in Chapter 5, controversy of a different nature surrounded the involvement of Scots migrants in industrial action. George Bowman Anderson had worked in a flax mill in his native Arbroath, and then served a year's engineering apprenticeship with the Caledonian Railway in Glasgow, where he also became involved in radical politics. In 1905 he went to Toronto to join his older brother, who already had links with the Socialist Party of Canada, which George also joined. Five years later he moved west to Winnipeg, where he worked in railway sheds and in his spare time met fellow radicals to study *Das Kapital*. It was therefore no surprise that he became involved in the Winnipeg General Strike in 1919, being appointed chairman of the central committee. Interviewed in 1973, at the age of 89, he recalled witnessing the fatal shooting of one of the strikers and the wounding of two others, but maintained that widespread violence had been prevented because of the insistence of the strike committee on a passive response to provocation.[68]

While George Bowman Anderson spent his leisure time studying Marx, the social lives of more Scots migrants probably revolved around the same mix of religious and secular associations that had occupied previous generations of expatriates. Although the overseas churches wielded less influence than in their 19th-century heyday, they still functioned as labour bureaux and cultural hubs where the migrants could tap into ethnic networks. In his first letter home from Toronto, for instance, James Lind referred to 'a very good Edinburgh minister' whose church he intended to visit the following week, and subsequently reported that the clergyman, despite a rather chequered background, offered a helping hand to new arrivals. 'I believe he took to drink and drugs in Edinburgh, it was always a bad town, and came out here to square himself up. He has been successful, and is well liked here, having done a lot for young fellows coming out from Scotland'.[69]

Some denominations still prioritised their evangelistic and pastoral role. The Free Church of Scotland in particular tried – through its overseas outposts – to ensure that migrants retained the faith in which they had been brought up, and its magazine, *The Monthly Record,* regularly appealed to ministers to answer the call of expatriate congregations, mainly in Canada. By 1924 the Toronto church was attracting up to 60 worshippers to its English-language morning service, and up to 120 to its Gaelic service in the evening. Attendances in Fort William (Thunder Bay) and Winnipeg averaged about 100 and 40 respectively, while between 40 and 50 families were connected with the Vancouver congregation.[70] Responsibilities to the 'loyal and devout' Scots of the diaspora were just as important as domestic commitments, and it was, declared the Reverend R. McLeod of Dunoon in 1930, 'the utmost folly on our part to think that *any* minister or licentiate of our Church is suitable for Canada, while we reserve the best for the home field'.[71] McLeod, like many other ministers, made his 'Macedonian Cry' shortly after returning from a lengthy preaching tour of the dominion, but mere 'coming and going', and the sending out of temporary deputies, was no substitute for the long-term or permanent settlement to which most Free Church clergy were reluctant to commit themselves.[72]

Ministerial delegates who were sent across the Atlantic generally stayed for about three months and followed a well-worn route. They sailed from Greenock to Montreal, a city which they repeatedly condemned for its Sunday entertainments and its dominant Roman Catholic influence. G.N.M. Collins of Greenock was dismissive of the renowned Dr Charles Gordon (aka Ralph Connor) when he heard him preach in Montreal in 1931. 'It was a rather rambling sermon, with some fine flashes of thought here and

Bird's eye view of Toronto, 1930s
(Archives of Ontario, RG 9-7-5-0-14, Ontario House photographs)

there, but altogether showing more of the genius of the novelist than of the insight of the theologian'.[73] Toronto, the hub of Canadian culture and commerce, and a focal point for Gaelic-speaking Highlanders from Lewis, was regarded more favourably: 'a high-toned city, and in the matter of Sabbath observance and morals… decidedly better than Montreal', declared Donald Mackinnon of Portree in 1935. Fort William, Mackinnon found, was also dominated by migrants from Lewis, mainly from Garrabost and Tong, while the Vancouver congregation, which dated back to 1911, was more cosmopolitan.[74]

Clerical rhetoric repeatedly emphasised the spiritual hunger of the migrants, their pleas for pastors, and the biblical mandate to nurture their faith. Exhortations were laced with warnings that, if neglected, 'the unstable and less-informed' migrants might be led astray, not only into other denominations, but – as Andrew MacDonell also feared – into 'the infidel and pernicious tenets of Moscow'.[75] Meanwhile, the complex relationship between tradition and faith was evident in the Free Church's persistent concern to secure Gaelic-speaking clergymen who would sustain the culture, as well as the beliefs, of their flock. In 1929 Neil Macleod, a theological student on a placement in Toronto, met a man who had allegedly sacrificed a better salary and prospects in New York for a position in Toronto, 'solely because there was a Free Church there, where he could worship God after the manner of his fathers'.[76] Macleod's assertion was corroborated seven years later by the Reverend James Mackintosh of Vancouver, when he urged the Free Church General Assembly to face up to its Canadian responsibilities. 'The Highland people', he told the gathering, 'were a special people, and they did not lose their specialisation when they went abroad. Some of the queerest traits of Highland character were developed to an amazing degree. They would not go to Church unless they could get the Free Church of Scotland'.[77]

The migrants' loyalty to the Free Church and their concern to maintain 'the doctrine, the mode of worship and the language of their upbringing' probably sprang as much from a desire to sink familiar ethnic anchors in unfamiliar environments as from theological conviction.[78] When the Reverend R.J. Macleod of Ness in Lewis visited an enclave of his fellow islanders at Dunrea, Manitoba, in 1924, he found the experience 'just the same' as in Scotland, as people gathered 'from far and near in cars and buggies' to hear him preside over a series of Gaelic services. They had preserved the traditions of the island they had left 37 years earlier to such an extent that Macleod observed, 'if they were to come back to Lewis to-day they would find more change of outlook in Lewis than Lewis would find in them'.[79]

The Free Church discouraged its expatriate flock from involvement with secular associations, but many migrants lived happily with a foot in both camps. By the 1920s ethnic societies were generally little more than a leisure-time adjunct to overseas settlement, but sometimes they reverted to their 19th-century profile of offering a charitable lifeline to those who had fallen on hard times. Usually this involved brokering or subsidising the repatriation of ill or impoverished Scots. From its inception in 1919, the Lewis Society of Detroit periodically took up collections to subsidise the repatriation of sick members. These included Joseph McDonald, who in 1924 was 'sick in New Mexico with malaria and tuberculosis' and was given a donation 'to help pay his expense to his home in Glasgow'; and Kenneth MacLeod, who in 1931, having been diagnosed with tuberculosis, was given clothes, 50 dollars and a transatlantic ticket from New York so that he could fulfil his wish 'to die in his native home'.[80] In 1924 the Society also co-operated with Detroit's St Andrew's and Clan Campbell societies to raise money to relieve distress in the Hebrides, as well as supporting a fund-raising appeal for the Lewis hospital.[81]

But some migrants believed that successful settlement depended on turning over a new leaf. James Lind blamed a colleague's restlessness on his wife's failure to leave her old life behind, and reflected on the importance of not making invidious comparisons:

One of the fellows a Structural engineer from Renfrew who works in this office used to work in the shipyards on the Clyde and go to the Paisley 'tec. He has been here 4 years and is as 'Paisley' in his speech as when he left home – and says he would go back to Scotland tomorrow if he could get a steady job at £5 per week. I think sometimes when a fellow marries an 'Old Country' girl he finds it harder to settle. His wife is always running back and forward across the Atlantic and I think, she is the unsettling influence.

When you go abroad you have got to forget 'what you did in the Old Country' and 'do as the Romans do' otherwise you are not so likely to get on.

You know how people at home don't like people who come back for a trip to say 'When I was in America' etc. Well the Americans & Canadians rightly don't like Old Country methods rammed down their throat so it does not pay to do it.[82]

The individuals who colour the canvas of the Scottish diaspora between the wars were steered by the familiar influences of precedent and propaganda that had inspired their predecessors. The background from which they emerged had many echoes of the years after the defeat of Napoleon a century earlier, when emigration became a common response to frustrated ambitions and looming destitution in a climate of post-conflict upheaval. By the 1920s, major strides in transport technology had transformed the mechanisms of moving, and the internationalisation of the employment market had created a much wider range of opportunities. Yet the personal contacts on which many emigrants still relied had changed little in the course of a century, and just as those who left Scotland in the 1920s drew heavily on informal networks, so they in turn reinforced those ethnic webs for the benefit of their successors.

But Scottish ethnicity was a badge that could be worn or discarded as circumstances dictated. Fellow Scots might help new arrivals to find work and a place to stay, and Scottish organisations provided an outlet for their social, spiritual and recreational needs. Except in explicitly ethnic enclaves such as Clandonald, however, migrants generally wove their Scottish identity into the warp and woof of their host societies, balancing practical integration and cultural distinctiveness. The tension was encapsulated by one 1923 migrant to the United States, Glaswegian Margaret Kirk, who in 1994 was interviewed for the Ellis Island History Project. At the age of 92, Margaret remained emphatic that she would 'never be anything but Scottish'. Even after 71 years in the United States, 'I'll always be Scottish', she repeated. 'I'll do everything all proper here in America, but, at heart, I'll always be Scottish'.[83]

In charting the history of the post-war Scottish diaspora in Chapter 5, we will consider whether the motives, experiences and sentiments of migrants after 1945 echoed or departed from the profile of Margaret Kirk and her contemporaries. Before that, however, we turn the spotlight on the broad theme of sponsorship, investigating 20th century manifestations of a phenomenon that has had a contentious, persistent and well-documented influence in the story of Scottish migration.

CHAPTER 3

Sponsored Emigration and Settlement

WOVEN CENTRALLY BUT controversially into the tapestry of emigration is the multi-coloured thread of sponsorship. Through initiatives undertaken by governments, charities and individuals, it has made its mark in various guises, and has already surfaced in the story of the inter-war exodus, when the Empire Settlement Act constituted part of Westminster's response to the challenge of retaining the loyalty and cohesion of the dominions in the stormy economic and political waters of the 1920s and 1930s. But the legislation lingered on the statute book for half a century, providing the backdrop to a range of assisted passage and settlement schemes operated either directly by the imperial and dominion governments, or by philanthropic institutions, some of which expanded their operations as a result of the increased funding. High-profile national experiments in political and social engineering, not least in Australia after 1945, but also including the emergency wartime phenomenon of seavacuation, operated alongside more obscure or low-key localised enterprises, including those that recruited specifically in Scotland.

Heritage and History

Twentieth-century sponsors and their recruits had a substantial heritage on which to draw, not least in a Scottish context. The 18th-century practice of rewarding military officers – including many Highlanders – with colonial land grants had been extended in 1815 to vetted civilians willing to settle on the vulnerable Canadian border with the United States. But if imperial security was the first priority, it was soon eclipsed by domestic concerns, as the economic depression that swept the British Isles after the Napoleonic wars transformed public and political attitudes to emigration. Previously denigrated by mercantilists as a nationally debilitating seepage of brain and brawn, colonial settlement began to be advocated as a weapon in the battle against massive unemployment, pauperism and potential unrest. For almost a decade, Westminster flirted with small-scale assisted emigration as a form of poor relief, responding patchily to petitions for passage costs or land from individuals and emigration societies. By the mid-1820s, when the government decided the policy was too expensive, almost 7,000 emigrants – including 3,083 Scottish handloom weavers – had been partially sponsored to settle in Canada and a further 3,569 (mainly English) colonists had been sent to the Cape of Good Hope.

From time to time throughout the rest of the century the case for state-funded emigration was argued by select committees, royal commissions, lobby groups and individual petitioners. But it was always a hot potato, which was never unequivocally endorsed by politicians, press or public. Portrayed as an opportunity in times of domestic crisis, it was soon re-defined as a threat when the economy revived, but even when it was first advocated seriously, during the post-Napoleonic slump, state aid was dismissed by some British critics as expensive and ineffective and resented by the recipients as a blatant device for dumping economic and social misfits on the colonies.

By the 1830s perceptions of emigration as a safety valve for the unemployed, destitute or disaffected were being replaced by the more positive policy of systematic colonisation devised by the frustrated politician and convicted child kidnapper, Edward Gibbon Wakefield. For more than three decades after 1840 the British government's sponsorship of migrants was indirect, as – under the scrutiny of the Colonial Office's Land and Emigration Commission – almost £5 million from colonial land sales was channeled into the selection, subsidisation and shipment of over 340,000 labourers and domestic servants, mainly to the Antipodes. But systematic colonisation did not escape censure either, as British critics accused it of a damaging exclusiveness that skimmed off the cream, while the host colonies complained about disparities between demand and supply and suspected that it was simply a dressed-up version of earlier, more explicitly negative policies.

When the case for direct government sponsorship reappeared on the agenda in the harsher economic climate of the 1870s and 1880s, as a remedy for the twin problems of British overpopulation and a colonial labour deficit, the simplistic arguments of its supporters fell on generally stony soil. Lobbying by the poorly funded National Association for Promoting State Directed Emigration and Colonisation produced a toothless advisory body, the Emigrants' Information Office and – in 1888 – the allocation of £10,000 towards the settlement of 100 crofter families from Lewis, Harris and North Uist on prairie homesteads in Manitoba and the North West Territories.

In sponsoring those one-off colonies at Killarney and Saltcoats, the government was reacting partly to the recommendations of the Napier Commission two years earlier that state-aided emigration was an 'indispensable remedy' for persistent overpopulation in the Highlands, reinforced by its own fear that six years of civil disobedience in the crofting counties would spiral out of control into a violent, Irish-style land war. The settlers' experiences were mixed. From a planning perspective, the venture was hastily conceived and poorly implemented, not least because the Scottish Office, in its haste to get things moving, failed to reach a specific agreement with the Canadian government about responsibilities for land allocation and loan retrieval. The land-locked prairie was also an alien environment for crofters who had been brought up with the sound and smell of the sea in their ears and nostrils, and the distances between homesteads only compounded their loneliness and isolation. While some settlers made rapid progress, it was not surprising that bad publicity about unprepared homesteads and paltry loans soon filtered back to Scotland, where they reinforced Hebridean antagonism against state-orchestrated emigration.

Resentment had already been at fever pitch in the Highlands and Islands for much of the century. With state funding the exception rather than the rule, private sponsors – in the shape of landlords – bore most of the responsibility for shipping impecunious tenants overseas, mainly to Canada. Among the first to dip into his pocket – in 1826 – was Maclean of Coll, who, having petitioned unsuccessfully for state funding to remove 300 tenants from the inner Hebridean island of Rum, financed their relocation to Cape Breton to the tune of almost £1,700.

Over the next 30 years landlord-sponsored emigration sent an estimated 14,000 Highlanders across the Atlantic, and in the 1850s a further 5,000 were shipped to Australia by the Highland and Island Emigration Society under a quasi-official tripartite funding scheme involving landlords, the Emigration Commission and the Society. In the 1880s the spotlight switched back to Canada, when Lady Emily Gordon Cathcart, who in 1878 had inherited her late husband's huge Outer Hebridean estate, sponsored the settlement of ten families from Benbecula at Wapella in the North West Territories.

Along with a vast swathe of land, Lady Gordon Cathcart had inherited the inflammatory legacy of brutal clearance, and, as we have seen in Chapter 2, her own attitudes and actions only added further fuel to the fire. In the eyes of Highlanders and their advocates, privately sponsored emigration had always been driven by profit rather than philanthropy. Stigmatised by landlord duress, clearance and exile, it was probably even more unpalatable than its sporadic, government-funded bedfellow because it operated at a local, personal level. Meanwhile in the urban Lowlands, where emigration was less directly associated with dispossession, charitable donations filled some of the gaps created by the government's parsimonious approach, although the funds raised by weavers' emigration societies in the 1820s and 1840s allowed only a small fraction of their members to leave Scotland.

By the 1870s charitable emigration schemes had begun to move into a different gear, developing a high-profile momentum that carried them well into the 20th century and – from the 1920s – into partnership with a much more coherent and consistent government strategy. It was the Victorian commitment to evangelical philanthropy that initially gave rise to a clutch of national and local emigration societies, whose mission was to rescue and relocate disadvantaged women, unemployed artisans and destitute children. By the end of the century the moral core of the evangelicals' rationale was being challenged by eugenic arguments about racial purity and an emphasis on secular imperialism. Not surprisingly, the philanthropists' philosophies and practices led them into controversial territory, especially in the heavily tilled field of child migration, where some specifically Scottish organisations – notably Quarrier's Orphan Homes of Scotland – shared the stage with the most prominent national institution, Dr Barnardo's Homes.

The rising tide of imperialism that marked the end of the Victorian age not only strengthened the resolve and filled the coffers of charitable emigration societies: it also brought the case for government-sponsored empire settlement firmly back under the spotlight, and led to the appointment of the Dominions Royal Commission in 1912. But it was only in the years following the final, 1,919-page report of that wide-ranging Commission in 1917 that the different strands of assisted emigration came together for the first time as an integral part of imperial strategy. Those years mirrored the post-Napoleonic decade not only in the economic dislocation mentioned in Chapter 2, but in the establishment's fears of social and political upheaval and its recourse to state-aided emigration as part of a package of responses. The difference was that in the 1920s the government shouldered a much more central role in sponsoring emigration than had been the case a century earlier, with access to significant, sustained funding that raised both its own profile and that of the voluntary societies with which it now liaised. The new strategy was, in the words of Leo Amery, Secretary of State for the Colonies, 'simply social reform writ large'.[1]

The soldier settlement scheme that assisted 86,027 war veterans and their dependents to relocate in the dominions between 1919 and 1923 was reminiscent – on a bigger scale – of the colonial military settlements of the 18th and early 19th centuries. But in the Empire Settlement Act of 1922, the government demonstrated a much more ambitious, and unprecedented, commitment to assisted colonisation, allocating up to £3 million a year in loans and grants to subsidise passages, land settlement and training courses in partnership with dominion governments or with public and private organisations in the UK or the dominions. The arrangements not only reversed the government's traditional non-interventionism, but also escaped the swinging 'Geddes Axe' which slashed so much public expenditure in the 1920s. Renewed at 15-year intervals, the legislation remained on the statute book, latterly as the Empire and Commonwealth Settlement Act, until 1972.

Inter-war Expansion, Innovation and Contraction

Chapters 2 and 4 evaluate some of the sponsorship schemes that were operated directly by the government as a result of guaranteed funding. But probably more significant was the way in which the legislation strengthened the hand of existing voluntary societies that had already dabbled in assisted emigration. The Salvation Army's rhetoric, for instance, had long been dominated by the moral and practical benefits of empire settlement. In 1903 it had established a separate Migration and Settlement Department under David Lamb (from the Angus village of Friockheim), to oversee its expanding provision of assisted passages and employment advice for single women, unemployed men and juveniles, and by 1911 it was advertising itself as the world's largest emigration agency.[2] Within a month of the Armistice it had received nearly 6,000 applications from would-be emigrants, and was singled out for special praise when the Empire Settlement Bill was introduced into Parliament.[3] Bolstered by the injection of government grants and loans, the Salvation Army was able by 1923 to launch a new Boys' Scheme which by 1930 had assisted 5,000 youths to relocate overseas, mainly in Australia.

Scots probably participated proportionately in the Salvation Army's emigration schemes, but the loss of records when the organisation's London HQ was destroyed during the Blitz is a major impediment to research. Officers were sent on recruitment visits to regional citadels: in January 1924, for instance, at least 24 boys were selected in Aberdeen, and in 1927 Colonel Lamb visited Inverness for the same purpose.[4]

Steamship lines paid it a commission on passages booked, and a snapshot of departures from Scottish ports in the first four months of 1923, captured by the *Scottish Emigration Database*, reveals that 255 individuals – 1.33 per cent of passengers – embarked under the auspices of the Salvation Army. A total of five Canadian Pacific liners and four Anchor-Donaldson vessels embarked 136 males and 119 females, including 45 infants or children.[5] Canada was the destination of 77 per cent, with the rest bound for the United States. Over half (almost 58 per cent) came from Glasgow and its hinterland, with a further 20 per cent from Aberdeen and just over 12 per cent from Dundee. Edinburgh was represented by only one emigrant, Elizabeth Brown, a 31-year-old biscuit factory worker from Leith, and rural areas did not feature at all. Most recruits were labourers or tradesmen, not least from the shipyards, but there were only two miners and one professional (an architect). Of the women, 68 were housewives, housekeepers or domestics, the latter crossing the Atlantic in three batches, on the *Metagama* and the *Montrose*. The average age of the adults was 25.8 (men) and 30.7 (women), the oldest man being a 61-year-old trimmer from Motherwell and the oldest woman a 64-year-old housekeeper from Dundee.

Despite the absence of records, we can clothe the statistical skeleton with a smattering of experiences. Not surprisingly, publications from the Salvation Army's own stable were positive and encouraging. But we should not take them at face value, and some recruits and observers sang from a more critical songsheet.

A Salvation Army official welcomes the first flight of immigrants to the gate of the Men's Immigration Reception Centre, 291 Sherbourne Street, Toronto, 1947
(Archives of Ontario, RG 9-7-4-4-27, Clint Melville)

In 1926 21-year-old Alexina Grewar emigrated from Glasgow to Ontario with two friends. While not financially assisted by the Salvation Army, or having any prior links with the organisation, these three girls chose to travel under its aegis because of its alluring advertising and the chaperonage that it allegedly offered. But not only did Alexina never see the escort who was meant to look out for them on board the

New immigrants enjoying breakfast at a men's residence run by the Salvation Army, Toronto, 3 August 1947 (Archives of Ontario, RG 9-7-4-5-60, D. Ottaway)

Montnairn; she also alleged that the Army in Scotland had a 'more kindly outlook' than in Canada, where its attitude was 'sharp' and the priority of those who ran the reception hostel in Toronto was 'to get rid of us so they didn't have to feed us'. Alexina's first job – secured within half an hour of arriving at the hostel – was a disaster. When her employer tried to pay her with an old fur coat instead of the promised wage of $22 a month ,the Salvation Army's after-care agent advised her to hand in her notice but did not help her to find alternative employment.[6] In similar vein, a year earlier, F. H. Mather of Winnipeg claimed that the Salvation Army had, for reasons of cost, 'cast aside' his Glaswegian employee, 15-year-old Kenneth Robertson, a year after bringing him out from Scotland. Robertson had allegedly been evicted from a Salvation Army hostel at Brandon at 10.30 pm and told to walk three miles across the prairie to his new employment.[7]

The lead taken by the Salvation Army in establishing a specific migration department in 1903 was followed six years later by the World Committee of the YMCA, although until the 1920s it confined itself to supervision and after-care of those who had gone overseas under other umbrellas. But after a London-based Migration Department was created in 1920 to harness colonial demand to British supply, the YMCA moved into a much more active mode, not least in Scotland, where it concentrated on helping unemployed youths and those in blind-alley occupations to fulfil their potential in Canada and Australia. Using funding released by the Empire Settlement Act, it advertised widely, using collective nomination to liaise with the YMCA and churches in the dominions to send out and follow up parties of boys whom it generally placed as farm labourers. The so-called Church Nomination Scheme aimed not only to function as an employment exchange but to strengthen international fellowship through such collaboration and prevent backsliding by the migrants. Those who went to Canada were processed by the United Church of Canada's receiving hostel at Norval, Ontario, which vetted their placements, ensured they earned a minimum of 10 shillings a week and maintained guardianship until they were 19 years old.

During the 1920s several hundred boys signed up, especially from depressed mining communities like Cowdenbeath, which in 1928 saw its first two parties cross the Atlantic, 'from shadow to sunshine'. Good reports from those pioneers allegedly led to the recruitment of a further 17 boys from Cowdenbeath in 1929, along with youths from other parts of the Central Belt, as well as Orkney and Lewis.[8] Successes were documented in the YMCA's monthly journal, *Scottish Manhood*,[9] and sometimes in the press, usually in the form of letters from satisfied recruits. But some reports were refreshingly realistic, not least an account by George Simpson, the welfare officer whose party of 46 in 1928 comprised a potentially explosive mix of

> unemployed lads from Lanarkshire, colliers from Cowdenbeath and Lochgelly, quondam Morningside message-boys, and the public schoolboy appareled in plus-fours – a conglomeration with the smouldering fires of local patriotism, class-consciousness, and snobbery ready to burst into flame at any moment'.

In fact, his job was made easier when virtually the entire contingent was almost immediately laid low by sea-sickness, the 'Great Leveller', which probably 'did more to produce an *esprit de corps* than all the exhortations which I periodically delivered during the voyage'. Simpson was also realistic about the challenges of home-sickness, alien rural environments and unfamiliar farm work, but despite his reservations, he assured boys that they would be treated as members of their employers' families, rather than hired hands, and he summed up his report by commending the nomination scheme as a 'wonderful opportunity' for youths with 'grit and determination'.[10]

By 1930 the YMCA was acting as agent and clearing house for a number of participating churches, including the Church of Scotland. But in the 1920s Scotland's national church also briefly operated a small-scale emigration scheme of its own. Cornton Vale at Stirling later became the site of Scotland's only women's prison, but in its first incarnation – from 1907 to 1914 – it was a rehabilitation centre for destitute men, mainly alcoholics, under the auspices of the Church of Scotland's Social Work Department. In 1924 it reinvented itself as a preliminary training centre for potential emigrants – young men between the ages of 18 and 30, and from 1926 to 1930 it utilised government funding to part-sponsor the testing of approximately 100 applicants per year, as well as the passages of eligible candidates who could not pay their own way. But the Church of Scotland's optimism that it was performing a valuable social service was short-lived. Its partnership with the parish authorities in Glasgow to train unemployed youths from the city before placing them with Canadian farmers led to a catalogue of complaints from Canada that the recruits were not only inadequately funded to reach their destinations, but also included many individuals who were physically and morally defective, and in 1930 the venture spluttered to an ignominious end.[11]

In their sponsorship of migration, all these organisations prioritised the training and placement of adolescent boys in overseas employment, although the Salvation Army had a wider remit that included girls, war widows and families. Other rescue organisations that had cut their teeth in the Victorian era confined their efforts exclusively to children and adolescents, and from 1922 they got a new lease of life when the shared funding legislation enabled them to claim a grant of £14 10s a head to assist with transportation costs, placement and after-care.[12] Longest-established and best-known of these institutions in Scotland was Quarrier's Orphan Homes, which between 1872 and 1938 sent a total of around 7,000 children overseas, mainly to Canada. Although only 836 of that number left after 1914, and recruitment was suspended entirely from 1917–19 and 1933–37, the emigration scheme as a whole accounted for about a third of the children taken into Quarrier's care. Like other child migration ventures, it also left a legacy that reverberated on both sides of the Atlantic long after its demise.[13]

When William Quarrier died in 1903, the mantle of responsibility fell on his daughter and son-in-law. Following the pattern established in the early days, separate parties of boys and girls were shipped once a year from the Clyde to Fairknowe, which since 1887 had functioned as Quarrier's reception and distribution home at Brockville, Ontario. From there they were sent to households that had applied for a 'home child' and had been vetted by the Fairknowe staff. The snapshot of departures from January to April 1923 captured by the *Scottish Emigration Database* includes that year's party of 57 Quarrier boys, travelling on the ss *Cassandra*. Four of the boys can also be traced in the Homes' case files, which give a flavour of the reasons for their admission, and sometimes of their subsequent experiences. As in the earlier decades of Quarrier's rescue work, many children had simply been orphaned, although some parents were casualties of war or the 1919 influenza pandemic as well as the ongoing scourge of tuberculosis. Children also continued to be removed from parents who were deemed unsuitable. One of the *Cassandra* party, Dugald McR, who – unusually for Quarrier children – came from the Western Isles, had been taken away in 1914 from a mother who was 'of immoral habits' and lived in the vicinity of the whaling station in North Harris, in a house that was 'frequented by men of all nationalities'.[14] Another carry-over from previous practice was the policy of sending several siblings overseas in different years: such was the experience of Thomas McH from Bonnybridge, one of the *Cassandra* party, whose four brothers were sent to Canada between 1922 and 1931.[15]

In charge of the contingent on the *Cassandra* in March 1923 was Claude Winters, superintendent at Fairknowe. He made the same round trip virtually every year, and was confident that the recruits he accompanied were destined for a bright future. He believed that most employers went beyond a simple business arrangement, offering their charges schooling and 'homes in the strict sense of the term', and in 1921, despite a 'critical' labour problem in Canada, he asserted that Quarrier's had 'no trouble in placing our boys and girls'.[16] Even in 1930, he claimed that 'our family is largely undisturbed by the unemployment situation', but his optimism was misplaced, since only four years later the Fairknowe premises were sold to the local Children's Aid Society, and the final curtain came down on Quarrier's Canadian work.[17]

For some children the transatlantic bridge undoubtedly provided an escape route from destitution and despair. Even the private case files, which highlight problem cases while remaining silent on the experiences of the uncontroversial majority, make occasional observations about successful placements and stellar careers, including the Quarrier child who ended up as the head of Toronto's library services. And at periodic reunions, the last of which was held in 2001, former home children were happy to reminisce about the hardships they had overcome, on both sides of the Atlantic.[18] When emigration was still ongoing, achievements were trumpeted more explicitly in Quarrier's highly propagandised annual reports, in the hope of touching readers' pockets, as well as their heart strings. But while not being unduly cynical, we need to be aware of the distortions created by various forms of selection: institutional selection, self-selection and the selective memories of participants. Such distortion is most evident in the formulaic nature of many of the published letters, in which children – probably copying from a template – voiced their debt of gratitude to the Orphan Homes, waxed lyrical about their Canadian experiences, and expressed a hope that siblings might follow in their footsteps.

But even Claude Winters was a realist, who – like the YMCA's welfare officer, George Simpson – freely admitted that his work was 'not all sunshine'.[19] He and his staff needed the wisdom of Solomon as they juggled the managerial challenges of maintaining a complex operation on an increasingly tight budget with the logistical problems of supervision over a wide area and the frequent need to arbitrate in workplace disputes. Case file reports did not mince their words in denouncing problem children, and demonstrate that at least some of the 284 individuals who returned from Canada during the six decades when Quarrier's emigration scheme was operative were sent back for reasons of unsuitability or misconduct, with at least five being deported. Moodiness and restlessness were recurring complaints. William A. was a 'dour moody lad' with 'an exaggerated opinion of himself' who could 'work if he wants to', but was 'too prone to run about and have a good time at the expense of his employers'.[20] In 1932 Frederick W. was sent back to Aberdeen, despite the efforts of three siblings – also in Canada – to dissuade him. His footloose attitude had driven Winters to his wits' end: 'How in the world this boy is going to earn his passage home I do not know when we cannot keep him more than two or three days in a place... in my time here we have never had a boy just like him'.[21] But almost as soon as he was back in Scotland, Frederick wanted to return to Canada, a proposal supported by the leader of the Aberdeen Lads' Club. 'I am certain,' he wrote to Winters, 'the only way of saving this lad from trouble with the Police and also of sending him to a life in the Common Lodging House is to remove him entirely from his Aberdeen surroundings, and I can think of no better place than Canada.'[22] Winters, once bitten, refused to comply, and Frederick stayed in Aberdeen where, by 1933, he had become dependent on public assistance.

Moral lapses were taken particularly seriously. In 1931 two girls were shipped back to Scotland after, respectively, becoming pregnant and aborting an illegitimate child. The first case involved a 20-year-old who had gone through three unsuccessful placements since being sent to Canada a year earlier. She and her brothers had been taken in by Quarrier's in 1915 after their father had been killed in action and their mother imprisoned for prostitution, and one brother had preceded her to Canada in 1923. The decision to return Margaret was based partly on Quarrier's damning assessment of the father of her unborn child – a Roman Catholic from 'a worthless family' that was mixed up with boot-legging – and partly on a desire to pre-empt deportation. 'Had Margaret's condition been caused by the right sort of people', it was noted in the case file, 'we could have sought redress but she herself was so foolish in her conduct and associations, and the man to blame of such an order that we could not take action and there was nothing to do but return her to Scotland in the way we did, as otherwise she would have been deported when she became a charge upon public charity'. In Claude Winters' opinion, she was 'neither mentally nor morally capable of taking care of herself' and the final entry in her notes indicates that she did indeed become a public charge – in Paisley. Margaret's travelling companion, also aged 20, who had been in Ontario for two years, had declared herself 'sick of Canada and the people too'. Reports from Fairknowe were mixed, one suggesting that she was to some extent the victim of another girl's bad-mouthing and was clearly 'trying to make amends' for her mistakes. She was, however, suspected of following her mother and sister into prostitution, and when, after her return to Scotland, her Canadian employer offered to fund her return to the province the following year, the proposal was vehemently opposed by Claude Winters as damaging to Quarrier's reputation and 'decidedly undesirable from the Canadian point of view'.[23]

It was not only girls who were sent home in disgrace. In the same year, concern for the Homes' reputation was also the criterion in the decision to repatriate a 19-year-old Glasgow boy, who repeatedly fell out with his employers and in 1929 had served a term of imprisonment for vandalising a railway track.[24] He was accompanied on the ss *Scythia* by a fellow Glaswegian, whose father was threatening legal action, alleging that his son was 'not a poor orphan boy whom they can exploit in Canada', but had been spirited away three years earlier without parental consent. He may well have had a case, for Quarrier's, like other child rescue institutions, was not averse to removing children overseas without the blessing – or sometimes even the knowledge – of their parent(s) and intercepting or blocking any subsequent letters between them. Since parental drunkenness was a recurring factor in triggering referral to the Homes, and the father was described in the case notes as being 'much given to drink and always in debt', he would have fitted the profile of an unsuitable parent, against whose corrupting influence the Atlantic offered a suitable barrier. His bellicose attitude and repeated urgings to his son to come home had an unsettling effect on the boy, so that 'no amount of persuasion... would induce him to give this country a fair trial'. On one occasion he wrote:

If they don't send you back you can walk away from your job, go to the authorities in the nearest town and demand to be sent back here as you are only a child in the eyes of the law and they can't compel you to stay there and work against your will. They can't eat you, they can't hang you or shoot you and if you can make things so uncomfortable for them they will be damned glad to send you back on the first boat.[25]

But the boy himself was also seen as a liability. After three years in Canada, he had reached the age of 18 without achieving a successful placement, and was reputedly 'altogether disagreeable... impertinent and self-willed', as well as being irreligious, foul mouthed and addicted to 'trashy novels'.

Other cases reflect misfortune rather than misconduct. Jeanie A, from Edinburgh, who was reportedly unsatisfactory in the performance of her work and 'not stable' during the six years she spent in Ontario, was, according to a medical report, suffering from extreme homesickness as well as anaemia, and 'her morale is broken'.[26] In December 1929 Norah A. from Glasgow was found in a distressed state at the CNR station in Montreal, having run away from the cousins who employed her but had paid her no wages for three years. And Robert A. from Edinburgh, whose employer had treated him 'like a son' during the seven years he spent in Osgoode, Ontario, and bought him a farm in anticipation of his marriage to a local girl, was killed in an accident on a level crossing in 1927.[27]

Interviews with former Quarrier children, broadcast by BBC Scotland and CBC in 1994, suggest that painful memories sometimes lingered into adulthood and old age. Lack of information and training meant that, instead of slipping effortlessly into the work patterns of the Ontario farms to which they were sent, they encountered 'culture shock with a capital C'.[28]

According to Peter Graham, who featured in both programmes, 'We didn't have a clue. We were greener than the grass in May. I never saw a cow in my life.' Graham had arrived in 1931, at the age of 17. Sent to a farm north of Kingston, where he was paid $7 a month and given room and board, he fell victim to the crushing loneliness that – not surprisingly – afflicted many children who had been brought up in the crowded, communal environment of the Orphan Homes. Graham recalled lying awake at night, almost overwhelmed by a longing to be back in his 'old familiar haunts' along the River Gryffe at Bridge of Weir. 'I don't think there's any feeling like it, homesickness. I don't think – if you've never experienced [it] you wouldn't know it. It's so, it's so overpowering, it's so something that you can't do anything about'.[29] He was also left on the sidelines at social events. 'Who wants to dance with you? You're an immigrant, or an orphan, or just a hired man, you know. So that was my case, I never danced'.[30]

Quarrier's difficulties in the late 1920s were not due entirely to the worsening economic situation. In his annual report for 1929, Winters alluded to an unprecedented 'measure of unrest' which he blamed on the bad influence 'of boys other than our own who will not settle'.[31] He may have been referring to a contingent of 'Cossar boys' who appeared in the Quarrier emigration register for 1927. Dr George Cossar was a Glasgow physician and philanthropist who had begun to send boys across the Atlantic before the war, to a training farm in New Brunswick that he purchased in 1910 and operated at his own expense. Then in 1922, thanks to a combination of the new government funding and private donations, he was able to purchase, for £2,000, the 36-acre Craigielinn estate near Paisley on which to train 'city boys of the poorer classes' for future careers as farm workers in Canada and Australia. Since Craigielinn was only a stone's throw from Quarrier's Homes, and operated on very similar principles (though confined to boys), it is not surprising that they co-operated, at least in a Canadian context.

Under the Empire Settlement Act Cossar was given a grant in return for testing 100 potential emigrants a year, although he encouraged boys to contribute as far as possible to their maintenance, training and examination expenses. By 1932, when financial difficulties led to the free transfer of Craigielinn to the Church of Scotland's Social Work Committee, Cossar had overseen the emigration of around 900 boys from all over Scotland to Canada and 200 to Australia. Like Winters, Cossar was in no doubt that his social engineering scheme was beneficial to all and he was pleased that 'a leavening' of rural boys had raised the overall standard of recruitment.[32] Launching an appeal for £2,000 in 1924, he claimed that boys who for years had been 'without the faintest prospect of work' were now earning good wages overseas and their cheerful letters were 'as good as a tonic in these depressing days'.[33]

Approximately half of the letters published in his annual reports came from Australia. From Victoria one correspondent in 1923 extolled the merits of the 'rubber udder' training in milking that he had received at Craigielinn, encouraged others to follow in his footsteps and claimed that the 'Scotch' were universally liked, 'no matter where you go in Australia'.[34] The picture painted from Canada was of a country that was 'as civilised as Britain', with abundant food and an attractive outdoor lifestyle. 'I will never regret coming here,' wrote one boy from Ontario in 1927. 'We have all kinds of fun all the year round. After work is over we go swimming or fishing, or go riding round the countryside horseback. No more running around the streets of Glasgow for me again'.[35]

These glowing assertions clearly have to be digested with the same pinch of salt as Quarrier's promotional correspondence. And Cossar's sponsorship scheme was marred by a similar undercurrent of criticism, from recruits, employers and immigration authorities. Writing to his mother in Glasgow in 1924, 14-year-old Hugh Paterson claimed that Cossar was only an agent for the British Immigration and Colonisation Association, which in turn was a tool of the Orange Order in Canada. He felt he was being dragooned into accepting a low-wage contract that would also prevent him and his brother moving from New Brunswick to Toronto, where three siblings were already settled and where his widowed mother was about to emigrate with two younger children.[36] Employers sometimes complained about undersized or feckless boys, such as John W., who in 1928 went to work for a farmer in Andover, New Brunswick. 'He is all arms and legs', complained his employer, 'and with the ever present cigarette, he looks like a centipede'. As well as spending all his wages on tobacco, he was 'very apt to tell lies', though the employer added, somewhat incongruously, 'He is of good manners and attractive personality'.[37]

In 1924 a former matron of Gagetown launched a scathing attack on the farm's managers, the Meiklejohns, claiming that the boys were poorly fed and ill clad, accommodated in cold, unsanitary premises, and subjected to bullying treatment.[38] The Meiklejohns' successor, John Jackson, may have paid more attention to hygiene, but was criticised by the immigration authorities for inadequate scrutiny of employers' references and total neglect of after-care. D.J. Murphy, the former Aberdeen agent, who by 1930 was the Immigration Department's representative in Saint John, alleged that many boys were 'farmed out without agreements' and were exploited by employers who overworked them and withheld their wages.[39] But criticism was also levelled at Cossar himself. As early as 1913, 60 citizens living in the vicinity of his New Brunswick farm at Gagetown had petitioned the federal immigration authorities to impose more stringent checks on his boys, too many of whom, they claimed, had criminal tendencies. Almost 20 years later, the enforcement of such checks was justified by Ottawa in terms similar to the criticism levelled at Glasgow parish council recruits trained at Cornton Vale: that there was a need to weed out the high percentage of 'runts and failures' who were being fished out of the 'gutter' and shipped to Canada.[40]

Cossar, meanwhile, hit back at his critics, claiming that restrictive regulations and inconsistent selection criteria were leading to the rejection of applicants simply on the grounds of underdeveloped physique. When the Australian authorities turned down three 'intelligent and physically fit' Craigielinn boys in 1926, he complained of a farcical recruitment system that summoned boys for interview at labour exchanges 'just for the disappointment of being rejected in this wholesale manner'. In similar vein, after Gagetown farm had become – at Cossar's own suggestion – New Brunswick's reception centre for *all* the province's sponsored juvenile immigrants in 1928, he accused the Canadian authorities of undue interference, particularly through the enforcement of stringent federal medical regulations and a preference for rural boys with a secondary education. Having operated independently in his early years, Cossar never accepted the need to cut his coat according to the cloth of government-sponsored migration, which he regarded as a two-edged sword, offering financial assistance with one hand while restricting his freedom of selection with the other.

The whole saga of institutional child migration is clothed in controversy and mixed messages. In the same month that the *Glasgow Herald* published correspondence which categorically condemned juvenile emigration as 'one of the most fatal mistakes that this nation ever made', it was happy to endorse the opportunities offered to demoralised city boys through Cossar's schemes.[41] Cossar himself was not alone among sponsors in regarding official intervention as a mixed blessing.

But much more vehement were those who, from a variety of perspectives, condemned the whole philosophy and practice out of hand, and whose criticism stands in sharp contrast to hagiographies of the philanthropists and the fund-raising publications of their institutions. To socialists, it was a device for shoring up the status quo by diverting attention from the need for state welfare provision. To psychologists, it drove a coach and horses through new child-centred ideas that stressed the importance of maintaining the family unit wherever possible.

Although most enterprises still claimed to be rooted in Christian philanthropy, the moral code that had inspired their founders had been eclipsed by an increasingly distasteful eugenic agenda. While British critics claimed that the real objective of the scheme was to secure cheap labour for Canadian and Australian farms, the host nations complained that they were being used as dumping grounds for destitute, degenerate or unemployable slum dwellers. That there was more than a grain of truth in at least one of those accusations is demonstrated in the recommendation by Frank Ogden, leader of the Aberdeen Lads' Club, that there was 'no better place than Canada' for returned Quarrier boy, Frederick W., if he was to be saved from the gutter or the police cell.[42]

In the midst of all these arguments stood the participants, some of whom were blissfully unaware that to emigrate was not the same as to take the orphanage's annual day trip to the seaside. Loneliness and homesickness were a common refrain in their recollections, while some fell victim to physical or sexual abuse which they were only able to articulate in later life. Over-stretched receiving homes put too much faith in the goodwill of employers who, in the absence of systematic inspections, could simply ignore written agreements about treatment, education and wages. It was only after the suicides of three 'home boys' in Canada and five similar deaths in Australia that the whole policy of juvenile emigration was investigated by a British delegation in 1924, leading a year later to new legislation that restricted the practice to the over-14s.

By the end of the 1920s juvenile migration had withered on the vine in the face of worldwide economic depression. Against a backdrop of new childcare policies after 1945, most, including the specifically Scottish institutions, did not resurrect the practice. Those which did – Barnardos, Fairbridge and some Catholic organisations – operated mainly in Western Australia, though a few hundred children were also sent to New Zealand and Southern Rhodesia. Child migrants continued to be shipped overseas until 1967, although numbers dwindled as opposition mounted. From the 1940s the Home Office, as the government agency responsible for child welfare in Britain, had wanted to terminate the practice because conditions in Australian institutions – many of which had been investigated and found wanting – did not conform to the requirements of the Children Act of 1948 in Britain. For two decades, however, it fought a losing battle against both the powerful participating institutions and the Commonwealth Relations Office, which was swayed by Australia's determination to recruit only white immigrants. The legacy is still with us today, as bitter experiences are revisited in a host of books, plays, dramas and documentaries.[43]

Antipodean Ventures: the Flock House Scheme

Not all sponsored child and juvenile migrants were the institutionalised products of dysfunctional or destitute families or plucked from the ranks of the unemployed. Nor were all inter-war sponsorship schemes reheated Victorian or Edwardian dishes. The mainly English Big Brother movement was founded in 1925 by Melbourne businessman Richard Linton. Initially seen as Victoria's version of the older Dreadnought scheme that brought almost 7,000 farm trainees – also mostly from England – to New South

Wales between 1900 and 1929, it soon spread further afield. Its main targets were teenaged public and secondary school boys, whose anxious parents were assured that their sons – the so-called 'Little Brothers' – would each be assigned a 'Big Brother', an adult British migrant from a similar background who promised to help the new migrant adjust, mediate between him and his employer, and generally keep an eye on him until he was 21. The Little Brother's part of the bargain was to follow his mentor's advice and maintain correspondence. By 1929, 1,515 boys had been brought to Australia under the scheme, which dipped during the depression, was terminated in 1941, but revived in New South Wales in the 1950s and 1960s. According to Australia House, 'excellent publicity' in Scotland led to 50 per cent of applications coming from north of the border in 1950, and 292 Scots in all (23 per cent of the UK total) between 1947 and 1953.[44]

New Zealand also got in on the act, with a more solid Scottish involvement. On 9 March 1915 the SS *Aberdon,* bound from Seaham in County Durham to Aberdeen with a cargo of coal, was lost in the North Sea, probably after hitting a mine. Among those who died was 27-year-old merchant seaman Alexander Fraser, who was looking forward to a reunion in Aberdeen with his pregnant wife, Jeannie, and infant son, John. Employment as a weaver and fish worker helped Jeannie to keep the bereaved family together, but by the time John and his younger brother Alex were in their teens she had married Thomas Rudd and acquired a stepdaughter. While it is possible that her decision to send John (16) and Alex (15) to New Zealand in 1931 was influenced by a desire to detach them from her new family, her grandson, Stephen Fraser, was always told by his father that it was a selfless, sacrificial decision. 'It can't have been easy for my gran sending her two sons away to the other side of the world,' he reflected in 2007. 'But the opportunity came up for them to have a better life – that's how dad always described it anyway.'[45]

The opportunity that Jeannie Rudd was able to invoke was part of another sponsored emigration venture that between the wars brought a total of 635 boys and 128 girls from Britain to New Zealand. The so-called Flock House scheme was funded from the marketing of wool and was masterminded by a Scottish emigrant and politician, Edward Newman. On leaving Partick in 1876, 17-year-old Newman had worked on sheep farms in Hawke's Bay and Katikati before acquiring a 3,000-acre property in Turakina in 1882. By the turn of the century he had become a prominent farmer and farmers' union official in the Rangitikei district, and in 1908 was elected to parliament. During and after the war his concern for veterans and their families was reflected in his support for soldier farm settlement and ultimately in the wool growers' trust which he established and chaired from 1920 until his death in 1946.[46]

Under a wartime arrangement all New Zealand's wool had been sold at a fixed price to the imperial government, but towards the end of the conflict a surplus was generated and sold by the government on the open market at a higher price. Since Newman felt strongly that this situation was attributable to the protection of sea routes, he proposed to the wool growers that their share of the profits should be invested in a fund to support the dependents of those who had suffered as a consequence of defending the empire at sea: 'men of the Mercantile Marine who had carried the wool Home through dangerous seas, and men of the Royal Navy who had helped to keep the trade routes clear'.[47] Along with civil servant T.R. Lees, head of the Department of Imperial Government Supplies, Newman prepared about 24,000 circulars and spoke at farmers' meetings throughout the country. Ten per cent of wool growers at all levels – over 2,600 individuals – agreed to support the venture and so was born the 'New Zealand Sheep Owners Acknowledgement of Debt to British Seamen Fund'. By August 1920, when the first meeting of subscribers was held in Wellington, Newman's efforts had generated donations totalling £237,000, and a London Advisory Committee was subsequently appointed under the chairmanship of the New Zealand High Commissioner to disburse funds, food parcels and blankets to bereaved families in Britain.

By 1923, after Lees had visited England, it was agreed that the bulk of the money could best be spent in bringing the adolescent children of deceased sailors to New Zealand for training in farm work and ultimate establishment on their own properties. The 1,000-acre Flock House farm near the town of Bulls in the North Island was purchased from a family of Scottish settlers, the McKelvies, along with almost 7,000 acres of adjoining land. It opened its doors in 1924, the same year that the Salvation Army established a training farm for migrant boys at Putaruru near Rotorua, on similar lines. The first contingent of 25 boys arrived at Flock House in June 1924, followed by a second party of 29 in September. Having secured the Prince of Wales as patron, the scheme also won the approval of Lord Baden-Powell, who was present when the Fraser brothers embarked for Auckland on the ss *Rangitata* in 1931. By 1925 assistance had been extended to girls, when a 30-acre property was acquired 25 miles from Bulls at Awapuni, Palmerston North, where the YWCA agreed to give female recruits a six-month training course in a variety of domestic and farm-based skills. A few parents were also assisted under the Fund.

Selection was in the hands of the London Advisory Committee, whose original remit was to identify suitable boys between the ages of 15 and 17. They were to be 'of good character and health, of suitable temperament, and desirous of learning and pursuing the occupation of farming'.[48] Alex Fraser's referees ticked almost all the committee's boxes, commending him as 'conscientious, honest and trustworthy, well-built and with good moral character'. He had, moreover, 'been dentally treated and tonsils removed'.[49] Alex and his brother were not the only siblings selected from Aberdeen. Three other sets of brothers and a trio of sisters also appear in the records, along with at least eight sets of brothers from other parts of Scotland. In six further cases a brother was followed by a sister, usually after a year or more.[50]

In November 1925 concern at the lack of Scottish participation prompted Frank Ivey, the Fund's London-based secretary, to give an illustrated lecture at the YMCA in Aberdeen, chaired by the Lord Provost. Ivey's exhortations were supported from the platform by Bishop Deane, who particularly commended the scheme to unemployed youths from Aberdeen, 100 of whom were in the audience.[51] In fact, Scotland was slightly over-represented among the Flock House recruits: at a time when only 9.3 per cent of the UK population lived north of the border, the 93 boys and 14 girls accounted, respectively, for 14.64 per cent and 10.93 per cent of the total number. The majority – 29 – came from Aberdeen, followed by Glasgow, with 25. Edinburgh, as in the Salvation Army sample from 1923, was poorly represented, with only seven recruits,[52] and the Marquis of Graham, the Fund's representative in Scotland, was particularly disappointed at the lack of interest shown by fishermen's sons from the islands, 'for they are undoubtedly the boys who are wanted in New Zealand'.[53]

Recruits were sent out in parties of between 25 and 30, supervised by a YMCA officer, and in the peak years of the mid-1920s, around 100 boys a year arrived at Flock House. Their passages, as well as two years' outfit, were covered, and after up to a year's training, they were apprenticed, usually on sheep farms, some of which were owned by the Fund's subscribers. The YMCA maintained its involvement by liaising with district committees in providing after-care through visits made by welfare officers to recruits on placement. Apprentices were paid two thirds of their wages, the other third being sent by their employers to the trustees, who, acting *in loco parentis*, invested the money in Post Office savings accounts on their charges' behalf.[54] Boys who were 'diligent and trustworthy', as well as competent, had their savings subsidised by the trustees at a rate of 15 shillings to the pound, to a maximum of £250, giving them a useful nest-egg when they

Three unidentified Flock House boys arriving in New Zealand on the *Rangitiki*, 1950
(*Evening Post* collection, Alexander Turnbull Library)

came of age and wanted to establish themselves on their own farms.[55]

Within less than a decade of its inception, however, the Flock House venture fell victim to the worldwide Depression. The girls' work was the first to falter, but in 1931 the New Zealand government terminated the migration of British boys, and the Fraser brothers were in the penultimate sailing party. In 1937 the Flock House property was sold to the New Zealand government, after which it operated as a training farm for New Zealanders (or immigrants who had arrived under their own steam) until its closure in 1988. Between 1949 and 1952 a brief and partial revival of the inter-war arrangements saw 49 British boys – the sons of airmen as well as seamen – brought out to Flock House, but the idea never really got off the ground, perhaps because of new British expectations following the Children Act of 1948. Concerns were expressed in Home Office circles about selection procedures, after-care and freedom to return to Britain, with disagreement surfacing over whether Flock House should fund the repatriation of homesick boys who could not adjust to farming in particular or to life in New Zealand in general.[56] As for the Fraser brothers, neither went into farming: John became a nurse and Alex a carpenter. They put down permanent roots, though Stephen Fraser recalls of his father (who made one return visit to his native city while stationed in Cirencester during the war) that 'a bit of his heart was always in the old country... After he'd had a tipple or two it was always "The Northern Lights of Old Aberdeen", memories of swimming on Aberdeen beach and big outings to Stonehaven'.[57]

War-time Emergency: Seavacuees

Those who sponsored the migration of children and juveniles to the dominions generally expected them to put down roots overseas. But the short-lived 'seavacuation' experiment of 1940 was a very different enterprise. Born out of the fear of imminent invasion in summer 1940, it came to an abrupt end following the sinking of the *City of Benares* in the Atlantic on 17 September with the loss of 87 children. By that time 2,662 recruits had been relocated overseas by the Children's Overseas Reception Board (CORB): 1,530 in Canada, 577 in Australia, 353 in South Africa and 202 in New Zealand. A further 838 – including the politician Shirley Williams and her brother – went to the United States under private arrangements. Some began to trickle back from 1942 when the threat of invasion receded, but most stayed abroad until the war was over. By May 1945, 25 per cent had returned to Britain, and when the CORB office was finally closed in February 1946 2,209 children had come home. Of the nine per cent who stayed overseas, several persuaded their parents to join them, with Australia registering the highest retention rate, 23 per cent.[58]

In contrast to domestic evacuation, which had a long gestation and predated the outbreak of war, plans for sending children out of the country were rushed through during June 1940 in response to the occupation of Britain's allies across the Channel and North Sea. Offers of hospitality by the four dominions prompted the government to act, and advisory, selection and implementation arrangements were hastily put in place under the chairmanship of Geoffrey Shakespeare, Dominions Under-Secretary. Previously opposed to overseas evacuation on the grounds that it was elitist, cowardly and emotionally damaging to participants, Shakespeare changed his mind as the security situation deteriorated. He also anticipated a beneficial legacy, hoping that on their return children would become 'evangelists of Empire' in a new post-war emigration, acting as informal agents who, in their homes, schools and communities, 'will talk Canada, Australia, New Zealand and South Africa, in season and out of season'.[59] His conversion was not shared by Churchill, who felt the proposal both reflected and encouraged a defeatist attitude. He was also dismayed at the 'hysterical' response from panic-stricken parents who bombarded the CORB office with so many enquiries that within a month its staff had grown from 30 to 620 to cope with the demand.[60] By early July over 200,000 applications had been received, despite the War Cabinet's determination to highlight the risks and suspend operations – a policy that was criticised for denying poorer children the escape route available to their more privileged counterparts who had already been sent overseas privately.

In an atmosphere of controversy, confusion and secrecy, a total of 19 parties was despatched over a two-month period, 16 of which arrived safely. About two-fifths were selected from Scotland and Wales, and four shipments comprised only Scottish children.[61] Escorts – 85 per cent of whom were female – included Salvation Army and youth organisation leaders, as well as teachers. One escort was allocated to every 15 children, whose ages ranged from 5 to 16 and who came from all over the country to embark at either Glasgow or Liverpool. Families were usually given a maximum of three or four days' notice, and goodbyes had to be said locally, as CORB did not permit parents to accompany their children to the ship. Nominated homes – usually the households of relatives or friends – accounted for 63 per cent of the placements, especially among the Scots sent to Canada, where, Geoffrey Shakespeare observed, 'every good Scottish family has a dozen relations'.[62] The driving force was usually parental, as with Betty from Edinburgh, whose parents had previously spent time in New Zealand, and hoped that their 13-year-old daughter's evacuation there would smooth the path for the re-migration of the whole family, including Betty's asthmatic younger sister.[63] But Shiela and Jessie Mackay from Grangemouth 'both wanted to go' and were among those children who persuaded their parents to apply to CORB.[64]

After the sometimes traumatic experience of leaving home, the children were billeted in embarkation hostels, usually schools, where – on top of earlier medical screening – they were subjected to rigorous examination by doctors appointed by the host dominions. About 11 per cent failed the test, primarily on medical grounds, although a few were rejected for other reasons. Miss G.B. Finlayson, a Glasgow teacher, had to return to their surprised parents a brother and sister who had been rejected because the girl was overwhelmed by the procedure:

> They were poorly clad. Their possessions were in one small attaché case and a brown paper parcel. They were from a slum area of Glasgow and, of course, they spoke the 'Glesca' lingo. The boy managed to tackle the doctor's questions not too badly. But the five year old girl had not a clue what he was saying. I could not interfere. She was so shy, timid and pathetic. And, of course, she was rejected out of hand. That meant the brother, too, was not accepted.[65]

Friction sometimes surfaced between CORB's English headquarters and its Scottish division, particularly over conditions in the Glasgow hostel. By early September so many complaints had been received that the Glasgow authorities were asked to discontinue its use, but they simply changed the name (though not the location) from Albert Road to Balgrave Road school. When that deception, and the ongoing problems, were reported to HQ by Roland Cartwright, a Yorkshire headmaster and escort, his bad experience there was blamed by his Scottish colleagues on his own inadequacies, a charge that was rejected by Marjorie Maxse, CORB's London Director, who was well aware of 'the antipathy of the Scottish Office' to English escorts.[66]

Shiela and Jessie Mackay were sent to CORB's Liverpool hostel on 12 August 1940, along with two other recruits from Grangemouth, Sylvia and Alex Winton. Jessie was 14, but the others were only eight years old, and they were escorted on the train journey by one of their school teachers, Miss Milne. For weeks their headmistress, Miss Martin, had been helping them prepare for their big adventure, including getting 'lots and lots of new clothes' and on the 'great day' of departure she sent them off with presents and sweets. After a journey on a train packed with other seavacuees they were marched to a 'miniature city' – the orphanage where they were to be billeted until they embarked on the Dutch ship the SS *Volendam*. On 30 August, however, five days out, the ship was torpedoed in the middle of the night. Shiela's diary documents how adventure suddenly changed to terror.

It was about half past ten that same night that I woke to find someone shaking me violently. When I sat up Jessie and the two Robertsons [their cabin mates from Galashiels] were up and fully dressed. Then I heard the alarm ringing. I got up and before I was half dressed Jessie and the Robertsons were away. I wasn't properly awake either. I just drifted along the crowded passage the way the rest were going. Then a big black sailor came up to me and asked me my boat station. I told him and I can remember he just hoisted me over his shoulders and took me safely to my boat station. By this time I was wide awake. I thanked the sailor and then got hold of Jessie. I bet you I gave her a right good row for leaving me. At first I thought it was another practice alarm at first. Then when we had to climb into the lifeboats I realised with a shiver it was no practise (sic). I've never seen the sea as rough in my life as it was that night. It was also pitch black. We got into the lifeboats then a man at each end began lowering it into the water. It seemed a long way down to the water and the boats kept swinging back and forward and smashing against the sides of the ship. But at last we reached near the water. The man cut one end of the rope and the one end of the boat fell with a splash into the water leaving the other end in mid-air. But the man at the other end cut the other rope and then we were rocking up and down in the very stormy seas. Then I discerned a man coming down the rope ladder into our boat. The iron thing that had held the rope was swinging about it went towards the man and crashed against his head. He was knocked unconscious and fell into the water and got drowned. I didn't realise how horrible it was at the time. I was just wondering if I would go the same way as him. Wondering if I would ever see dry land again. Wondering if I would ever come out alive.[67]

In fact, all 231 CORB children on board the *Volendam* survived the experience. On being returned to Gourock they were feted by the newspapers, and Geoffrey Shakespeare, for their bravery and resilience. By her own account, Shiela's first words to her mother when they were reunited in Glasgow were 'could I go back?' and a local Grangemouth newspaper – doubtless sniffing a propaganda coup – claimed that all four children from the town were 'unanimous' in their desire to make a second attempt. 'A torpedo seems to make them all the more anxious to get to their destination', it observed, adding that neither Mrs Mackay nor Mrs Winton had changed their opinion 'that getting the children out of the country was the best thing possible'.[68]

A group of British children who were sent to New Zealand under the Overseas Reception Scheme (CORB), 27 September 1940

(*Evening Post* collection, Alexander Turnbull Library)

Less than a month later, two of the *Volendam*'s passengers found themselves at sea again, aboard the ss *City of Benares*, en route to Montreal, but this time they were not so fortunate. Three days out into the Atlantic, Michael Brooker and Patricia Allan were among the 77 CORB children (and 171 other passengers and crew) lost when the ship sank within 20 minutes of being torpedoed. Thirteen children survived, and were brought back to Gourock, along with the other 145 survivors. There they were met by Geoffrey Shakespeare and Edith Sowerbutts, a CORB port embarkation officer who was already in bomb-blitzed Glasgow when her boss arrived with the devastating news. It was she who was responsible for returning survivors to their families, as well as children whose embarkation had been cancelled when the plug was pulled on the whole CORB operation.[69]

By the end of October all the seavacuees had arrived at their destinations. The motives of their hosts ranged from family obligations to patriotism, and supervisory arrangements were left largely to local authorities in the dominions. Sometimes everything worked out well and both sides had a positive experience. Mrs J.R. Osbaldistone from Aberdeen, but settled in Wellington, New Zealand, was delighted to host two boys from her native city, and felt that her ability to converse in Doric 'must have made the settling-in so much easier for them'.[70] Another CORB boy compared his two-roomed tenement home in Scotland with the material and educational advantages of life in New Zealand, a sentiment confirmed by the mother of two brothers, also sent to New Zealand, who heaped praise on the host family, firmly believing that 'their lives and ours were enriched by the relationship with these wonderful people'.[71] On the other side of the world, Moyra Paterson from Glasgow and Eric Bell from Aberdeen both stayed on in Canada to complete university courses.[72]

In 1944 Margaret Bruce wrote to the Premier of Ontario, seeking advice on how to effect a family reunion in Canada. CORB wanted to repatriate her three children, who had been sent to an uncle in Aurora in 1940, and had told the parents that if they did not agree to their return in the summer of 1944 they would have to make their own arrangements and foot the bill. But Mr and Mrs Bruce, while 'longing to see the children', had good reason for not wanting them to return to Glasgow. 'We were bombed out in March 1941', Mrs Bruce explained, 'and lost absolutely everything we possessed and since then have been living in a dull basement room'. With no prospect of being rehoused, they had 'no home to bring the children back to', had applied to emigrate themselves, and wanted to know how long they would have to wait. The children, who had 'got on exceptionally well in Canada' and 'really do not want to come back', were anxious for their parents to join them in Ontario.[73] The reply she received was not particularly encouraging. Although there was no bar against British subjects settling in Canada as long as they were fit and had enough funds to keep them until they found work, the British government had imposed an embargo on the transfer of money from Britain to Canada, exit permits were not being granted, and shipping companies had a two-year waiting list. The prolonged separation of families was 'just one of those things parents must put up with'.[74]

Isa, Robert and Gordon Bruce were happily settled on their uncle's farm, but some children were undeniably lonely, ostracised or abused, or were themselves disruptive influences. In disturbing echoes of some of the institutional child migrants' stories, an unhappy minority moved from placement to placement, while others' plight was reflected in bed-wetting. One seavacuee recalled experiencing 'no love after I said goodbye to my parents in Edinburgh', and carried the pain of parting with her throughout her sojourn in New Zealand.[75] Siblings were not always kept together, homes were not always inspected, and paperwork did not reach the dominions until long after the child had arrived. Winifred F. from Glasgow was considered a 'problem child', who left her first placement in British Columbia because of lack of space in the host's home, and her second because she was a 'difficult child to manage'. Thomas L., also from Glasgow, was removed from his first placement in Winnipeg for 'bad behaviour', and after three more placements joined the Canadian army, but in 1944 was arrested for 'vagrancy and forgery'.[76]

Geoffrey Shakespeare claimed that problems were more common in nominated homes than when children were sent to strangers, perhaps because expectations were higher and misunderstandings more likely to arise. Four cases in CORB's Canada files seem to bear out that statement. Catherine B. from Uddingston was 'not happy' in her grandfather's home in Glen Leslie, Alberta, and left almost as soon as she had arrived; Mary R. from Glasgow 'did not fit in' to either of her placements in Vancouver, the first of which was with a relative; Hazel and Violet S., sent to William S. in New Westminster, BC, left within a few months because they were 'not wanted'; and William W. from Dundee was removed from his first placement in Toronto at his aunt's request. Having allegedly given 'too much trouble' in three subsequent placements, his parents agreed to his return to Scotland in 1943.[77]

In the case of Harry and Douglas M., it seems to have been the parent rather than the children who created the problem. Like all placements in the United States, the boys' evacuation to Chicago in 1940 was privately arranged, following a chance meeting in Edinburgh the previous year between their mother and an American couple, the Claspers, who had agreed to pay the outward fare and board the boys. CORB only became involved when in 1943 the mother – who had been widowed and bombed – started to write a series of impassioned letters to all and sundry, including Churchill and the king. Claiming that the Claspers had reneged on their promise to look after the children, she demanded either that a priority permit to be issued to allow her to visit them or that the boys should be returned to her at CORB's expense. Following investigations by CORB's American representative and the British Consulate, the consensus of opinion was that the Claspers had been ideal foster parents, who had 'made admirable arrangements for the children's care and wellbeing', including spending large sums of money on medical care.[78] The mother's unreasonable demands had, however, driven them to despair, so that in 1943 they seized on advice from the American Committee for the Care of Evacuated Children that the way was now open to have the boys returned to Scotland. In December 1944, after a short and unhappy interlude in the care of the Edwin Gould Foundation in New York, the Committee for Overseas Children of the English-Speaking Union funded their equally unhappy repatriation. Both boys pined for their American foster parents, to whom they longed to return, and the older boy refused point-blank to live with his mother, lodging instead with his infirm and impoverished maternal grandmother, who had a very low opinion of her daughter's parenting skills.

Geoffrey Shakespeare's early concern about the emotionally damaging consequences of overseas evacuation seem to have been borne out in this sad case. But Harry and Douglas were not the only children who missed their foster parents or longed to return whence they came: there is plenty anecdotal evidence that returning home could be almost as dislocating as leaving. In some cases, the excitement of reunions soon turned to disillusionment with poverty, food shortages and lower living standards, while parents who had saved their rations to provide special reunion treats were unprepared for children turning up their noses at the 'awful' food. Before long, their unfavourable comparisons began to irritate not only families but also schoolmates, some of whom accused the seavacuees of having run away from the war. Readjusting to the academic and social environment of school was a further hurdle, not least when children were ridiculed for the strange accents they had picked up.

The spectre of potential problems can be read into a generally upbeat account in the *Glasgow Herald*'s account of the arrival of 111 former seavacuees at Glasgow's Central Station in July 1945. The 'small, timid children' of five years earlier, it observed, had turned into handsome adults who 'astonished their parents with their Canadian voices, self-possession, and sartorial smartness. Tall, sophisticated young women rushed up to throw their arms around parents who hardly recognised them, while boys shook hands firmly with fathers who could only stare at their eccentric hats, sports jackets, and neckties'.[79] Although the *Herald* added that 'the young people forgot their Canadian self-possession in the delight of being one of the family again', in some cases the excitement of reunion soon gave way to strained relationships, as different family members faced the challenge of getting to know each other again. Parents had become strangers – sometimes elderly strangers – and siblings who had stayed behind were often jealous of the attention being lavished on the returners.

Despite its short life, the CORB venture was extensively documented in home and host countries. Like institutional child migration, it also highlighted emotive cases which in turn fuelled debates about its underlying philosophy, as well as its practice. Such dramatic but unrepresentative experiences meant, however, that the part played by child migrants in the wider story of sponsorship has been distorted by the ongoing controversy in which it has become enmeshed. Assisted emigration may be most commonly – and pejoratively – associated with children and adolescents, but they did not have a monopoly on sponsorship, the bulk of which involved adults, and attracted little public attention.

The Hudson's Bay Company

Sponsorship of adults in the second half of the 20th century was often tied to specific employment opportunities. One venture in which Scots were disproportionately involved had a much longer history than even child migration. Its final fling was highlighted by a BBC documentary in December 2011 which brought together four of the last remaining 'Bay Boys' who in the 1960s and 1970s signed up for a life of adventure with the Hudson's Bay Company.[80] John Todd from St Andrews, Jim Deyell from Shetland, John Graham from Lindean near Selkirk, and Donald Mearns from Aberdeenshire stayed on in the Canadian north after the fur trade collapsed, and Todd became finance minister in the North West Territories legislature. Others, as we shall see, came back to Scotland.

It was in the late 1700s that Orcadian labourers in particular had first been targeted by the HBC on five-year, renewable, terms of service. Before long these sojourners became the backbone of the Company, which in the 19th century cast its recruitment net more widely across the Scottish geographical and social spectrum. From Governors George Simpson and Donald Smith down to an army of anonymous factors and labourers, Scots dominated the HBC, decided policy and kept open the arteries of the fur trade throughout the Canadian north.[81] Their involvement persisted until the 1960s, but by the early 20th century the emphasis had begun to shift from unskilled labourers to school leavers with initiative and leadership qualities, harnessed to book-keeping skills. Just before the First World War there was an enthusiastic response to press advertisements for teenaged junior clerks who were willing to engage for three years to work in the Athabasca and Saskatchewan districts. The Company was looking for 'either those who have just left school with training on the Modern Side or those with some experience of office work... of robust health and... able to withstand the rigours of a Northern Canadian winter'. As well as paying for their passage, plus board and lodging, they would earn £30 in their first year, rising to £40 and £50 in years two and three, plus a £20 bonus on satisfactory completion of their contract, and a premium of 10 dollars per annum once they had mastered the local language.[82]

Early generations of recruits had been driven primarily by a need to support family incomes through the monies they remitted home. In the 20th century, however, economic imperatives were replaced by a thirst for adventure, which was the dominant recurring theme in the flood of applications, both before and after the war. By the 1920s the Company was hiring its labourers *in situ*, but still preferred to source its apprentice clerks and store managers from Scotland, especially the north-east corner in the hinterland of Aberdeen. George Fowlie from Alford, Ernest Hampton from Banchory and Taylor Third from St Fergus were recruited in 1923, 1924 and 1926 respectively, and all subsequently served together at York Factory, the post that had once housed the Company's Governor. Fowlie brought to his new employment valuable accounting experience gained through his employment in a local bank, while Hampton and Third were alerted to opportunities in the sub-Arctic because close relatives were already working for the HBC.[83] Perhaps Maud-based agent, William Craighead, had also had a part to play, by his regular appeals throughout the 1920s for fit young men 'of good education and some business experience' who, as the pre-war advertisements had also emphasised, could cope with the challenging environmental conditions.[84]

A generation later ex-Harrovian Angus Pelham Burn was attracted rather than deterred by the northern environment. It was in 1951 that he joined the HBC, not directly from school, but after studying at the Northern

Angus Pelham Burn in the Hudson's Bay Company store, Lac Seul, Ontario, 1951
(© Angus Pelham Burn)

College of Agriculture in Aberdeen. Having seen two local press advertisements, encouraging readers to 'Go lumbering in Queensland' or 'join the romantic fur trade', he applied to both, but only the Hudson's Bay Company replied to his letter. Summoned to Glasgow for an interview, he was one of just two successful applicants from a batch of between 20 and 30, and in due course found himself on a flight to Winnipeg, from where he was initially transferred to Lac Seul, Ontario. But most of his seven-year sojourn was spent as manager at Big Trout Lake, the major trading post in northern Ontario. During that time the Company paid for two fortnight-long round trips back to Scotland, before he returned permanently in 1959 to pursue a career in business and public life.

Opportunities in the Canadian north were broadcast mainly through press advertisements, though personal encounters also had a part to play. Jock Gibb, having performed badly in his school examinations in Aberdeen in 1948, was doing unskilled work in a local paper mill when his interest in a fur-trading career was triggered by an encounter with an acquaintance of his father who had returned from the sub-Arctic to start his own business. By the end of the year Jock had joined over 500 applicants for interview in only the second hiring drive in Scotland since the mid-1920s and became one of 12 successful recruits chosen from the north.[85] In retirement in British Columbia – and despite a heart transplant – he has made a name for himself as an author. Gordon Brown from Inverkeithing – a post office telegram boy – opted to apply to the HBC in 1950 after his parents had refused to allow him to go to Australia. Like most of his generation of recruits, he responded to a newspaper advertisement, as did 17-year-old John Wallace a decade and a half later. By that time a lower age limit was in force, and John was initially rejected after being interviewed in Aberdeen along with 200 other hopefuls. His mother, speaking in April 2010, recalled his determination not to wait:

> We were interviewed on our own without John, and then John was brought back in, and Mr Phillips [the HBC's personnel officer] basically said, 'How do you feel about his going?' So I says, 'He's determined to go, so there's no point, if that's what he wants to do, he's got to do it'. And when he brought John back in he said, 'I really would like to take you – I will take you next year' and John said, 'Well, if you won't take me now, somebody else will.'[86]

John Wallace had started to think about Australia as an alternative when, a fortnight later, Phillips telephoned to say that the rules were being waived in order to take him on to the Company's books in August 1966, two months before his 18th birthday.

According to Jock Gibb, recruitment of Scots persisted into the mid-20th century not only because of their heritage of service, but on the pragmatic grounds that homesick Scots could not 'bail out and run for home', unlike the Canadian employees whom the Bay had been forced to hire after the Depression.[87] On the other hand, Gordon Brown, who worked for more than a decade on Indian reservations in the North West Territories, and now lives in Saskatchewan, recalled a high turnover of Scots, with only two of the companions from his cohort of recruits still being on the Company's payroll after five years.[88] In the late 1970s, when Scots could no longer be employed, retention of local employees became even more difficult, but by that time the Company's fur-trading wing was in terminal decline, so the problem was less acute.[89]

The men who have been willing to write or speak about their experiences in the 20th-century Canadian fur trade belong to a self-selecting group with positive recollections. We know much less about those who struggled, or about the female or Aboriginal perspective. Drowning and the loss of limbs from frostbite were still occupational hazards, and communication remained a challenge despite improved technology. In the 1950s and

Angus Pelham Burn. Trout Lake, Ontario, 1953
(© Angus Pelham Burn)

'60s, contingents of new recruits were generally billeted at Winnipeg's Marlborough Hotel, close to the HBC's headquarters, where they were subjected to further medical and dental checks before being scattered to the Bay's trading posts to learn the retail part of the trade. As well as being the only person on his flight who was going to work for the Company, Angus Pelham Burn recalls being the solitary resident in the Marlborough, where he slept round the clock after a gruelling, five-stage, 37-hour flight from Scotland. He then spent his orientation period marking and pricing stockings in the basement of HBC House, periodically falling asleep over the task as jet-lag took its toll. Trainee clerks were usually transferred every six months, but managers had longer postings. Jock Gibb, like Angus Pelham Burn, found himself at Big Trout Lake, where supplies arrived by tractor-drawn sleigh trains in winter and by float planes in summer. At Pangnirtung, where John Wallace was based, the year's supplies were delivered, and the furs collected, by the HBC boat, the *Pierre Raddison*. 'If you ran out, that was it, you ran out', he recalled. 'We had no fresh milk. Eggs, they came in a can. Bacon too – quite nice bacon – but it came in a can. There was milk that was called klim – that's milk backwards – powdered milk'.[90]

A key part of the trainee managers' work was trading furs with the Aboriginal trappers, whose living conditions were similar to those of their 18th- and 19th-century predecessors. In winter families lived out on the trap lines in large teepees (or occasionally log cabins) and in summer they moved closer to the trading posts to pitch their tents. They brought in their pelts of mink, beaver and stoat, along with their shopping lists, about every three months, and in return for furs would be given supplies and hunting equipment. Angus Pelham Burn's personnel and business skills were developed as he negotiated with over 1,500 Cree at Big Trout Lake, and he has particularly warm memories of his interpreter, Henry Frogg. Reflecting on his time with the HBC, Angus was emphatic that his experiences were enjoyable and instructive in equal measure:

> I had the time of my life. It was the best thing I ever did. I learned to look after myself; how to sort of drive a dog team; how to sort of fly an aeroplane; how to help pull teeth. I learned all sorts of things that you'd never do nowadays... Everything that I learned out there has been useful to me, and without that experience I wouldn't have achieved a quarter of what I think I've achieved.[91]

Sponsored emigration under the auspices of the Hudson's Bay Company was restricted to young men who fancied the good wages and adventurous lifestyle associated with the northern Canadian fur trade. Government-assisted relocation to the other side of the world, in the shape of the £10 passage, was open to a much wider range of people pursuing a more varied spectrum of occupations. That latter-day manifestation of the Empire Settlement Act, which persisted until the early 1970s, forms part of the story of post-war emigration told in the next chapter.

CHAPTER 4

Post-war Impulses, Initiatives and Identities

'IT SEEMED LIKE the obvious thing to do.' That was the response of
Arthur Russell, a Baptist minister from Stirlingshire, when asked in
2006 why he had gone to New Brunswick 54 years earlier.[1] He was one
of 147,000 Scots to arrive in Canada between 1946 and 1960,[2] many
of whom would have echoed the sentiments of the Reverend Russell.
For the first generation, the decision was made against a backdrop of
economic hardship, housing shortages and a lingering war-weariness,
interwoven with the lure of lands whose high-profile recruitment campaigns promised work, wages and amenities that were unreachable in
their homeland. By the next generation, when the legacies of war had
receded, the quest for betterment more emphatically and deliberately
eclipsed the flight from austerity. It was also accompanied by an unspoken but clear shift, particularly in North America, from the traditional perception of emigration as a collective activity – where even
individuals tended to reach their decisions within a structure of state or
voluntary sector corporatism – to an atomistic and private process that
became almost always the preserve of individuals or nuclear families.

In this chapter we explore several separate but complementary
strands in the tapestry of almost 30 years of post-war emigration. Con-
tinuities from earlier periods are part of that fabric, but equally prominent are the new principles and practices that emerged as migrants in
different guises – settlers, returners, serial migrants and transilients –
exploited their mobility and sold their skills in an increasingly sophisticated global market-place. Domestic dead-ends were headed off by official initiatives in host countries, as empire settlement schemes entered
their second, Australia-focused phase, and the Canadian government
turned its attention to the selection of professionals. It was also an era
in which new technology shaped attitudes and actions, as well as employment opportunities, for just as the silver screen, the cathode ray
and the airwaves became increasingly influential tools of persuasion,

Men off a flight from Scotland show Ontario Premier George Drew how to wear
a tam o'shanter, 1947 (Archives of Ontario, RG 9-7-4-4-36, Gordon H. Jarrett)

so the mechanism of movement shifted from sea to sky, with profound
implications for the physical and psychological markers of migration.

Paradoxically for an era that often seemed to be drowning in statistics, quantifying migration from Scotland in the second half of the
20th century is particularly problematic. We are confronted with an
incomplete patchwork of statistics riddled with inconsistencies and con-
tradictions because of frequent changes in classification methods and
the different criteria of a variety of collecting bodies, making it impossible to compare like with like. Movement to other parts of the UK
was difficult to disentangle from overseas migration, and by the early
1960s separate Scottish figures had been absorbed into UK-wide returns.
Since 1964 estimates of overseas migration have been based on a small,
statistically unreliable sample from the International Passenger Survey.
Accuracy was distorted further by the exclusion of early air travel from
the figures, even though it was increasingly utilised – especially by Scots
– from the mid-1950s. In 1960, for instance, official Canadian statistics

recorded that 3,043 individuals (67 per cent of all Scottish arrivals that year) had entered the country by air, compared with 46 per cent for the UK as a whole.[3]

The basic framework can, however, be deduced by scrutinising a range of publications: census returns in donor and host countries, the UK's annual abstracts of statistics, the annual reports of the Oversea Migration Board (1953–65), the annual reports of the Registrar General for Scotland, and (for some years in the 1960s) the reports of the Scottish Economic Planning Board, along with its consultative and advisory body, the Scottish Economic Planning Council.[4] Overall, the second half of the 20th century saw a reduction in the levels of net out-migration, particularly in the 1980s and early 1990s, when Scotland sometimes gained more people than it lost. In the post-war generations with which we are concerned, however, levels remained high – between 30,000 and 40,000 a year – with the greatest loss in the 1960s, peaking in 1966.[5]

There are different estimates of the overseas component of that migration: the 1961 Scottish census claimed it constituted about half of the exodus during the 1950s, rising to two-thirds in 1957, while the Office of National Statistics put the figure at 60 per cent during the 1960s, and 55 per cent in the 1970s.[6] But in 1965 the Scottish Economic Planning Council, in highlighting a total net loss of 385,700 over the previous 13 years, claimed that two-thirds of the migrants were bound for England and Wales (mainly the Midlands and south-east) and one third for overseas destinations.[7]

Four years later the Planning Board reinforced and amplified those figures through the report of its Working Group on Population. Between 1951 and 1966, it claimed, 90 per cent of Scotland's natural increase had been lost through migration, compared with about 33 per cent in Wales and northern England, with departure rates in the seven years up to 1967 having been exceeded only during the 1920s. In response to fewer opportunities in England, the emphasis had shifted also from cross-border movement – about 22,000 a year in the early 1960s – to overseas migration, which rose from 9,000 in 1961–12 to 29,000 in 1966–67.[8]

The Scottish Economic Planning Council's assertion that emigration was 'far more significant in Scotland than in any other part of Great Britain' echoed the Oversea Migration Board's claim in 1961 that 'for some years Scottish oversea emigration... has continued at a higher rate

Group of Scottish emigrants leaving for Canada, 1947
(Archives of Ontario, RG 9-7-4-4-10, Ontario House photographs)

proportionately to her population than for Britain as a whole'.[9] This, of course, was nothing new: Scotland had always punched above its weight throughout the history of emigration, though by the 1960s the punch was losing some of its power. In the 1950s, when Scotland contained about 10 per cent of the population of Great Britain, Scots represented an average of 12 per cent of overseas departures, but by 1964 they accounted for 10.9 per cent, and by the 1970s and 1980s for 9.4 per cent.[10]

Throughout the period with which we are concerned, their favourite destinations, like those of their counterparts in the rest of the UK, were the traditional ones of the Commonwealth, followed by the United States. In the first decade after the war, when 80 per cent of British migrants went to the Commonwealth, Canada and New Zealand received respectively 88,336 and 10,161 Scottish migrants. Between the Australian census of 1947 and 1954 the number of Scots-born in the country had increased by 20,630, to 123,628; in the 1960s and 1970s Scots, says Richard Finlay, constituted between a quarter and a third of the British exodus to Australia, and as late as the 1970s, as many as 15 per cent of Australia's immigrants were Scots.[11]

In 1930 there were 250,000 people of Scottish birth in the United States, as well as a further 649,591 of Scottish parentage. Located mainly on the Atlantic seaboard and in the mid-west and north-west, in the first half of the 20th century they consistently represented about 2.4 per cent of the USA's overseas-born whites.[12] In the 1930s, interest began to wane, and the US census of 1970 recorded only 170,000 Scots living in the Republic, fewer than at any time since 1860.[13] But by that time the United States had relaxed its immigration restrictions, and as Scots' interest was rekindled, they began to account for between a quarter and a fifth of the country's immigrants.[14] Taking a broader statistical perspective, when a total of 10,049,000 Americans (4.4 per cent of the population) was recorded in the 1980 census as having either single or multiple Scottish ancestry, Scotland occupied seventh place in a 'league table' of hyphenated American ancestry.[15]

Legacies of Conflict: the War Brides

We will return later to the significance of these figures, but in putting flesh on the statistical bones, we begin with a much scrutinised category of migrants, whose experiences embrace both war and peace. If war widows – 1,769 in all – were part of the mosaic of assisted migration to the dominions after the First World War, then the many shiploads of war brides who left Britain in the 1940s have captured a much more prominent place in the public imagination. Although the trail had been blazed by a few thousand Great War brides, they were eclipsed by more than 100,000 women who followed in their wake almost three decades later. Of the 100,000 or so Second World War brides from Britain, 40,353 went to Canada, accompanied by 20,997 children, and 33,849 went to the United States, accompanied by 14,078 children.[16] Most of the rest were distributed between New Zealand and Australia. Their stories – mainly self-selected tales of success, told in old age through the inevitably distorting lens of hindsight – have given rise to an industry of books, oral collections, websites, plays, films and school projects, which reflect both the vibrancy of women's history and an ongoing fascination (particularly since the 1970s) with this short-lived but significant migrant stream. By contrast, virtually no attention has been paid to those couples who returned to Britain, to the women who retraced their steps when their marriages failed, or to the brides from around the world who, after marrying British servicemen overseas, took up new lives in the UK. The challenge for the historian is to identify significant themes from anecdotal evidence, and to root the brides' personal narratives in the wider historical context of migration in general and female migration in particular.

Corporate organisation and individual outcomes were woven together in the war brides' experiences. Permission to marry men on active service was enmeshed in red tape, and the women's relocation, which was funded by Commonwealth governments and overseen by Red Cross personnel, often saw them travelling together on chartered ships, their husbands and fiancés having preceded them. Women and children following in the wake of husbands and fathers who had gone ahead to find work and accommodation was a familiar part of the mechanism of migration, particularly to urban-industrial locations in North America. The difference lay in the exceptional wartime circumstances in which couples had met, the preponderance of rushed courtships, and the publicity accorded to the new arrivals. The brides were highly visible, not only on the quayside, but in the new communities into which they had to integrate, especially in rural areas. Some coped with the loss of the family support networks they had left behind by forming or joining overseas clubs or war-bride organisations, although others were wary of aligning themselves with associations that they feared would perpetuate their 'otherness'.

Links were maintained individually as well as corporately. Doreen Stewart from Newton Stewart, who disembarked at Fremantle, Western Australia, in 1946, corresponded for more than half a century with her cabin-mate, who was instrumental in forming an Overseas Wives Club.[17] The Australian YWCA, Red Cross and Country Women's Association provided after-care and advice. In an effort to prepare Canada-bound brides for their new lives, the Canadian government set up a Canadian Wives' Bureau in London, which for almost three years from 1944 until January 1947 also organised passages and oversaw internal transport arrangements to ports of embarkation. Meanwhile, for the America-bound, *Good Housekeeping* magazine in June 1945 published, at the request of the US Office of War Information, a pamphlet entitled *A Bride's Guide to the USA*. It included a glossary, and readers were urged to familiarise themselves with American terminology. At the same time they were encouraged to retain their 'English' accents, which were 'regarded in America as charming'.[18] Scottish brides – most of whom came from Glasgow or Edinburgh, though with a significant smattering of Highlanders who had married men from the 3,700-strong Newfoundland Forestry Unit – were not offered any elocutionary advice.

Despite these aids, many brides had little idea of what to expect. Some took cold feet before they left British soil, and May Comrie from Glasgow, who sailed from Southampton to Halifax in 1946, recalled being locked into her railway carriage en route to the port because on previous journeys some distraught war brides had thrown themselves from the trains.[19] Helen Piggott, also from Scotland, and her young son, spent their last night in Britain billeted in Holloway Women's Prison.[20] Embedded firmly in the memory of those who left after hostilities ended were the 'amazingly good food' and other shipboard luxuries, but those who sailed in wartime convoys encountered overcrowded accommodation, daily lifeboat drills, and sometimes inadequate rations. Stella Higgins, who sailed from Glasgow with her baby in 'a terrible old former frozen mutton ship' in January 1945, recalled a slow transatlantic crossing to Halifax and food of steadily deteriorating quality. Another Glaswegian, Jenny Zorn, who sailed to Halifax two months later, slept 12 to a cabin on the ss *Britannic*. As the ship steered its course out of the Firth of Clyde into the open sea, she described the convoy of 80 vessels as 'a wondrous sight... all those ships surrounding us in their designated positions travelling in a huge group across the face of the ocean' but added that 'after Fastnet it seemed our last link with home had gone for ever'.[21] Seasickness – a hardy perennial in the long saga of migration – often took its miserable toll, and on the wartime ships medical facilities were minimal.

Rose-tinted romance might be transformed into unpalatable reality as soon as the ship docked. Poor communications meant the women were not always met, and a handful – like one of Jenny Zorn's travelling companions – faced the heartbreaking news that their husbands had been killed in action while they were crossing the Atlantic. Onward train travel was usually less comfortable than the voyage, and some women were nervous about reunions with husbands whom they had never seen out of uniform, as well as new relatives and neighbours whom they feared might be unwelcoming. As Eleanore Coburn from Edinburgh travelled as part of a contingent of over-dressed, perspiring war brides in a non-air-conditioned train from Halifax to Toronto in

April 1945, she became painfully aware of their vulnerability. 'We were in a new country, didn't know the customs, and our husbands were the only persons we knew. It was really terrifying', she recalled.[22]

In 1834 Susanna Moodie had 'gazed... in perfect dismay' on the 'miserable hut' in Douro township where the family was about to settle in the midst of a desolate forest as pioneer farmers in Upper Canada.[23] More than a century later, her dismay was echoed by some war brides, who found that conditions at their destinations bore little resemblance to the idyllic lifestyle they had anticipated. Former city dwellers – the vast majority of the brides – sometimes found they had exchanged the intimacy of the tenement for the loneliness of the prairie or 'backblock' farm, where they had to develop a new set of domestic skills, cope with livestock, and learn to do without the cinemas and dance halls that had framed their social lives.

Vera McIntyre from Kirkliston, who was, by her own admission, 'completely undomesticated', had come from a household that employed a maid, washer woman and gardener, and could not admit to her mother that in Pukeatua, New Zealand, she was living in a farm cottage with an outside toilet.[24] Isabella Horvath from Kilmarnock, who had organised a War Bride club in her home town, read all the history books sent from the Canadian Wives' Bureau and 'ogled' the fashion pages of the Eaton's catalogue in advance of moving to Canada, was shocked to find herself living 'in the middle of nowhere'. Although she admitted in retrospect it was a character-building experience, she admitted to having been home-sick for 40 years.[25] Christina Sharpe from Edinburgh 'had no idea of what a farm was like' when, with their young son, she joined her airman husband at Picton, Ontario, in August 1946. And in Nova Scotia, where Dorothy Blaikie from Glasgow formed a long-running Overseas Club with 14 other war brides in and around Brookfield and Stewiacke, the absence of running water and indoor sanitation made her early years a challenge, not least when premature twins arrived in 1947.[26] On the opposite coast, Margaret Brown had two babies and two miscarriages during her first three years in Vancouver, when her husband struggled to find work and they were given grocery vouchers by the Salvation Army after hitting financial rock bottom. Like Vera McIntyre, she at first kept her (much worse) circumstances from her mother in Glasgow, but eventually succumbed to homesickness, and spent two-and-a-half years back in Scotland with one of her children.[27]

High visibility was sometimes coupled with resentment, particularly in small communities, that the war brides had stolen the most eligible bachelors. 'You would have thought I had married the only son of the town's multimillionaire,' declared Kathy, a Scottish war bride who arrived in Brandon with her husband in November 1945. Although she seems to have encountered only curiosity, rather than hostility, she found the attention stifling and prairie culture alien. After three weeks, and having had too much to drink at a party thrown in her honour, she gave vent to her frustration in a drunken tirade:

> They sat there with stunned looks on their faces, and I went on, and I guess it was all the frustrations of being a bride but not having a husband for a year and then coming five thousand miles away to this dump of a town on the prairies where everybody thought a grain elevator was gracious architecture.
>   I told them about the war, what it was like to live on rations and no new clothes for five years, and no fresh fruit and one egg a week and The Blitz and then the v2 raids, and here they were in Canada, selling everything they could grow and good jobs and big money, and talking about how the Americans were a bunch of no-goods and, oh, it went on.[28]

In fact, Kathy's outburst cleared the air, although her self-painted profile would not have endeared her to organisations like the Imperial Order Daughters of the Empire, which had anticipated that the war bride phenomenon would bring 'a fine type of English or Scotch settler' to Canada and reinforce positively the country's British identity.[29]

Particularly painful were the experiences of women who arrived to find they had been deserted, or those whose husbands proved unfaithful. 'Sally', from Edinburgh, fell into the latter category. Pregnant with twins soon after arriving in New Brunswick, she rarely saw her philandering husband, and when after a few years he told her she could go back to Scotland, it was on the unacceptable condition that she left the children behind. Although she had the support of her sister, who settled nearby, she tried to hide her plight from her parents and 'didn't feel that I should go whining home'.[30]

Some homesick war brides, like Margaret Brown, did go home, at least temporarily. While Mary Ash from Ayr found that contacts made through the YWCA and the Rose and Thistle Club in St John's, Newfoundland, helped many women to cope with loneliness, she recalled that for the first three months the main topic of conversation at their weekly meetings was 'how much does it cost to go home?'[31] A few were able to put their thoughts into action. In what became known as the 'thousand dollar cure', the husbands of disillusioned brides funded them to go back to the UK for a visit, not least in the hope that, once reminded of the drudgery, smallness or poverty of the country they had left behind, their homesickness would be assuaged and they would be cured of any lingering desire to return permanently whence they had come.[32]

Threats and Opportunities

The thousand-dollar cure was not confined exclusively to war brides. The term was applied more widely to unsettled migrants of the post-war generation who returned to Britain, only to discover that they preferred life on the other side of the Atlantic. The austerity and limited horizons that had contributed to their initial decision to leave, but had been forgotten in their disappointment of punctured expectations, often struck them more forcibly when they came back to a low-wage country where rationing did not end until July 1954, and where social life as well as the economy seemed to be becalmed in the doldrums. Disillusionment characterised much of the exodus in the 1950s: a letter to *The Scotsman* in 1950 drew attention to the dozens of merchant seamen who had deserted their ships in Australian ports to avoid returning to a land where it was no longer worth living. Pointing the finger at an out-of-touch government that poured its energies into the abortive Tanganyika groundnut scheme and assured the ration-hit people of Britain that they were the best fed nation on earth, W.S. Cruickshank added sarcastically, 'every time I open *The Scotsman* I expect an announcement by the Tailor-in-Chief to the Board of Trade to tell us we are now the best-dressed people on earth'.[33]

Despite Harold Macmillan's confidence that full employment, rising living standards, exports and investments had created 'a state of prosperity' unprecedented not only in his lifetime but 'in the history of this country', there was by no means universal agreement with his declaration in 1957 that 'most of our people have never had it so good'.[34] A Gallup poll at the beginning of the year – in the midst of Suez-induced petrol rationing – found that 41 per cent of the British population had expressed a wish to emigrate if free to do so, and we have seen that the overseas component of Scottish migration rose to two-thirds in 1957.[35] As well as highlighting Britain's declining international position, the canal crisis added complaints about national humiliation to existing concerns about high taxation, inflation and overcrowding, and triggered what the Conservative politician, Angus Maude, described as an 'ugly rush to the High Commissioners' offices'.[36]

Macmillan's optimistic rhetoric had a particularly hollow ring in Scotland, where – despite some evidence of better living standards and job prospects – the economic glass was for many more than half empty and its contents increasingly unpalatable. Press and politicians had been fretting for almost a decade about disproportionate migration, which they attributed not only to general war weariness but to specific disadvantages in the shape of overcrowded and insufficient housing, persistent unemployment and distance from markets – or even the lack of rural bus services and village pubs.[37] As in the 1920s, there was an overriding air of defeatism in a country which was seen as having only a past and not a future. Long-standing structural weaknesses in the Scottish economy had not been addressed: pre-war deindustrialisation had not been stemmed or reversed, and there was little sign of investment in the sort of new enterprises that were creating jobs south of the border, where wages in some sectors were about a fifth higher than in Scotland.[38] Disgruntlement and pessimism were reflected in the disproportionate flight, not simply of the economically active in general, but of the particularly aspirational skilled and professional workforce within the 20–44 age range. The significance of single professional females among the leavers in the 1950s suggests, says Richard Finlay in his book *Modern Scotland*, that the 'endemic sexism of Scottish society' impelled such women to seek 'more enlightened environments', but the exodus of professionals continued into the 1960s and '70s, when about 50 per cent of Scottish graduates – male and female – still anticipated having to leave Scotland to pursue a career.[39]

Some of these statistics had their origins in an official investigation of the Scottish economy in 1960–61. The Toothill Inquiry drew attention to the 'substantial' net outflow, which had risen from 44 per cent of Scotland's natural increase from 1931–51 to 76 per cent of the natural increase between 1951 and 1960. It also highlighted the selective nature of the exodus, including graduates seeking employment in industry and commerce: a survey undertaken by Glasgow University

Appointments Committee on Toothill's behalf had found that about two-thirds of arts graduates and three-quarters of science graduates had left Scotland for their first job.[40] It claimed, however, that the heavy outflow had prevented unemployment in a context where industrial expansion could not have kept pace with the existing population, a depressingly negative comment which gives weight to Finlay's assertion that 'the idea of emigration as a form of social policy by default had a lot of currency in Scotland'.[41]

Toothill counselled against alarm or despair, pointing out that mobility was built into the Scottish psyche, and that instead of applying any sort of tourniquet Scotland should make positive efforts to attract replacement labour from elsewhere:[42]

> Emigration generally means the loss of the more skilled workers and of the younger parts of the population and in some ways may aggravate the difficulties of the economy. But it is not possible to frame a policy to stop it and indeed it would be short-sighted to do so even if it were. It has gone on at as high proportionate rates through some of the most prosperous periods of our history and is we think likely to continue in some measure for we could find no direct relationship between it and unemployment rates. The sensible aim is to make the economy buoyant enough to attract as many people in as out.[43]

But the economy did not become buoyant, and the inflow, especially from overseas, amounted to little more than a trickle. Within a few years the issues were being revisited by the Scottish Economic Planning Board and its consultative council, in a series of detailed reports which explored the causes and consequences of migration, near and far. In 1965 the Planning Council claimed that inadequate deployment of Scotland's workforce was to blame for Scotland's 'high rates of unemployment and emigration and her lower than national rate of economic development', and warned that the depletion of the 15-44 age group would have serious long-term consequences for those left behind.[44] The baton was then taken up by the Board, which reiterated that Scotland was suffering 'a disproportionately large loss of younger men', especially from the skilled and professional labour force.

A survey by the Ministry of Labour in August 1965 which solicited the views of 208 medium-to-large Scottish manufacturing companies about the reasons for migration among their staff during the previous year found, unsurprisingly, that career prospects and higher salaries influenced 77.7 per cent of the 429 individuals who had left both their employment and their native country, although employers suggested that decisions were also shaped by 'the wish to share in a better social and domestic life'. For many, that meant moving south of the border, for there was 'a general belief that life in England was more pleasant than in Scotland' in terms of 'general amenities, the weather, levels of prices, entertainment, better housing and a less restricted way of life'.[45] If the 1950s had been a decade of monochrome disillusionment across the UK, the 1960s was a multi-hued era of 'pleasure and leisure', when, in the words of another Prime Minister, Britain was also 'burning with the white heat of technology'.[46] But some Scots felt this exciting new world was eluding them, existing only in England or North America: indeed, transatlantic migration was thought to offer England's economic, social and cultural attractions 'but to an even greater degree', and 25 per cent of (a slightly larger version of) the 1965 sample had gone overseas.[47]

In the Highlands, of course, migration had for long been stalked by the malign spectre of clearance. The Free Church of Scotland, which between the wars had highlighted the damaging effects of depopulation, returned to the fray in 1951. Lambasting unsympathetic government policies that it claimed were tantamount to modern clearances, it warned that 'many are responding to the call of the British Dominions for young emigrants, and will continue to respond until they feel they can secure a livelihood and some measure of social and economic security at home'.[48] It subsequently welcomed the formation of the Highland Fund in 1953, at a time when the Highlands was described as 'Britain's most gravely depressed area',[49] from which 'the life blood of vast areas [was] ebbing away'.[50] But the Fund's efforts to reverse depopulation were unsuccessful, and – in the face of hopes 'so often dashed' – more than a whiff of clerical cynicism greeted the formation of the Highlands and Islands Development Board in 1965.[51]

It was in 1965 that an Advisory Panel on the Highlands and Islands, working under the auspices of the SEPB, tentatively recommended encouraging people to move away from 'declining localities'. The panel had concluded that some communities had ceased to be viable and that the economic policy of the last two decades 'of spreading the jam as widely (and therefore thinly) as possible has met with insufficient success to justify its continuance'.[52] Two years earlier the STUC *Bulletin*, intimating that a forthcoming conference in Inverness would address the economic plight of the Highlands, had reminded readers that a similar conference 39 years earlier had condemned the requirement for High-landers 'to cross the seas in search of work which could be found at home if the natural resources of the Highlands were fully exploited'.[53] Almost two generations on, nothing seemed to have changed, and the special conference in February 1965 revisited problems of unemploy-ment, emigration, absentee landlordism, low rates of natural increase and an ageing population.

The gloom extended further. In the south-west too, jobless figures were higher than the Scottish average in the 1960s,[54] and in 1969 Pro-fessor Max Gaskin of the University of Aberdeen was commissioned by the Scottish Office Regional Development Division to investigate and report on the economic prospects of the north-east region. He pro-nounced the area economically stagnant, as a result of net outward migration, above-average unemployment rates, and decreasing oppor-tunities in the male labour market. Unaware of the implications of the oil bonanza peeping over the North Sea horizon, Gaskin predicted that unless the traditional industries of fishing, farming, forestry and tex-tiles were revitalised, new industries encouraged, and tourism boosted, economic dislocation would ensue.[55] The economic planners realised, however, that migration was shaped more by policies and opportuni-ties in the migrants' destinations than by disillusionment or down-turn in Scotland. So what were these incentives? Did they repre-sent a conservative continuation – or resumption – of established programmes, or was there an in-jection of radical new initiatives? And did they appeal to existing, or different, constituencies?

Assisted passages to the do-minions were resurrected after 1945. The Empire Settlement Act, which in 1922 had initiated an unprecedented era of state subsi-dies, had been renewed for the first time in 1937, with its maximum

Emigration poster, 1949
L I Box 155 22/2/14 Pt I Archives New Zealand
The Department of Internal Affairs Te Tari
Taiwhenua

Australian Immigration Department officer Graham Gillespie processing applicants at Edinburgh regional office, 1962 (National Archives of Australia, A12111, 1/1962/14/35, 7471848)

annual allowance slashed by half to £1.5 million. That cut reflected disillusionment with the practice of state-aided emigration – the annual grant rarely being used up – and the fact that in the 1930s the movement of migrants shifted firmly into reverse gear. The rehabilitation of state subsidies after the war, in the amended clothing of the Empire and Commonwealth Settlement Act, was evident in the repeated renewal of the legislation – in 1952, 1957, 1962 and 1967 – only coming off the statute book in 1972. The major difference was that the policy agenda was now set in the dominions, and although British taxpayers still helped to subsidise migration to Australia, their contribution was steadily revised downwards, with an annual ceiling of £150,000 being imposed in 1952.[56]

It was, of course, Australia that occupied centre stage for the post-war generation of sponsored migrants, as well as being the only dominion to enter into an agreement with the UK government on assisted migration.[57] Ever since the 1830s assisted passages, in various guises, had – of necessity – been part and parcel of antipodean migration, and Australia had made considerable use of the Empire Settlement leg-

Scottish immigrant, Sandra Wright, arriving in New Zealand on the *Atlantis*, 6 June 1951 (*Evening Post* collection, Alexander Turnbull Library)

islation in the 1920s. The outflow during the Depression, coupled with Australia's vulnerability to Japanese attack in the war, reinforced the Commonwealth government's determination to resurrect sponsored migration to an under-populated and under-developed country. The result was 'the most sustained, ambitious, and expensive' of all the post-war sponsorship programmes.[58]

The initial offer of free passages to veterans and their families, reminiscent of the 1919 soldier settlement experiment, was followed by the famous 'Ten Pound Poms' scheme, launched in 1947 by Australia's new Ministry for Immigration. Under the slogan, 'populate or perish', roving interviewers from Australia House recruited around 1.5 million Britons over the next quarter century, two-thirds of them under the assisted passage scheme. Adults paid £10 for a one-way trip, 14-to-18-year-olds £5, and children nothing, with free passages subsequently being extended to the under-20s.[59] In 1957, after interest had dipped during an Australian depression, the 'Bring Out a Briton' campaign encouraged individuals, employers, churches and institutions such as rotary clubs to nominate candidates, then two years later the Nest Egg scheme extended assisted passages to families with more than £500, provided they arranged their own accommodation. Australia House presided over advertising, the distribution of application forms and recruitment, with preliminary selection devolved to labour exchanges and from 1959 to regional offices in Edinburgh, Belfast and Manchester.

Scots were not backward in responding to these initiatives. In August 1950 *The Scotsman* reported a turnout of over 80 people – many of them women – at a meeting in Edinburgh where an official from the

Immigrants arriving off the *Atlantis* in Wellington, New Zealand, 6 June 1951
(*Evening Post* collection, Alexander Turnbull Library)

Australian Department of Immigration had explained the new scheme of depersonalised nomination. In E.C. Morgan Dean's opinion, 'Scots are inclined to be independent in matters of this kind', and would appreciate the new opportunities for work and hostel accommodation.[60] Nine years later, the newly opened Edinburgh recruitment office was besieged with over 1,000 enquiries in its first three days of operation. These probably translated into about 300 applications, although the selecting officer, W.H. Macmillan, felt that greater success might have been achieved if the office had been located in Glasgow, which was the hub for most of the skilled labour that Australia desperately needed.[61]

Various other schemes operated outside the scope of the Empire and Commonwealth Settlement legislation. Between 1947 and 1975 New Zealand funded a less publicised and more selective version of the £10-passage scheme, which brought in almost 85,000 migrants, 91 per cent of them from the UK.[62] Recruitment was overseen by the New Zealand Labour Department, guided by an Immigration Advisory

Council. Two officers were sent to London to establish an office just opposite New Zealand House on the Strand, and for the first five years, the post-war shortage of shipping was circumvented by the Labour Department chartering its own ship, the *Atlantis*. Advertisements sang the praises of a five-day, 40-hour week and a comprehensive State social security scheme, and particular efforts were made to recruit women. Interest was keenest in the 1950s, and in 1951 five selection officers from New Zealand House conducted an estimated 5,000 interviews. When the target intake of assisted migrants was raised from 5,000 to 10,000 a year (soon dropped to 7,500 because of housing shortages) the £10 migrant contribution was abolished, the age limit extended from 35 to 45 and all occupational quotas for single migrants were abolished.[63] But although Scots were well represented among the migrants, one New Zealand civil servant clearly expected more, at least in 1955, when 14 per cent of the year's 6,320 applicants scheduled for interview came from north of the border. His marginal annotation in the final monthly report of the Migration Branch expressed surprise that the Scottish figure was 'not as high as we would expect in view of [the] traditional Scotch attitude to migration', and the report also recorded that 144 of the Scottish applicants had failed to report for interview, with a further 93 interviewees being rejected.[64]

Meanwhile Canada, traditionally the most popular of the dominion destinations, was falling behind Australia in the migrant league table. The axis of interest shifted in response to the perception that Australian doors were opening as Canadian ones were closing: in other words, Australia's aggressive, all-embracing and long-lasting government-funded recruitment campaign was set against Canada's much more selective and cautious courtship of skilled, professional recruits, and its distinct lack of enthusiasm for extensive immigration in the late 1940s. The Labour Department's reactive 'tap approach' to migration – which determined the annual intake on the basis of employment levels – was a response to memories of inter-war joblessness, and it was coupled with fears among young professionals that their careers, already blighted by depression and war, would be further hampered by competition from migrants. The shortage of transatlantic shipping was another obstacle, while the devaluation of the pound in 1948 was accompanied by a reduction in the amount of capital that migrants could transfer to Canada. Sterling-area countries like Australia were not affected by the ruling, which saw the

Potential emigrants viewing poster for the
Ontario Air Immigration Plan, 1947
(Archives of Ontario, RG 9-7-4-1-1, Camera Talks)

allocation slashed from £5,000 to £1,000, spread over four years. It was 'absurd', declared one British politician in 1950, to expect whole families to make a fresh start in Canada under such financial constraints, while the Royal Empire Society claimed that since 'the financial consideration dictates his destination', it was no wonder that the young married man with small children was turning away from Canada and towards Australia.[65]

These discouragements were countered – and soon eclipsed – by a determined and persistent campaign to recruit migrants, particularly to Ontario. Canada did not fall into recession, and it soon became clear that all sectors of the economy were crying out for labour. Advertisements depicted a land of abundance, in the shape of food, cars and domestic appliances: one incredulous newly arrived Scot in the luxury-starved 1940s described herself as 'fair drooling' over the cosmetics and clothes in Eaton's catalogues, and declared that her well-dressed Canadian counterparts 'must have put half their salaries on their backs'.[66]

As early as 1947–48 the Ontario Premier, George Drew, frustrated at the shipping bottleneck and the influx of European refugees under bulk labour schemes, organised an airlift of over 7,000 Britons, primarily to work in the province's factories. His initiative was then adopted and adapted by the federal government, which by the end of 1950 had negotiated with Trans-Canada Airlines to fly settlers directly to Montreal or points east at the heavily subsidised rate of £55 – a sum that was also slightly lower than the tourist-class ocean passage of approximately £60.[67] The journey took approximately 15 hours from London, via Prestwick and Labrador. One Scot who arrived in 1952 recalled that when the plane was refuelled at Goose Bay in sub-zero temperatures, the 100 passengers were rushed into an old wooden building with 'guards on the door to see we didn't go outside, in case we got frostbite'.[68]

Various employer-sponsored schemes, as well as intermittent government subsidies, were available to those who could not afford the fare. Even the migrant who arrived 'with only a shilling in his pocket' was welcome,[69] at least if he or she had a reliable ethnic pedigree. As the Minister of Immigration told the federal Parliament in 1955, 'We try to select as immigrants those who will have to change their ways least in order to adapt themselves to Canadian life and to contribute to the development of the Canadian nation'.[70] Canada's selection criteria resonated with the conservative objectives of many British migrants: as a BBC broadcast had alleged seven years earlier, 'the sahib goes to the Colonies but the workman goes to the Dominions, each to find a white society with the same social structure as he's left at home'.[71] And even though in the post-war decades Canada was playing second fiddle to Australia, especially after the introduction of the points system in 1967, it was still a key player in the premier league of destinations, and was regarded as a serious competitor by its Commonwealth rivals. Over a third of its 2,500,000 migrants between 1945 and 1967 came from the UK, not least from Scotland, where networks built up during more than two centuries of migration and settlement helped to reinforce the claims of a new generation of advocates. It is to the structure and substance of the recruitment business that we now turn.

Spreading the Word

'Wish you were here?' On 7 January 2012 an advertisement with that heading took up two-thirds of a page in *The Scotsman*. 'Make it happen with an exciting new online emigration portal', the strapline urged readers, pointing them to a website that outlined opportunities in Australia, Canada, France, New Zealand, South Africa, Spain and the USA, and urged them to pay £8 for advance tickets for spring 'emigration shows' in Glasgow or London. Stripped of the European locations and the high-tech format, the advertisement could have been plucked from the 1950s or '60s, even down to the assertion that 'Australia, Canada and New Zealand are still desperately seeking skilled people'.[72]

Organised recruitment had been part of the migration business since the days of pilgrimage and crusade, but developed an increasingly prominent profile in the half century before the First World War. As host countries gained more control over their immigration policies, battalions of professional agents swarmed across the British Isles and Europe, competing with each other in singing the praises of their particular country, province or state through a variety of written, oral and visual media. Policy and funding were dictated in their homelands, but their day-to-day activities were generally overseen by a head office in London, presided over by an Agent-General or (later) a High Commissioner, who also had wider responsibilities for the promotion of trade and industry and the conduct of diplomatic relations. While Australia and New Zealand maintained a centralised structure, liaising with a nationwide network of 2,000 employment exchanges in advertising, interviewing and initial selection, Canada preferred some devolution of responsibility, stationing agents at regional headquarters in strategic cities across the country and collaborating with part-time ticket offices in arranging their lecturing itineraries and in booking the passages of recruits.

As we saw in Chapter 2, these structures and practices continued into the inter-war era, although by the early 1930s tighter budgets and falling demand had led to the closure of most of Canada's regional offices, as well as New Zealand's London-based Department of Immigration. Agents had always set a premium on personal appearances, especially in remote rural areas, but from the early 20th century they had been able to illustrate their lectures with an increasing array of lantern slides: by 1912 New Zealand, for example, had a stock of about 3,000 such visual aids, which were constantly on loan during the key winter lecturing season. By the 1920s still images could be supplemented by newsreels and other movie films. Sponsored by government immigration departments as well as transportation companies like the CPR and Cunard, they depicted migrants in training, departure and transit, and at work and play, and were shown in cinemas as well as village halls. The British – especially the Scots – were avid film-goers: by 1938 there were 4,967 cinemas in Britain, and during the 1930s Glasgow had the most cinemas per head of population in Europe.[73] Since the late 1920s the Imperial Institute had also been building up a substantial slide and film library, with contributions from private individuals, dominion governments, railway companies and other commercial businesses. Its

New Zealand House, London, 1964
(AAQT 6401 A76017 Archives New Zealand
The Department of Internal Affairs Te Tari
Taiwhenua)

collection was regularly borrowed by schools, uniformed and religious organisations, hospitals and film societies, as well as by its own travelling lecturers, who by 1944 could make use of 15,000 prints and 900 films.[74]

Even before the war, migrants who appeared on the screen talked as well as moved, and by the 1950s film-makers were becoming more ambitious. Some portrayed fictional characters, as in *The Seekers* (1954), an imperialist tale of English settlers in 19th-century New Zealand.[75] Other films portrayed real migrants acting their parts in docudramas, notably in a clutch of promotional films produced by the New Zealand Labour Department.

One of them, *Journey for Three* (1950) wove a romantic story into its portrayal of the experiences of three young settlers, two of whom were played by migrants from Aberdeen and Edinburgh. Along with its stable-mates, this information-cum-propaganda film – which showed the newly arrived migrants being handed their envelopes with job and accommodation details – was distributed through labour offices, tourist bureaux and schools and was favourably reviewed.[76]

Romantic opportunities were peddled by the *Daily Mail* when it reported in 1955 that New Zealand was in desperate need of between 30,000 and 40,000 'good home-loving girls under 30' to be soul-mates to lonely Kiwi men. 'We have had such a flood of inquiries', one of the London migration officers commented, 'that you would think there weren't any marriageable men left in Britain'. The staff at the Migration Office, while toeing the official line that they did not operate a 'matrimonial agency', secretly reveled in the unsolicited publicity – 'the greatest fillip our drive for immigrants has had'.[77]

More than half of Canada's immigrants in the post-war decades settled in Ontario, including over 350,000 from the British Isles.[78] George Drew's airlift initiative was succeeded by a vigorous advertising campaign, particularly in the 1960s, and not least in Scotland. Expectations on both sides had changed considerably since the provincial government had first begun to woo settlers in 1873 and by now reflected the emphasis on the recruitment of professionals and skilled tradesmen to meet Ontario's commercial and industrial needs. Instead of land grants and assisted passages, 'the emigrant of today requires advice and expert counselling. He needs information on employment prospects, education, housing, cost of living, climate, social services and a host of other subjects'.[79] This targeted information was provided through the 'situations vacant' columns of professional and trade journals, and special features in the daily press such as the well-paid opportunities for registered nurses that were advertised in three Angus newspapers and the *Scottish Daily Express* in 1967. At a time when staff nurses in the UK were earning between £32 and £40 a month, migrants were offered £112, rising to £130 after registration in Ontario. Other attractions were good holidays, insurance and pension plans, and if necessary, an advance of the fare.[80]

Enquiries were handled by 'trained immigration counselors', based at Ontario House, who also selected specific personnel on behalf of Canadian employers. North of the border, the latest promotional films often formed the centerpiece of recruitment drives. In November 1968, for instance, filmgoers in Glasgow, Edinburgh and Dundee were told about Ontario in general, and the steel town of Hamilton in particular, through the films *Ontario Today* and *Sights and Sounds of a City*. Extensive advance press advertising helped to swell attendances, with 850 turning up to one of the Glasgow venues, the City Halls. At the event, billed as a 'film and facts evening', attendees were given an information kit about life in Ontario, as well as a general application form for employment, to be returned to the Ontario government's Glasgow immigration office. The film was followed by a discussion period, chaired by immigration counselors, with travel agents and representatives of transportation companies 'stationed at the rear of the Hall... to answer your questions about transportation and the shipment of household effects'. Those who wished to reflect a little longer or who preferred to ask their questions in a less public forum could drop in to the Glasgow office for an impromptu interview, as could those who had not attended, but whose interest was piqued by subsequent newspaper coverage – through photographs and interviews – of individuals who had attended the shows and were thinking of emigrating.[81]

The post-war generation, however, also had access to a powerful new recruitment medium in its own home: the BBC. The corporation's imperial ethos remained strong until the early 1960s, and was imparted through royal broadcasts and coverage of royal tours, as well as through productions such as 'Children of the Commonwealth', a 1950s series for *Children's Hour* in which the Imperial Institute collaborated with the BBC.[82] If recruitment was a tangential outcome of these broadcasts, it was a more direct consequence of two decades of radio programmes, beginning in the mid-1940s, which focused particularly on opportunities in the dominions. A live BBC broadcast from the New Zealand stand at the 1951 Schoolboys' Own Exhibition generated 'a large number of enquiries' to the High Commission and was commended by the New Zealand Immigration Branch's public relations officer in glowing terms: such publicity was, he declared, 'of greater worth than many hundreds of pounds spent on Press Advertising'.[83]

While radio was the normal medium, television made an occasional contribution to the recruitment campaign: after 'a solid plug for migration to New Zealand' – targeted on the under-21s – had been given in a 45-minute 'Teleclub' programme in January 1955, the High Commission in London was deluged with 4,600 letters in six days, along with enough counter enquiries to occupy four desk officers.[84] Scrutiny of the BBC written archives has yielded the scripts of 37 relevant radio broadcasts between 1947 and 1968. Most were produced by the Home Service but 15 were *Woman's Hour* features. The destination most frequently covered was Canada (ten dedicated programmes), followed by New Zealand (eight dedicated programmes), Australia (five) and South Africa (four). There were seven general surveys, and two programmes that each coupled two dominions together. Migration to the United States featured in only one broadcast.[85]

If the medium had moved on, what about the message? The notable neglect of the United States reflected both the BBC's entrenched imperial loyalties and the interests of the post-war generation. It was, however, paradoxical in an era when seductive images of America were filling cinema and television screens. Furthermore, while most broadcasts were positive, the BBC was not a propaganda arm of the Commonwealth Relations Office: aware that some migrants were not doing well, policy makers in the late 1940s instructed that negative case histories be injected into programmes, as a warning to listeners that migration was not an easy option, with a successful outcome guaranteed.[86] Some broadcasts were simply descriptive or historical, two featured New Zealanders coming to Scotland, and another discussed concerns about the emigration of scientists in the 1960s. One *Woman's Hour* broadcast dealt with readers' correspondence, including a letter that criticised misleading information allegedly given in a recent feature on New Zealand. Only one of the broadcasts was unequivocally negative, but several urged listeners to research their decision thoroughly and not entertain unrealistic expectations. Three programmes featured migrants who had resettled in Britain. Although the broadcasts did not target particular parts of the country, a few Scottish case histories were woven into the narratives.

Radio coverage took off in earnest in 1948–49 with a seven-part series of 15-minute programmes hosted by the Conservative politician Bernard Braine. *Lands in Search of People* was rooted unequivocally and explicitly in imperial soil. It began by reviewing the historical context and reflecting on current debates about the politics and economics of emigration. Braine conceded that Britain could ill-afford to lose the 'young, keen, alert artisans and craftsmen, experienced trainees and professional men' who were 'once again taking the Empire trail', and acknowledged that labour shortages were being met by 'thousands of foreign workers' who were taking up jobs shunned by Britons. But demographic realignments should, he argued, be viewed in a wider strategic context: a redistribution of population to match resources would strengthen both the British hub and the Commonwealth spokes, and dispersal would have security benefits as well as raising living standards in donor and host countries alike.[87]

Having made the strategic case, Braine and a variety of guests spent the next five programmes scrutinising opportunities in specific destinations. First to come under the spotlight was the 'Colonial Empire', a series of locations – mainly in East Africa – where the recommendations were hedged about with more caveats than for the dominions. While there were opportunities in farming, mining, commerce and the colonial service for the 'instructor class', migrants without significant capital should be prepared to rough it, and were strongly advised not 'just to go out and hope for the best'.[88] In the dominions listeners were warned to expect housing shortages and were reminded – as they had been for centuries – to pull their weight, work hard and adapt to their new surroundings and neighbours. The long-standing preoccupation with climate re-emerged in warnings about the health hazards of West Africa, but commendation of the energising, healthy and spacious environments of all the dominions where, moreover, the shops were full to overflowing, the people willing to help those who were prepared to help themselves, and high living costs were cancelled out by generous wages. In Canada they were directed specifically to Ontario, the country's 'industrial heartland', but away from the Maritimes, Quebec, the prairies and the far west, where, according to Braine, 'there's not much scope for them'.[89] His Aberdonian interviewee in Johannesburg – a former paper mill worker from the city's suburb of Stoneywood – had extolled the working conditions, industrial relations and educational system in the Transvaal, while Braine reminded women listeners (or a certain constituency among them) that there were 'few countries where a woman's life can be as easy and carefree as it is in South Africa – because this is a country where native servants are plentiful'.[90] The final programme addressed the possible accusation that the series had painted too rosy a picture by using two interviewees – from Canada and Australia respectively – to reinforce the importance of perseverance, 'temperamental adaptability' and a willingness 'to work with your hands as well as your head'.[91]

The advice given in Braine's series was reinforced, amended and challenged over the airwaves during the next two decades. *New Lands for Old*, broadcast in 1952, explored policies and opportunities through a series of interviews with government officials and migrants, and came to the conclusion that 'almost everybody who emigrates to any of the Commonwealth countries settles in pretty well'.[92] John Stubbs, a naval architect from Glasgow, had no regrets about relocating his family in 'the heart of French Canada'; another interviewee claimed that Australia offered 'any number of jobs' for anybody, at 'colossal' wages; New Zealand was crying out for immigrants to meet its labour shortages; and in South Africa too the expanding economy offered good openings to skilled artisans, professional men and industrialists.

There were, however, caveats. Housing shortages persisted across the

Commonwealth. While migrants to South Africa would find it easy to settle down among the 'many South Africans of British stock', integration was more difficult in Afrikaans-speaking areas, and 'an atmosphere of uncertainty' about constitutional and race relations had in the previous two years led to a net emigration of Europeans from South Africa. And although interviewees who had gone to Southern Rhodesia waxed lyrical about the open spaces and high living standards, listeners were warned that the country offered 'no opening for the unskilled white worker', with the arrival of 'every family' creating an extra strain on the infrastructure. A limited cultural life was the problem in New Zealand, where many settlers found 'the long weekend is

Scottish papermaker, Tony Taylor from Bucksburn, Aberdeen, checking the watermark at Shoalhaven paper mill, Bomaderry, New South Wales 1957 (National Archives of Australia, A12111, 1/1957/16/46, 9759454)

dull'. Migrants to Canada and Australia were advised not to entertain overblown expectations, and – in the words of an interviewee from Alberta – to 'make sure you're mentally able to take the shock of finding that being British is not a passport to instant success'.[93]

A few years later, further cautionary advice was offered in the reflections of two returners, Maurice Whitbread, who left Canada in 1957 after an 11-year sojourn, and E.L. Black, who returned from Australia in 1963. Whitbread had been unable to find either a niche or a regular income. 'What I did,' he told listeners, 'was to make a combination of the old-style grand tour, post-war readjustment, growing up and gaining life experience all in one. It is not a thing which necessarily commends itself to Dominion governments. They want immigrants who will bring their skill and strong right arms to the country and use them. People like me are a bit of a nuisance.'[94] E.L. Black was a more embittered returner. In his 40s when he was appointed vice-principal of a teachers' training college in Australia, he blamed his failure to settle on a combination of his age, workplace jealousy, the climate and the housing situation.[95]

The pros and cons of emigration were given most frequent and thoughtful coverage on *Woman's Hour*. Different destinations were compared, advice and practical information dispensed. In a broadcast in January 1947, during a notorious winter that played its part in triggering subsequent emigration, Marian Cutler was captivated by the 'enormous pictures' of sun-soaked cornfields, groaning fruit trees and gleaming towns that decorated the walls of the (unnamed) dominion office into which she stepped 'out of the snow and fog, sleet and slush'. But she went on to remind listeners of the hurdles that had to be overcome and warned that recruitment officers wanted only responsible migrants, young men and women with perseverance, skills and enough capital to make a start, not those 'whose only qualification was wishful thinking and whose enthusiasm was born of a restlessness – an aftermath of war'.[96]

At the end of the same year, opportunities were covered in more detail in three features by Christine Cook, who assuaged concerns about the climate in Canada and South Africa, observed that Australia was 'a country which will give back what you put into it', and suggested that in New Zealand 'women who feel a little nervous of the heartiness of Australia might find the right niche'.[97]

Finding the right niche was a recurring theme in the *Woman's Hour* broadcasts. Perhaps this was because, as Christine Cook suggested, 'from a woman's point of view, somehow emigrating seems a much bigger step than from a man's', and women were more concerned with the emotional impact of that step than with its material implications. Homesickness was 'inevitable', declared Joyce Thom in 'A Letter from New Zealand' in 1957. 'It does take a while to make friends,' she added, but 'New Zealanders on the whole are friendly and easy going' and migrants who were adaptable and willing to work soon settled down.[98] In a broadcast two weeks later, concern that she would 'have to start all over again' in making friends in Canada was uppermost in the thoughts of an imminent migrant, while in 1968, an interviewee who had gone to Australia, when asked to explain the high return rates, reiterated the advice to adapt to the host culture and 'submerge your own personality a little bit'.[99]

Migrant Lives and Identifications

Radio broadcasts, promotional films, newspaper reports and corre-spondence embellished advice to migrants with glimpses into the new worlds of those who had taken the plunge. How did their experiences compare with those of their predecessors in the 1920s? Did the cir-cumstances that triggered post-war migration produce a new range of achievements, failures and attitudes, or did migrants measure satisfac-tion and disappointment by timeless criteria, that were as relevant in the 1760s as they were in the 1960s?

Unfulfilled expectations were a recurring cause of friction and disap-pointment down the ages, although Geoffrey Nunn, a former colonial administrator who made a guest appearance on Bernard Braine's radio series in 1948–49, claimed that modern migrants were less resilient and more demanding than the pioneers.

> People's ideas today are entirely different from what they were in the old days. In the old days whole families of people were prepared to get into a wooden ship, spend three months or whatever it was in the most ghastly conditions, going across to America, say, then arming themselves with hatchets and knocking a forest down. Well, I don't know whether it's change in habit or a change in outlook or what it may be, but I don't think there's any doubt about it that people nowadays seem to want everything on a plate before they get there.[100]

By the mid-20th century, few migrants anticipated having to blaze a trail through the forest before making a settlement. Products of an industrial society, many Scots were encouraged to believe that their skills would be welcomed with open arms overseas. A failure to find or retain work was therefore – as in the troubled inter-war years – a major destabilising factor. In 1949 a letter to the editor of *The Specta-tor* warned that in British Columbia, where unemployment was 'very bad', the writer had 'never come across so many disappointed workless men of all classes', and he was making a beeline for Canada House 'to tell them it is utterly useless to encourage emigrants to come out here unless they have a good job to come to'.[101]

Eight years later, Swansea magistrates gave a conditional discharge to two penniless and disillusioned Scottish miners who had 'in desperation' stowed away on a transatlantic cargo ship, after a fruitless five-month search for work in Montreal or Toronto. John Christie (22) and Gerald O'Neill (20) were 'experienced miners' from Twechar in Dunbartonshire and Kilsyth in Lanarkshire, when they left Scotland as assisted and self-funding migrants respectively. But, like the harvester-miners of the 1920s, they had found only high unemployment rates, no assistance for the workless, and a scramble for return passages. From the dock of a Welsh court, they were sent back to Glasgow with the aid of travel warrants issued by the National Assistance Board and a loan of ten shillings each from Swansea Justices Court Fund. Both declared that they would now return to the Scottish pits. Having not been able to get even a day's work in a country where they had been assured of 'great opportunities', Christie 'would not advise anybody to go to Canada', while O'Neill described how 'we slept in six police stations and in fields' before being charged 30 cents for a night in a Salvation Army hostel.[102]

On the other side of the world, some migrants who had taken up assisted passages complained about the lack of after-care. The New Zealand Labour Department had, according to one disgruntled migrant, 'sponsored, transported and dumped' her in New Zealand, where some of the psychiatric nurses recruited in 1947 also resented the demand that they should surrender their passports until they had fulfilled their bond, were dismayed when they were treated as 'charwomen and prison attendants' rather than trained professionals, and disliked the remoteness of the institutions to which they were sent.[103] Opportunities in Australia were tempered by intermittent recessions and – as we shall see in Chapter 5 – by resentment of the allegedly inflated expectations of 'whingeing Poms'. But Australia had taken cognisance of a previous generation's accusations that its government's misleading claims, coupled with 'indifference and failure', had left migrants unemployed and in some cases suicidal,[104] and post-war passage assistance was often coupled with supplementary programmes to identify job vacancies and select appropriate recruits.

In fact, across the dominions, migrants' complaints about unemployment and destitution were exceptional and much less common than during the hungry thirties. Targeted recruitment of professionals and skilled tradesmen in a context of tightening immigration controls resulted in a much closer correlation of demand and supply, in an era when migration became an increasingly fluid, reversible and expandable phenomenon that defied simple definition. The migratory process had always been characterised by temporary sojourning as well as permanent settlement, incorporating seasonal, serial and step dimensions, and multiple relocations. But for the post-war generation, that sense of permanent impermanence and diluted leave-taking became more prominent, thanks to the advent of mass intercontinental air travel and a globalising economy. A rolling stone mentality and return migration were encouraged not only by better technology and higher incomes, but by the opportunity, until the early 1970s, for a wide spectrum of individuals and families to enjoy a subsidised two-year working holiday down under. Even those 'ten pound Poms' who did not admit to such a deliberate strategy were probably more likely to view the experience as an experimental sojourn than migrants who had ploughed their own savings into a new life overseas.

While disillusionment and despair clearly brought John Christie and Gerald O'Neill back to Scotland, failure was – and always had been – the trigger for only a minority of returning migrants. The post-war generation gave birth to a new phenomenon, the so-called 'transilient', a highly mobile and often rootless individual who played the international labour market, responding to a demand for his or her skills wherever they were required.[105] Itinerant career migrants – not least Scots – had always been part of the tapestry of mobility, but until the mid-20th century they had formed a numerically modest elite. As we have seen, the loss to Scotland of a skilled and professional workforce was a constant cause of concern to policy-makers, but it's an ill wind that blows no good, and the growing constituency of well paid, mobile expatriates and their families gave a much-needed boost to the Scottish tourist industry. Not only was it able to capitalise on the ebb and flow of family reunions: as the industry tuned its ear to the fascination of the multi-generational Scottish diaspora with the land of its ancestors, selected parts of Scotland began to be marketed as a mecca for genealogical pilgrims. Building on the 'tartan tourism' of the 1920s and '30s, heritage holidays were promoted in the clearance (and golfing) hotspots of the Highlands, while Shetland launched the first of its 'hamefarin' excursions in 1960.[106]

Equally significant in post-war migration was the emergence of the professional female. Young, single domestic servants had always been a highly visible – and well documented – part of the exodus, while their more invisible sisters left in family groups, as daughters, sisters, wives and mothers. Victorian charities like Maria Rye's Female Middle Class Emigration Society had subsidised governesses and teachers to relocate, particularly in Canada, while missionary service offered an early outlet for women doctors, as well as teachers. But it was the post-war era, with its shaking off of long-held traditions, that saw the independent, initiative-taking female migrant begin to eclipse stereotypes of menial employment and passive domesticity. One adventurous young Scot who preceded her fiancé to Alberta spoke, in an interview, of how she had been 'lured to big old Wild West Canada by the Alberta government, who promised me the world'. For a year her particular corner of that idealised world lay in a one-room, all-age school at Nanton in the foothills of the Rockies. 'Culture shock! I could write a book about it,' she declared, recalling her first day. 'It was September and I was wearing a smart mauve and brown suit. The finest Scottish wool, and made by a dressmaker. It was for curtseying to the Queen. Not for your first day in a one-room version of hell on earth.' By the time she left for Calgary to marry her newly arrived fiancé from Kilmarnock, and take up an urban teaching post, she had learnt to ride western style, shoot and generally live the outdoor life. She had also developed an ambivalent relationship with an environment which could simultaneously attract and repel, relishing her 'wonderful experience' but hating 'what that cold and lonely land did to some of the women'.[107]

That feisty teacher's sentiment reminds us that, even in an era of increasing freedom from the shackles of tradition, migration could still have a particularly dislocating impact – practically and psychologically – on women. First impressions were crucial, and, as we saw with the war brides, culture shock was often associated with their introduction to rudimentary accommodation in isolated areas. But complaints about inadequate housing were not confined to war brides in the 1940s. Just as Andrew MacDonell's Hebrideans had shivered in draughty cottages in northern Alberta in the 1920s, so many 'ten pound Poms' sweated through the searing heat of Australian summers in the cramped, corrugated iron Nissan huts that constituted the government-provided hostel accommodation during the 1950s and '60s.[108] In a *Woman's Hour* interview in 1967, Ida Jenkins, an Australian broadcaster who sat on the Commonwealth Hostels' Appeals Committee in Sydney, defended the hostels as a temporary measure, but conceded that 'I wouldn't want to live in them myself.'[109]

Even if migrants bypassed the hostels the initial experience could be unpalatable. In 1951 Ina Watson emigrated from Glasgow with her husband, a boilermaker, and their two children. They went in search of better employment prospects and housing than the west of Scotland could offer, and they sailed a year after her husband had replied to an advertisement for boilermakers with the State Electricity Commission in Moe, Victoria. Ina's knowledge of Australia was minimal. 'I didn't even know how far away it was. They said that it was a land of sunshine because we saw it advertised all over Glasgow, "Come to sunny Australia".' The reality came as a shock.

> Finally, we came in at Victoria Dock in Melbourne. There were two men from the State Electricity Commission to welcome us. And then they told us that there was no sewerage where we were going, no footpaths, no roads. We hadn't been told that before we left.
> I felt a bit cheated and very, very disappointed when I got there and found mud right up to the front door because the weather was so wet. You get a lot of rain in the La Trobe Valley. Everything was strange. They were lovely little houses but right in the bush. The kangaroos up at your front doorstep sometimes. It was pretty hard. I was very homesick.[110]

Homesickness – allegedly felt most acutely by women – was identified, in a 1967 study of post-war immigration to Canada, as the single most powerful reason for returning to Britain, and its findings were corroborated by similar investigations of Australian returners in 1967 and 1973.[111] It is highly improbable that the homesickness recalled by Ina Watson, which also gave rise to the 'thousand dollar cure' and to considerable debate over the airwaves, was not an equally painful – and recurring – experience among earlier generations of migrants. What is different, however, is the frequency and frankness with which such sentiments were articulated, and the palliative measures that were taken. Were previous generations simply more stoical and – as Geoffrey Nunn implied – less likely to make a fuss? Or were expectations of instant adjustment linked to the technology that was demolishing many of the traditional hurdles of travel and communication? Was lingering homesickness, paradoxically, a consequence of the communications revolution that by the post-war period was starting to bring cheap air travel within the grasp of ordinary individuals and families? If the migrants could keep in easy touch with the worlds they had left behind – by airmail letter, phone and the ready availability of a return flight – were they less likely to put down roots in the new worlds into which they had been parachuted? The much more recent advent of internet facilities such as email, Skype and social networking have, arguably, further intensified rather than assuaged homesickness, isolation and displacement. Migrants who spend more time with their computers than their new communities are surrounded by visual and verbal reminders of an alternative existence, from which they are never liberated to leave their old life behind.

This brings us to the final thread to be woven into the post-war tapestry: the migrants' pursuit or abandonment of their Scottish heritage, and the extent to which their perceptions of the role of ethnicity matched or departed from the stance of their predecessors. Eighteenth-century Scots had become (in)famous for manipulating ethnically based patronage networks in pursuit of occupational and social advancement: in British Guiana, for instance, they had allegedly carried this 'principle of cohesion' so far that the large local shrimps were described as 'Scotchmen... because of the habits of these creatures in clinging one to the other'.[112] In the 19th-century diaspora they commonly made use of churches and ethnic societies to scratch each other's backs in finding a livelihood, lodging and – in hard times – a lifebelt, as well as in framing their social lives, and their distinctiveness had attracted comment. By the 1920s, however, these institutions had become much more marginal to the migrants' wellbeing, as their relevance retreated to the cultural sphere, and in the post-war decades they were further eroded by secularism, the domestication of leisure and the privatisation of migration. The Lewis Society of Detroit, for example, founded in 1919 on the cusp of extensive migration from the Western Isles, had, as we saw earlier, commonly offered financial support to destitute or sick members before the war. That there was less enthusiasm in later years for making disbursements to individuals who had fallen on hard times was exemplified in the Minute of a meeting in 1963, at which 'a discussion took place regarding a delinquent member who is now re-cuperating from a broken hip whether she is eligible for a gift from the Lewis Society'.[113] The harder line reflected dwindling membership and monies: as those who had arrived in the great Hebridean influx of the 1920s began to die off, they were not replaced by a big enough infusion of new arrivals, and membership, which had stood at 339 in 1936, had dropped to 84 by 1967.[114]

From the start, the constitution of the Lewis Society of Detroit offered membership to natives of the island, their spouses and descendants. Some Scottish associations, which had initially been more exclusive, responded to falling rolls by extending its embrace, first to non-Scottish spouses, and then to anyone who was interested, so that eventually the ethnic component of these organisations became purely cosmetic. Scottish migrants, like their counterparts from other parts of the British Isles and beyond – and especially in cosmopolitan environments – moved in a variety of ethnically based social circles that might encompass Morris dancing, Eisteddfods and St Patrick's Day parades, as well as Burns' suppers and Highland Games. Rigid, distinctive identities had, we might argue, been transformed into a more malleable menu of optional ethnic identifications.

Whether this change reflected a wider, unspoken acceptance of a pan-British identity is more debatable. Bernard Braine's presentation of the appeal of the dominions in 1948 had certainly been couched in terms of their Britishness. The objective of the series, he declared in his introductory salvo, was to show listeners 'that those who leave Britain for the dominions are not really uprooting themselves at all, for Britain is to be found wherever the King is sovereign, wherever the writ of British freedom runs and wherever the British way of life prevails'. He returned to the theme four weeks later, when, in commending 'Canada's industrial heartland' of Ontario, he reminded listeners that 'great cities like Toronto, with its skyscrapers' might be American in appearance but were 'intensely British in outlook'.[115]

Some migrants whom we will meet in Chapter 6 deliberately avoided playing the tartan card. Others, like New Zealand journalist Oliver Duff, found even a partial, second-generation Scottish heritage to be a prison from which they could not escape. Duff, who was born in Waitahuna Gully, Otago, in 1883, to an English father and Scottish mother, reflected in a 15-minute radio broadcast in 1948 on the love-hate relationship he had with the culture which had dominated his life. On the farmlands of Otago, he claimed, settlers from Scotland

> not only remained Scots themselves but put Scots labels on everyone else. I have been out of Otago for forty years, but they still make a Scot of me in Wellington. In other words I can't help being a Scot... I can't write a page about anything, could not prepare this script, without slipping into sentimentalities and preachings which I hate but can't shake off. It clouded the last years of Captain Cargill and the Reverend Doctor Burns that their Free Church settlement did not remain Free Church; that the alien crept in, was needed, and could not in justice or

commonsense be kept out. But their sorrow was premature. The door had to be opened, but the intruder was completely assimilated.[116]

The Free Church of Scotland that had pioneered the colonisation of Otago in the 1840s had by the 1940s shrunk to a small remnant of 'wee Frees' whose doctrines remained rigidly reformed and whose power base was confined mainly to parts of the Highlands. It did, however, retain some overseas outposts, particularly in North America, where its determination to fight a rearguard action against liberal theology, Catholicism, secularisation and the dilution of its Highland culture reminds us that not all Scottish institutions in the diaspora simply rolled over and relinquished their identity without a fight. The Free Church presence was sustained primarily through congregations in Detroit, Toronto, Thunder Bay, Winnipeg, Vancouver and Prince Edward Island, but it also had a presence in eastern Australia, where by 1950 it was keen to step up its efforts in response to an increasing flow of migrants.[117] In 1955, when the Presbyterian Church of Eastern Australia was suffering a serious shortage of clergy, it launched a scheme to pay the passages of outgoing ministers, who would also be given a stipend of £600 a year and a £100 bonus (£200 to married men) at the end of four years. They were expected to be men of 'robust health' who would stay for at least four years. More importantly, in the light of the recent secession of two ministers sent from the Free Church, they were reminded of the importance of retaining their spiritual identity, since the Australian denomination 'would rather receive no minister at all than one who would forsake them whenever it suited him to do so'.[118]

Meanwhile in Canada, the Free Church was grappling with the challenges of an ageing membership that was receiving few infusions of new blood as young, Canadian-born people drifted away; the tension between cultural preferences and relevant practice as Gaelic-language ministry became increasingly unsustainable; and the difficulties of persuading clergymen to cross the Atlantic, even for six-month secondments. We saw in Chapter 2 how the Reverend James Mackintosh of the Vancouver congregation, in making a recruitment pitch at the Free Church General Assembly, had been able to claim that Highlanders in Canada 'were a special people' who would not countenance worshipping within another denomination.[119] By the 1950s that cohesive spiritual and cultural identity was fast disappearing, except on the other side of the border in Detroit, where in 1954 a new Free Church was opened under a settled ministry, 11 years after the city's Hebridean population had begun to meet, first in private homes, and then – as numbers grew – in a hired hall.[120] A year earlier, however, a delegate to the General Assembly had suggested that the Canadian outposts should reconfigure their identity and prioritise the spiritual needs of a new generation. 'Are our missions to live "unto themselves" or become missionary vantage-points from which to bring our witness to the people of the New World?' asked Professor David MacKenzie. 'Are they to make an impact on the life surrounding them – or continue as a bit of Scotland in a far-away land?' To cling to their cultural heritage at all costs would, he argued, sideline their evangelistic opportunities and their very presence in an increasingly multi-cultural, multi-ethnic Dominion.[121] By the mid-1970s, after two decades when congregations – often pastorless – continued to dwindle, and the arrival of Gaelic-speaking migrants slowed to a 'mere trickle', the parent church eventually admitted the financial and cultural impossibility of maintaining the status quo, and the remaining North American churches affiliated with doctrinally likeminded indigenous denominations.[122]

Across the border, the 1970s saw the beginning of a revival in Scottish ethnicity, at least among older immigrants and (especially) those of Scottish ancestry. The steady erosion of Scottish associational activity since the 1920s had begun to move into reverse as early as 1956 with the inauguration of Grandfather Mountain Highland Games, the formation of the Clan Donald Society USA and the establishment of the commercially and culturally focused American-Scottish Foundation. Two decades later it accelerated dramatically as part of the American love-affair with genealogies, which was itself partly attributable to the success of Alex Haley's novel *Roots*, and its television adaptation.[123] But not only did new Scottish societies appear and old ones gain a new lease of life: these associations also reflected 'an invention of tradition within the diaspora community', embracing indigenous traits that would have been unknown, or anathema, to their predecessors.[124] This symbolic ethnicity has been manifested in such practices as the Kirkin' o the Tartan and the pageantry of Tartan Day, although an increasingly commercial element has been injected into the events of Tartan Day's offspring, 'Scottish Week'.

Similarly, the commercial possibilities of ancestral tourism have given rise to a modern reincarnation of the transatlantic trips sponsored in the 1920s and '30s by the Order of Scottish Clans.[125]

As we saw earlier, the pursuit and reconfiguration of identities were not always confined to the new world. Nor were the controversies and tensions associated with them. Some 'homecoming' migrants still came back in the expectation of re-engaging with a country that only existed in their imaginations: a land that remained frozen in the image they had created at the time of their departure, and which became more and more divorced from reality the longer they were away. Descendants of the migrant generation were increasingly likely to be genealogical tourists searching for an invented identity, often in the ruins of cleared Highland townships. As the anthropologist, Paul Basu, has demonstrated with reference to early 21st-century 'returners', this can involve the manipulation of ancestral lines in order to highlight the most distinctive associations, particularly those which speak of victimhood, thereby giving the descendants' visits the extra dimension of pilgrimage.[126]

Such sentiments, and the disillusionment or displacement experienced when Scotland proved to be unrecognisable and its people indifferent to their quest, are not unique to roots tourists. Throughout the 20th century – indeed, throughout the history of migration – sojourners, transilients and boomerang migrants, as well as settlers, sometimes struggled with issues of belonging and definitions of home. Perhaps the unease and sense of impermanence in the Scottish (and wider British) diaspora became more acute in the post-war era, as technology revolutionised travel and communications; as frequent farewells and reunions became the norm; as the payout from the 'colonial dividend' shrivelled and finally died;[127] and as multiculturalism reshaped the familiar institutions and cultures of an anachronistic British world. But their discomfiture was also a consequence of persistent prejudice in the sending and receiving countries. It is to the causes and consequences of this hostility, and to the wider phenomenon of the dysfunctional migrant, that we turn in the next chapter.

A 1920s poster emphasising the ease and affordability of family emigration
(CP Archives, A-6343)

Promotional posters stressed the benefits of farming
(Library and Archives Canada, C-126302k)

The Canadian Pacific Railway highlighted opportunities on the prairies
(CP Archives, BR 194)

Above: The longer-settled East was not neglected in advertisements
(Library and Archives Canada, C-144748)
Right: Women were a prime target for recruitment agents
(Library and Archives Canada, C-137978k)

WHITE STAR
LINE
CANADA'S
CALL
To WOMEN.
For full Information apply to—
SERCOMBE & HAYES, 9, South Street, DORCHESTER

Abundant harvests were a recurring theme (Library and Archives Canada, C-137960)

CANADIAN PACIFIC

THE BEST WAY TO
YOUR OWN FARM IN CANADA

PASSAGE MONEY ADVANCED.

LOANS FOR FARM PURCHASE.

BRITISH SETTLERS ON THEIR CANADIAN FARMS.

THREE THOUSAND BRITISH FAMILIES WANTED FOR CANADA.

A SPLENDID OPPORTUNITY:

FOR the family farming a holding too small to adequately provide support or for the future of their children;

FOR farm workers and married sons and daughters of farmers having no occupation other than farming, and unable to secure land at home;

FOR any family in which either the husband or wife has had farm experience, and one or more of whose children are of working age.

FARMS READY FOR OCCUPATION IN SETTLED DISTRICTS near RAILWAYS, MARKETS & SCHOOLS

FREE PASSAGES FOR CHILDREN.

For Further Particulars **APPLY WITHIN.**

The prospect of ready-made farms was a powerful incentive (Library and Archives Canada, C-55446)

Customs House Quay, Greenock, was the point of departure for many Scottish emigrants

(© 1993 Robert Baumgardner)

CHAPTER 5

The Dysfunctional Diaspora?

THE COURSE OF MIGRATION, like that of love, has never run smoothly. Its tempestuous history is brought to life with striking eloquence in poetry and songs, old and new. Runrig's 'Rocket to the Moon' contrasts the unequivocal bleakness of the Clyde's silent shipyards with the apparently endless horizons of the Canadian prairies.

> There's a town in Manitoba
> They say the windows touch the sky
> But across the brine the shipyards close
> In this garden flowers die.[1]

Examples of disillusionment, controversy, fraud and failure have so far punctuated the narrative intermittently, but the persistent undercurrent of opposition to migration and migrants, which periodically erupted into visible waves of hostility, warrants expanded identification and analysis. In this chapter we turn the spotlight initially on the sources of disquiet: institutions and individuals in the UK in general and Scotland in particular who at different times opposed the haemorrhage of population on economic, political and cultural grounds. We then look at similarly negative constituencies in the host countries that complained about being saddled with the degenerate, unemployable or militant detritus of British orphanages and dole queues. The scene then shifts from paper debates to painful practical outcomes, demonstrated in the fate of migrants whose expectations of acceptance and integration had been shattered by experiences much more devastating (and externally imposed) than the run-of-the-mill disappointments described in earlier chapters. Here we are concerned primarily with the fate of those individuals who were regarded as so dysfunctional by the host societies that they were denied entry, detained in hospitals, asylums and jails, or deported. All these strands contribute to the darker side of the tapestry of migration – a dimension that, despite changing emphases over the generations, presents us with recurring patterns of paradox, tension and contention.

A Tradition of Tension

Anti-migration sentiment in the 20th century had a long pedigree. Many of its roots were firmly embedded in Scottish migrants' clashes with authority two centuries earlier, when it became very clear that the wanderlust associated with Scots since time immemorial was moving into a higher gear, at least in the Highlands. In a mercantilist age, such a trend was anathema to government and landlords for whom national health and wealth were synonymous with the retention, not the release, of population. Setting a pattern that would be followed by many others over the next 200 years, they turned their fire on recruiters, whose seductive promises, they claimed, drained Scotland of money and manpower and threatened the effective implementation of estate modernisation policies. The threat was not purely economic, for deteriorating relations with the American colonies by the early 1770s meant that migration posed a serious threat to national security. Fears that migrants might take up arms against the Crown once they arrived in America had led, in September 1775, to legislation that effectively banned transatlantic emigration for the duration of the revolutionary war.

The loss of the American colonies undermined the government's unequivocal opposition, as it began to see the strategic sense of populating the redrawn frontier with loyal settlers, not least Scottish Highlanders. No further recourse was had to direct statutory prohibition, although the solid wall of landlord opposition, manifested in practical terms through the disingenuous Passenger Act of 1803, was not undermined until the collapse of their grand designs after the Napoleonic wars. A resurgent 'spirit of emigration' in the 1790s was noted with regret by several ministers in their submissions to the *Statistical Account of Scotland*, and recruitment agents continued to bear the brunt of criticism. When at the turn of the century Thomas Telford was commissioned by the government to advise on how to promote Highland development through communications, fishing and the prevention of emigration, he blamed the 'evil' outflow on unwise estate management, reinforced by 'artful Persons, who hesitate not to sacrifice these poor ignorant People to selfish Ends'.[2]

Even when overseas migration was embraced by devotees of Malthus in the 1820s and during the more positive era of systematic colonisation that succeeded it, neither strategy was unanimously endorsed. Malthusian policies were criticised as expensive and ineffective from a British perspective and by the recipients as a blatant expulsion of unwanted paupers to the colonies, accusations that re-emerged during the depression of the 1870s. Systematic colonisation was condemned at home for its damaging selectivity that exported the best and left behind the neediest, while overseas critics saw it in very different terms: as a dressed-up version of a negative policy whose objective was to ship out the unwanted to a reluctant empire.

Antagonism to emigration had a particular resonance in the Highlands, where it was inextricably entangled with the legacy of the clearances. Even though from the 1860s a clear and increasing majority of emigrants had come from the urban-industrial Central Belt, dark images of loss and longing continued to dominate public perceptions well into the 20th century, within and beyond Scotland, and not least in enclaves of Highland settlement. The exilic lament of the *Canadian Boat Song* echoed down through the generations, and was reinforced at different times in the 20th century by the novels and short stories of Ralph Connor, Hugh MacLennan and Alistair MacLeod, the passionate poems of Gaelic bards and the popular songs of Runrig or Cape Breton's Rankin Family.[3]

The suspicion of recruiters that had surfaced in the 18th century persisted into the era of professional agency activity. Dr David Boyter, the ship's surgeon and New South Wales government's recruiting agent who took his campaign to the Highlands in the 1830s, was welcomed in some quarters for relieving overpopulation but criticised in others for skimming off the cream. Those who were lured to Australia in those early days of free settlement were advised that 'the emigrant who settles in these distant countries generally bids adieu to comfort and peace of mind', and would exchange civilised society for a convict-blighted community where 'robbery, violence, and indolence, stalk through the land'.[4] While most trade unions in the 19th century operated emigration funds in the belief that the relocation of surplus labour, especially during market downturns, would benefit those who went and those who stayed alike, they also warned members against overseas agents who sought to recruit strike breakers, and by the 20th century they had become concerned about the correlation between emigration and the loss of workplace solidarity.[5] Employers, meanwhile, deplored the loss of manpower from both factory and farm and the inflated wages created by the departure – often the union-sponsored departure – of the cream of their workforce. These views found an outlet in Conservative newspapers such as the *Aberdeen Journal*, and led John Maclennan, the Canadian federal government agent for the north of Scotland from 1907–11, to complain in 1908 of the difficulty in generating enthusiasm for Canada because of the way in which the local press had 'poisoned the public mind'. Two years later he warned his employers in Ottawa of the dangers of antagonising unduly the 'large farmers' who constituted such a 'powerful force in the community'.[6]

For a generation after Confederation, relations with Canada were also soured by the tendency of the British press to portray the senior dominion as a snowbound wilderness. As a result, illustrators employed by the federal government and the railway companies were instructed to omit even the minutest snowflake from their promotional posters.[7] But warnings against settling in Canada were much less vociferous than those issued against its republican neighbour to the south, where 19th-century migrants were told they were likely to fall under the evil spell of land sharks, cheats and secularists.[8]

Pitfalls and perils also allegedly awaited those who opted for more distant destinations. Warnings against Australia's scorching sun might be avoided by heading for New Zealand, but Kiwi recruiters battled with the accusation – sometimes levelled by rival agents – that their goal was 'to allure people to lands the heritage of Maori cannibals'.[9] More realistic criticism was directed at the economic effects of mass recruitment under New Zealand's national development programme in the 1870s, which provoked a backlash of criticism from pundits and participants. A migrant from Dundee, for instance, writing from Canterbury in 1873, asserted that the 'lying handbooks of New Zealand' had lured him to a colony with an 'almost universally overstocked' labour market, minimal arable land and a journey of over 80 miles to his nearest market.[10] As for South Africa, recommendations were often eclipsed by warnings about limited opportunities and high living costs, and in 1881 a Shetland-based agent was reprimanded by his employers for over-egging the Cape as 'the fairest land to be found in any country'.[11]

Reactions Against Recruitment: 20th-century Controversies

Pot shots continued to be taken at recruiters during the 20th century. In 1925 Andrew MacDonell cited 'persistent adverse propaganda in the press' as one of the two main reasons for several families withdrawing their applications to emigrate (the other being delays in the interviewing process).[12] In 1926 W.J. Egan, Canada's deputy minister of immigration, defending the Canadian government's female agent in Inverness against a claim that she lacked the credibility of a male agent among the 'douce farmers of north east Scotland', reminded his London-based superintendent of emigration, J. Bruce Walker, that those farmers had always opposed Canadian agency work.[13] Perhaps he had in mind the criticism directed at John Maclennan before the war, or a more recent letter published in the *Scottish Farmer* which warned that the Canadian government's Aberdeen-based agent, D.E. Lothian, was making unsolicited recruitment visits to farm workers in the county without the knowledge or permission of their employers.[14] Then in 1930, as opportunities were eroded by the deepening depression, the *John O'Groat Journal* published a letter from Ontario claiming that recruiters were 'telling people about a country they know nothing about from actual experience'. Those with any sort of job should avoid jumping from the frying pan into the fire, advised Alexander Sutherland, since 'with all the unemployed in Canada there are enough people here to do all the farm work and the other work too without taking over more to be stranded in a country with six months of winter and no work at all'.[15]

Antipodean recruiters were also tainted by press criticism, not least in the *Scottish Farmer*. In 1926 claims of exploitation were at the centre of an epistolary spat between the Conservative politician Lord Apsley, and a former migrant, one P. Marshall. Having just returned to Stirling after 12 years in Victoria, Tasmania and New South Wales, Marshall was scathing of the glowing recommendations Apsley had made in a lecture to an 'overwhelmingly crowded meeting' in Glasgow.

Having disguised himself and secured an assisted passage as an unskilled farm labourer, Apsley had spent a month travelling across three Australian States, a venture which, according to Marshall, was an 'immigration stunt' that would serve only to drive down living standards in Australia. The noble lord and his friends, he alleged, 'have scarcely had time to relish a piece of roast kangaroo... let alone be in a position to give a sound opinion of the prospects of anyone on the land'. It was, he continued, 'a disgrace to this country that young men should be enticed out to Australia with specious promises by well-paid immigration officials', only to consign them to such 'rotten conditions' on farms that they ended up as a half-starved, unemployed, urban underclass in a country where there was no 'dole'. Apsley retorted by leveling accusations of destructive criticism and sour grapes, but Marshall had the last word. 'You have often to destroy before you can construct,' he retorted, 'and I cannot do better service to my young countrymen than see to it that they are under no illusion as to the true facts.'[16]

Much of the hostility to recruitment agents had deep roots in widespread political and socio-economic opposition to emigration. Scottish nationalists had long been scathing about an exodus which they attributed to Scotland's inability to control its own affairs and the failure of politicians to accept that the country was under-worked rather than over-populated. 'If emigration is the cure for unemployment, how comes it that Scotland is in such a plight?' demanded the *Scots Independent* in 1927, in the context of an attack on Westminster's support for emigration rather than the reconstruction of Scottish industries.[17] Writing to the Secretary of State for Scotland in the same year, Lewis Spence, President of the Scottish National Movement, articulated the increasing alarm of 'patriotic Scotsmen and Scotswomen' at the 'continuous and disastrous stream of emigration from Scottish soil'.[18] The emigrants themselves were also blamed for abdicating the responsibilities of nationhood by chasing overseas rainbows, exporting their skills and talents to the benefit of foreign competitors while Scotland continued to languish in the political and economic wilderness.

Some politicians pulled no punches. 'Flatulent humbug and pernicious nonsense' was the verdict of veteran Highland Land Leaguer and NPS member, Angus Clark, on pro-emigration policies which he claimed constituted one of the greatest scandals in Europe and had resulted in Scotland being only a 'half developed... weakling'. His opening salvo in a letter to the editor of the *Weekly Herald* in 1936 set the tone for the denunciation that followed. 'Emigration,' he wrote, 'has but one result, an impoverished nation. It never solves a nation's problems nor cures its ills. It is a poisonous fallacy, which none but Scotland's enemies will support, a policy of despair, which every friend of Scotland will oppose.' He went on to urge that lessons should be learned from past mistakes and, in a glancing blow directed at both Labour and Conservative opponents, advocated that policy-makers stop thinking about internationalism and imperialism, but instead concentrate on developing Scotland's internal resources under self-government.[19]

Nationalists continued to address the 'very serious problem' of emigration after the war, when they strove to 'direct attention to its causes and cure'. Part of that strategy involved, in 1956, sending a questionnaire to all Scottish MPs and peers. When no replies were received from Highland constituencies, the relevant politicians – particularly Labour's Malcolm Macmillan in the Western Isles – were berated by John Smart, Honorary National Secretary of the SNP, for their lack of interest. 'Or are they ashamed of their opinions?' he asked, rhetorically, before urging that cash and confidence should be channelled into persuading the Highlander – allegedly the world's best pioneer – 'to do his pioneering at home'. Success, he maintained, could not be achieved under an 'alien government' but only under self-rule, when 'those exiles whose hearts are still Highland will come home, not just to die and be buried, but to live and to restore life to our country'.[20]

The *Scots Independent* kept up a regular onslaught on the depopulation of Scotland as a whole. Throughout 1956, for instance, reports and correspondence regularly bewailed the 'curse to Scotland's future', which – despite relatively full employment – was running at a 'dangerously high' level.[21] Two particularly assertive letters came from Francis Gilroy, an expatriate in Australia. On returning to New South Wales after a visit home, he had filled his suitcase with copies of the *Scots Independent* and other nationalist literature which he distributed at the Sydney Highland Gathering and through a variety of Scottish societies. In his opinion, 'if Scotland must be free the fight should be carried on far from her shores', and he argued that second-generation Scottish exiles – or those who had been 'practically a lifetime away' – were more likely to sympathise with independence than the newcomer who 'usually... wants to forget Scotland and its frugality'.[22]

Some post-war nationalists sang from an even more radical song sheet than Angus Clark had done in 1936, and militant opposition to the recruitment of Scots for overseas settlement was occasionally akin to the intimidatory approach of Irish republicans.[23] The Scottish Patriots, under Wendy Wood, burned assisted emigration forms outside the Australian consulate in Edinburgh and danced an eightsome reel on the ashes.[24] A 15-minute wonder in January 1956 was the case of the allegedly poisoned pie, when Australian selecting officers based at Tollcross Employment Exchange in Edinburgh handed over to detectives a steak pie that had been delivered by post to an unidentified 'enemy of Scotland', but addressed to 'The Australian Emigration Officer'. Two days earlier the BBC in Scotland had broadcast a warning after an anonymous call to a newspaper had claimed a poisoned pie had been mailed to 'a person with anti-Nationalist views', but the story fizzled out when the public analyst reported that the suspect pie had contained 'no poisonous matter'.[25] Three years later one of those selecting officers recalled that the steps of the office had also been painted with abusive slogans, and several travel agencies in Edinburgh and Glasgow which displayed emigration posters had bricks thrown through their windows.[26]

In December 1956 Sidney Holland, Prime Minister of New Zealand, received an extraordinary plea from the blunt-speaking Douglas Henderson, then President of the Edinburgh University Nationalist Club, but who claimed he was 'National Secretary' of the 'Nationalist Party of Scotland'. His xenophobic letter – which displays an anti-English sentiment reminiscent of the hostility directed against Irish immigrants to Scotland in a previous generation – merits quoting *in extenso*.

> At the request of my Executive, I am writing to draw your attention to the serious effects caused by the activities of your Emigration Officers in Scotland.
>
> We are happy to think that many Scots have played such a prominent part in the development of your country. Nevertheless we cannot shut our eyes to the fact that these benefits to New Zealand have been gained at the cost of a disastrous drain of many of the finest and best of Scotland's youth...
>
> It is our considered opinion that the English government is actively and deliberately fostering a large-scale clearance of our people although, as a nation, we are considerably under-populated. To add to our difficulties there is an incredible and dangerous influx of English people into Scotland. This we can only regard as a threat to the survival of our country.
>
> I ask you in the name of the Scottish people to give this problem your personal attention and issue the appropriate instructions to your officials to cease forthwith their emigration activities in Scotland and concentrate on our grossly over-populated neighbour, England.[27]

Opposition to emigration was articulated across the political spectrum and produced some strange bedfellows. In the 1920s critics ranged from the shipping magnate Sir Alfred Yarrow, who complained that £400 was being squandered on the education of every young emigrant, to the Communist Party, which demonised emigration as a capitalist phenomenon that turned a blind eye to domestic unemployment and aggravated labour problems overseas. Wal Hannington, a founding member of the Communist Party of Great Britain, was a familiar figure on Canada-bound vessels in the Clyde, particularly in the winter of 1923, as he and other members of the National Unemployed Workers' Movement preached their anti-emigration gospel to passengers, who should not, they argued, be 'shipped off to an uncertain future', simply because the system had failed them.[28]

Most socialists deplored sponsored emigration as an immoral weapon that inhibited the extension of state welfare. They were particularly antagonistic to the Conservative government's Empire Settlement Act, on the grounds that it was a short-term expedient with unacceptable eugenic and economic implications. In the peak year of 1923, as emigrants – 'lured by sunlit posters' – packed the transatlantic liners, the Glasgow ILP newspaper, *Forward*, launched a barrage of criticism against the circumstances that had triggered such a remarkable flight from 'poverty and struggle'.[29] Two years later, it was still directing its fire at disingenuous advertising, warning readers against both

Immigrants sending postcards home from Gander Airport (Library and Archives Canada)

the CPR's 'alluring' recruitment propaganda and the troubled 3,000 Families programme, one of a number of 'shady and spectacular schemes' that had, it claimed, been 'concocted' by the British government.[30] A recurring concern among politicians as well as journalists was that the emigrants were – as Dumbarton MP, David Kirkwood, pointed out in 1928 – far from being the 'ragtag and bobtail of city life', but 'the best blood of our land, the young and vigorous', many of whom fell victim to fraudulent offers of employment and ill-thought-out land settlement schemes.[31] Brickbats continued to fly after the war. Although less vehement, Scottish Labour MPs were still vocal in the debates that surrounded the renewal of the legislation in the 1950s and '60s. In the second reading debate in 1952, Western Isles MP, Malcolm MacMillan, claimed that advice to emigrate – peddled by the Conservative government in the interests of the cohesion of the Commonwealth – was 'something of a counsel of despair'. As chairman of the Highlands and Islands Advisory Panel, his goal was to stem depopulation and stimulate regeneration of the region, and he was 'very concerned with the danger of making emigration a substitute for a solution for unemployment'. His concerns were echoed by William Ross, MP for Kilmarnock, who argued that the £1,500,000 a year being earmarked for developing emigration should instead be spent 'in getting some of the Scots back into Scotland', particularly the Highlands. Ten years later, while the Labour opposition supported the renewal of the legislation, the MP for Dundee, G.M. Thomson, pointed out that Scotland was still contributing disproportionately to UK emigration, without receiving its fair share of immigrants from the Commonwealth.[32]

From a trade union perspective, Scottish Miners' Union president, Abe

Moffat – addressing a meeting in Toronto in February 1957 – expressed 'great concern' that each week Canada and Australia were attracting around 6,000 young people, adding that in his own industry, the average age of miners had risen from 36 before the war to 41 in the mid-1950s.[33] Two months later the annual conference of the Scottish Trades Union Congress commissioned an inquiry into the reasons for Scotland's 'disproportionate weight of emigration', which it estimated had been 16 times greater than that from England and Wales over the last century and was currently exerting a 'dangerous influence' on the future health of the economy.[34] And at a specially convened conference in February 1965, the STUC was preoccupied with the 'problem' of an ongoing exodus from Scotland in general, but particularly from the Highlands, where 'prolonged selective emigration of the reproductive age groups', particularly young women, had resulted in a markedly low rate of natural population increase.[35]

But there was also a degree of opposition to emigration from the other end of the political spectrum. While most Conservative and Liberal politicians in the 1920s supported the imperialist agenda enshrined in the Empire Settlement Act, some were uncomfortably aware that rural recruitment campaigns, by taking away the best farm servants, were alienating many of their natural supporters. From time to time contributors to the right-of-centre *Spectator* magazine fretted about the implications of losing youthful and enterprising migrants and struggled to reconcile such a loss with 'the desirability of increasing the population of the dominions with men and women of our stock'. Emigration, wrote St John Ervine in 1947, 'should be from surplus, not from insufficiency', and he highlighted the paradox of almost one million people wishing to emigrate with a British labour shortage that required the immediate immigration of at least 250,000 European 'foreigners', including 125,000 from recent enemy nations.[36]

In 1950 the former Registrar-General for Scotland, J.G. Kyd, added a civil servant's voice, and a Scottish perspective, to the debate. While acknowledging the need to 'develop the lands of the Commonwealth' with 'British stock', he claimed that if Scotland's recent disproportionate contribution were to continue, then 'the economic and industrial prosperity of our country will be very hard to maintain'. The net outward loss of 32,400 Scots in 1949 – a year of apparent industrial prosperity and full employment – exceeded total departures in 1930–39, and the problem was compounded by the youthful profile of the migrants.[37] Kyd's intervention was followed by a brief flurry of politically driven letters to the editor of *The Scotsman*. For W.S. Cruickshank the haemorrhage of primary producers was creating a seriously unbalanced population in skills as well as age; he maintained that 'the only way to stop them going is to make this country of ours once again a land worth living in'. George Dott, on the other hand, claimed that the root cause of migration was 'simply the lack of a Scottish Government' and suggested that if the dominions needed immigrants, then they should seek them exclusively in England.[38] The issue was still pertinent 15 years later when Sir Duncan Sandys, Commonwealth Secretary in Harold Macmillan's Conservative government, commissioned an enquiry into the economic consequences of overseas migration. The resulting report introduced a specifically Scottish dimension into the question, pointing out that not only had Scotland's persistently high levels of unemployment and migration continued into the post-war period: like the STUC at the same time, it concluded that the highly selective and youthful nature of the exodus was going to have a 'serious effect' on Scotland's prospects of long-term economic recovery.[39]

Political posturing was, as these examples demonstrate, fuelled by economic arguments and in the press ideology battled with expediency, editorial opinion blowing hot and cold according to whether the emigrating public was perceived as a liability or an asset. In some rural constituencies between the wars, the loss of farm servants was bewailed while the departure of skilled artisans was seen as a means of shrinking the dole queues. For post-war critics the main issue was the 'brain drain', a term coined in the 1960s with reference to the loss of skilled scientific, engineering and medical personnel. Yet it was not a new phenomenon – as a survey published in 1969 points out, the lack of robust statistics on which to base these concerns meant that the controversy tended to generate 'more heat than light'.[40] Nonetheless, it is clear that specific occupations were being targeted from time to time, a strategy that had some echoes of artisan recruitment in the 18th century. In 1966, for instance, *The Times* reported that senior police officials in Scotland were 'seriously worried' that the attractive remuneration being offered by the Toronto Police Department had attracted more than 600 Scottish applications from a UK total of 1,200. Already struggling with 'a severe manpower shortage', the Scottish forces could not compete with salaries of between £1,874 and £2,160, which were more than double a police officer's pay in Scotland.[41]

There was also a cultural dimension to domestic opposition, which was targeted on both emigration and immigration. Within the Scottish Presbyterian churches in particular, the orchestration of colonisation schemes often sat uneasily with periodic – and pejorative – outbursts of anti-emigration sentiment. In 1911 the General Assemblies of both the Free and United Free Churches had complained about the 'menace' of an 'exceedingly onerous' tide of emigration that was sweeping Scotland, claiming that national stability and the future of Protestantism were at risk because of the disproportionate departure of Presbyterians. If political nationalists in the 1950s turned their fire on English influences, the religious establishment between the wars was preoccupied with Ireland. In the 1920s the xenophobic flames were fanned by the Church of Scotland's notorious call for the wholesale repatriation of Irish Catholic immigrants, who, it was alleged, were filling the vacuum left by stalwart Presbyterian Scottish emigrants, exacerbating both employment and the erosion of Scotland's religious identity.

More than ten years later the Free Church of Scotland was still declaiming against depopulation on the same sectarian grounds. While Highlanders should not be debarred from pursuing their 'irresistible' and 'hereditary' tradition of worldwide wandering, they should – in the opinion of the Reverend G.N.M. Collins – be steered to the Central Belt in order to stem the influx of Irish Catholics. He complained to the 1935 General Assembly that after the war

> they had the spectacle week after week of liners carrying away the very flower of their youth to the Colonies in search of employment and a livelihood, and at the same time cross-channel steamers from the Irish coast were dumping on the Clydeside hundreds – thousands, indeed – of Irishmen who spread across the industrial belt of Scotland and supplied the demand for cheap labour. If these emigrants had been co-religionists they would have received them with greater readiness, but they were not, they were aliens whose loyalty was first to the Pope, with whom the canon law of Rome was paramount, and not the civil law of the land. These Irish people were at the present time in occupations which ought to be available for Highland people. One eminent politician quite recently expressed the pious hope that the economic depression would so lift in the Colonies that shortly they would be open to receive more emigrants. That was a remedy they did not desire to see applied.[42]

Free Church terriers were still gnawing at the same sectarian bone in the 1940s and 1950s, although their efforts were now directed to ensuring that new employment opportunities in the depopulated Highlands would not attract 'an alien population' of men from 'the good old Highland clans of Flannagan and O'Reilly'.[43] And even in 1972 Irish immigration continued to draw their fire, as part of a wider opposition to unwelcome cultural influences on the British nation.

> The troubles in Ireland have given rise again to the question of the immigration policy of the Government, reminding us that lack of

care in the admission of aliens to this country may well involve us in serious difficulties, not only from the influx of Asiatic[s] and others of equally alien culture and religion, but also (and perhaps especially) from incomers from Eire who are eager to enjoy all that Great Britain has to offer, and, at the same time, to use their privileged position for the destruction of the British way of life.[44]

'A vicious and soulless propaganda': the Highland Perspective

The Free Church's concerns about migration did not revolve only around anti-Catholicism. The denomination's main constituency lay in the Highlands and Islands, where since the 1840s it had spoken out consistently against clearance and emigration. In the 20th century it continued to champion the crofters' cause through the denunciation of economic policies which had triggered out-migration and supported initiatives which promised to reverse that trend. In 1906, it petitioned the House of Commons to promote land reform and the development of infrastructure, fishing and hydro power in order to stem the outflow, and just after the war the church became involved in the 'Highland Betterment Association' to deliver similar objectives.[45] Although in 1924 it admitted that it sometimes gave grants to individuals to help them emigrate, since 'this kept them from morally deteriorating while they were waiting for a Small Holding', it continued throughout the inter-war period to advocate revitalisation through farming and fishing.[46] In 1946 Dr A.M. Renwick felt the new hydro-electric schemes offered a 'ray of hope... that industry would return to the Highlands' and reverse the area's 'pitiable condition' that was a consequence of 180 years of depopulation; in 1953 he welcomed the formation of the Highland Fund as a means of stemming the tide by injecting capital into the region.[47]

Despite its ambivalence and occasional practical support for emigration schemes as a Hobson's choice, the Free Church was firmly in the camp that equated Highland depopulation with impoverishment rather than enrichment. Much more unambiguously in that camp was Dr Lachlan Grant of Ballachulish, who in the 1930s added his voice to the chorus of protest. The slate village's long-serving GP – also a journalist, scientist and medical officer of health – denounced emigration because it undermined his scheme for the economic and social rehabilitation of the Highlands. A Liberal who was also active in the early days of the SNP, he echoed the

Dr Lachlan Grant of Ballachulish
(National Library of Scotland)

nationalists' concern about the endemic haemorrhage from the north. Two years before he co-founded the Highland Development League in 1936 with the Reverend Thomas Murchison of Glenelg, he wrote to his friend, Ramsay Macdonald, at that time the tenant of 10 Downing Street, claiming that depopulation was associated with an increase in the number of pauper lunatics in the Highlands. It was a controversial eugenic argument, which Grant subsequently revisited in public lectures, and in an article in the *Caledonian Medical Journal* in 1937, in which he claimed that physically and mentally strong Highlanders had been steered overseas, leaving behind a disproportionate residue of the old, infirm and degenerate.[48]

Grant's main assertion, however, was that stemming the 'abnormal' human tide of outbound Highlanders was an essential prerequisite for land reform. He predicted that if this were not tackled, a distinctive people, language and culture would become extinct. Writing in the *Northern Times* in 1935, he claimed that the Highlands had suffered disproportionately from emigration, and maintained that 95 per cent of those who had left would have been as well, or better off, at home. His intervention was triggered by a report presented to the recent General Assembly of the Church of Scotland, which had recommended emigration, particularly of young women and boys, as the remedy for unemployment. Grant hit back by accusing the Church and Nation Committee of 'either a woeful ignorance, or flagrant audacity' in recommending such a 'myopic policy', which he compared unfavourably with the commitment of the recent Free Church Assembly to stem depopulation. 'Too long,' he continued, 'has this vicious and soulless propaganda been going on, and its advocacy by the Church is, as it were, "the last straw".'

Like Angus Clark, he believed that the future of Scotland – and the Highlands in particular – called for 'less glorification of overseas countries', and urged people with pioneering spirit and vision to put those attributes to use to improve their own, and their countrymen's, lot in Scotland.

Reminding readers of the warning in the Book of Proverbs that 'The eyes of the fool are on the ends of the earth', Grant maintained that the eyes of the Scot were 'too often bent in the same direction'.[49]

For more than a century biblical analogies had been woven into the narrative of Highland migration, often in poems, songs and sermons that portrayed an enforced diaspora similar to that of the ancient Israelites. Also maintained into the 20th century was the bardic tradition of imprinting an exilic motif on the experience of migration. The final verse of Iain MacLeòid's poem, 'Bàs Baile' ('Death of a Township'), an earlier section of which has already been quoted in Chapter 2, offers a poignant perspective on the departure of the *Marloch*.

> Lìon gach màthair ciste le aodach blàth
> air son talamh fuar, is bìoball anns gach seotal.
> An oidhch' a dh'fhalbh iad
> dhìrich sinn an cnoc a b' àirde
> is shuidh sinn gun fhocal, sàmhach,
> gus an deach ás ar sealladh
> solas crann-àrd a' *Mhàrloch*.
> Sin thòisich glaodh taigh-fhaireadh
> aig tiodhlacadh daoine beò.
> An oidhch' ud bhàsaich am bail' aggain.

> Each mother filled a kist with warm clothes
> for a cold land, with a bible in each shuttle.
> The night they left
> we climbed the highest hill
> and sat wordless, silent,
> till the *Marloch*'s mainmast light
> disappeared from our sight.
> Then the wake-house cry arose
> for the burial of the living.
> That night our township died.[50]

In writings spanning the entire 20th century, the exilic theme was also taken up by novelists such as Ralph Connor, Hugh MacLennan and Alistair MacLeod. Connor's Glengarry Highlanders in Eastern Ontario, having been 'driven from homes in the land of their fathers', had 'set themselves with indomitable faith and courage to hew from the solid forest, homes for themselves and their children that none might take from them'. MacLennan's Cape Breton miners, whose forebears had left the Highlands 'with the pipes playing laments on the decks of their ships', belonged to 'a race of hunters, shepherds and warriors who had discovered too late that their own courage and pride had led them to catastrophe'. And at the heart of MacLeod's novel *No Great Mischief* – which takes its title from General Wolfe's scornful attitude to Highland soldiers on the Plains of Abraham – are the MacDonald pioneers who left Moidart for Cape Breton in 1779. Their 20th-century descendants, like MacLennan's characters 50 years earlier, find themselves unable to lay the ghosts of their Highland heritage, an indelible clan *duchthas* that, even in the diaspora, remains simultaneously a blessing and a curse.[51]

Of course, literary or musical laments were not focused exclusively on the Highlands. *Scottish Journey,* Edwin Muir's bleak inter-war reflection on national alienation and its industrial roots, decries the southward march of brains and brawn, and the reciprocal importation of English ways.[52] More than half a century later, in 1987, a similar sense of industrial dereliction lies at the heart of the Proclaimers' 'Letter from America' which compared the wastelands of the industrial Central Belt to the cleared Highland landscapes created in a previous generation. To a refrain of 'Lochaber no more', 'Sutherland no more', 'Lewis no more' and 'Skye no more', they add a litany of the post-war victims of deindustrialisation: 'Bathgate no more, Linwood no more, Methil no more, Irvine no more'.

Hostile Hosts

If the haemorrhage of population was opposed in the migrants' homeland on the grounds that it was bleeding Scotland of her brightest and best, host lands wrung their hands for diametrically different reasons. Ethnicity was sometimes perceived to be a factor in mental, physical or moral defectiveness, and although ethnic markers were used primarily to discriminate against central and eastern Europeans or Asians, allegations were also made about the export of Britons who were already of unsound mind.[53]

The hostility was fuelled by a mixture of moral outrage and financial sensitivity. In 1906, for instance, 21-year-old Jeannie Caldwell was deported from Toronto back to her home in Dennistoun. She had been sent out the previous year by the Glasgow Prisoners' Aid Society after a string of convictions for theft and fraud in Glasgow, Edinburgh and London, but her career in Canada, her deportation form records, 'has been almost continuously that of a criminal'. The most recent of her four convictions was for stealing a gold watch from the matron of the Hamilton YWCA, but since she could not be compulsorily deported under the existing legislation, the immigration department had to fund her return transportation.[54]

In the eugenics-dominated decade before the First World War, Canada was preoccupied with the idea that not only criminals, but also weak-minded immigrants from Britain – particularly 'English defectives' from the metropolitan slums – were polluting their society and draining their economy because they did not fall under current deportation laws. Statistics from the Toronto Asylum were used in an article in the *University Monthly* in 1908 to suggest that immigrants made up a disproportionate part of the province's asylum inmates: while 20 per cent of Ontario's population was foreign-born, between 40 and 50 per cent of those in asylums had been born overseas.[55] Alongside the mentally ill, 'home children' were also favourite targets. They were victims not only of public prejudice in the communities where they were placed but in the 1920s they were stigmatised by Canadian child-care professionals, who claimed that British child migrants were disproportionately depraved – eugenically contaminated – and therefore posed a financial as well as moral threat, since they tended to end up in hospitals, asylums and prisons, where they became a drain on Canadian taxpayers. Physical and mental impairments or illnesses and criminal or immoral behaviour seem to have been the main reasons for the enforced repatriation from to Canada to Scotland of five migrants from Quarrier's Homes between the wars.[56]

On the whole, Scots were not singled out for particular criticism, although we have seen in Chapter 2 how Canadian optimism in 1923 about the arrival of Hebrideans who were 'just the right type, physically and mentally, to make good in this country' was soon transformed into disappointment, and then hostility.[57] The mental calibre of the *Marloch* migrants was challenged even before the ship had sailed, in a letter sent to the Canadian immigration authorities in February 1923. Denouncing the forthcoming arrivals from the Hebrides on the grounds that the assisted immigrants were cast in the same mould as their countrymen who had settled in Cape Breton a century earlier, the letter-writer alleged that the pioneers' descendants were 'absolutely unreliable citizens' who by the 1920s were crowding the asylums, 'living in poverty, and content to do so'.[58] In fact, a comparison of the different ethnicities of patients in the Nova Scotia Hospital with the census records does not justify that assertion, at least in the brief period for which comparative figures are available. In 1892, a year after the census in which Scots-born had made up 1.6 per cent of Nova Scotia's population, they constituted a slightly higher profile (2.7 per cent) of admissions to the Nova Scotia Hospital, but in 1900, when there was only one Scot among the 124 admissions, Scots constituted approximately an equivalent 0.8 per cent of the province's population.[59] But perhaps the resentment articulated in 1923 was why J.V. Lantalum, the immigration agent at Saint John, New Brunswick, was ordered not to broadcast the arrival of Andrew MacDonell's party. 'Do not give any newspaper publicity to the movement' was the unambiguous (but ineffective) instruction sent down from Ottawa HQ.[60]

As we also saw in Chapter 2, booking agents came under fire from the Canadian immigration authorities for allegedly careless selection, and from dissatisfied employers who were saddled with unsuitable recruits. But the inter-war era equally saw increasing hostility to immigration *per se*, rather than simply to the problem of the wrong type of immigrant. As economic conditions deteriorated, new arrivals were stereotyped as impoverished and incompetent rejects from Scottish society, an unskilled, idle urban army that was more likely to seek handouts in the towns than roll up its sleeves on the land. It was a sentiment picked up by Lachlan Grant, who, in the course of his attack on the Church of Scotland's support for overseas migration in 1935, suggested that such a policy would not be welcomed by the dominions, at least not by Canada, which by then was struggling with farming unemployment, and where migrants would suffer 'certain disillusionment'.

Scots were also disliked and feared on account of their militancy in the workplace. Following two syndicalist-style general strikes on the Rand in 1913 and 1914, nine trade union and labour activists were deported from South Africa. Among the five Scottish deportees was James Thompson Bain, 'the father of the South African Labour Movement', and ten Scots in all were named on a list of '27 Dangerous Strike Leaders' compiled by Johannesburg Police Deputy Commissioner K. Vachell.[61] At the same time ex-members of the Lanarkshire Miners' Union were involved in a lengthy and bitter strike on Vancouver Island. According to *Forward*, the 300 United Workers' Union members 'arrested and clapped into prison' on the island included Joseph Mairs and his father, 'well known unionists', who had arrived from Airdrie two-and-a-half years earlier. Young Joseph, despite allegedly playing no part in the disturbances, had been given a 12-month sentence but had died in prison – effectively murdered, claimed *Forward* – as a result of neglected peritonitis.[62] Six years later Scots like Robert Boyd Russell, Thomas Clement Douglas and Danny Schur featured prominently in the six-week Winnipeg General Strike of 1919, while the chairman of the Central Strike Committee was George Bowman Anderson, whom we first met in Chapter 2.[63] Most of the hostility Anderson encountered was, he recalled, not from management or the state, but from xenophobic foremen and fellow workers who 'wanted all the best jobs, and what was left was good enough for you, if they could get away with it'.[64]

Three years after the Winnipeg strike, emigrants from Clydeside were all tarred with the same brush of militant, work-shy trade unionism by Clifford Sifton, former Minister of the Interior. Writing in *Maclean's Magazine*, he declared:

> A Trades Union artisan who will not work more than eight hours a day and will not work that long if he can help it, will not work on a farm at all and has to be fed by the public when work is slack is, in my judgment... very bad quality... Such men are not wanted in Canada, and the more of them we get the more trouble we shall have... We do not want mechanics from the Clyde – riotous, turbulent, and with an insatiable appetite for whiskey.[65]

Meanwhile, on the east coast, James Bryson McLachlan, from Ecclefechan, had already made his name as an official of the United Mine Workers of America, playing a leading part in the achievement of collective bargaining in Nova Scotia's coal industry during the First World War. He then led the Cape Breton coalminers in the strikes of the early 1920s until he was convicted of seditious libel in 1923, and sentenced to two years' imprisonment.[66] He was, says Billy Kenefick, 'the driving force behind the formation of the Canadian Communist Party'.[67] Kenefick – in making the case for a serious study of the working-class Scot abroad – also speculates that the decline of Scottish left radicalism in the 1920s was due partly to the emigration of 'some of the country's most experienced and politically active workers'.[68]

It was the recruitment of prairie harvesters, however, that was to produce a particular rift in British–Canadian relations. In 1923 almost 12,000 British harvesters were brought to Winnipeg by the CPR and CNR, but exaggerated promises of work and wages left many stranded, unable either to send money home or to bring their families to Canada. Five years later there was strong Canadian opposition to the Ministry of Labour's proposal to resurrect the scheme by offering subsidised one-way tickets to the prairies to 8,500 unemployed miners, many of them Scots, in the hope that they might find permanent work once the harvest was over. It was a mismanaged fiasco which led to many deportations, the discrediting of assisted colonisation and the premature demise of land settlement schemes amid bitter recriminations. Canadian criticism of a work-shy army of the 'unwashed, unshaven and unshorn', many of whom were militant trade unionists and 'professional trouble-makers', was matched by recruits' complaints about poor wages and farmers reneging on contracts.[69] By late 1929 the Ministry of Labour had admitted its mistake in taking industrial workers who, as well as being 'quite ignorant' of Canadian farming methods, 'go out with all kinds of ideas about Trade Union rates of wages and hours of work'.[70]

Canada was not the only hostile host. Across the border, violation of the American quota legislation was the charge levelled at a number of Scots, usually after they had entered the United States illegally from Canada. Some of the Hebrideans who had arrived on the *Metagama* in April 1923 fell into that category.[71] In some cases there were multiple transgressions. In 1926, for instance, the American authorities threw the rule book at 15-year-old Mary T. who, 'by false and misleading statements', had crossed the border at Buffalo, a year after arriving in Montreal from Glasgow. She was, moreover, an unaccompanied minor, deemed to be of 'constitutional psychopathic inferiority' and likely to become a public charge.[72] She was one of 10,904 individuals deported from the United States in 1926.

A year earlier 27-year-old Clara G. had been deported as a 'likely public charge', on the grounds of mental instability. She had arrived from Glasgow in 1923 to join her father in Philadelphia, but when he worked his way back to Scotland as a seaman a year later, she moved to New Jersey. After staying briefly with an aunt, she found work in service, but left after a disagreement with her employer, and was subsequently admitted to hospital with 'gland trouble'. By late 1925 her case had come to the attention of the immigration authorities, and at a hearing on Ellis Island a year later she was slated for deportation, the warrant stating that she was 'unstable mentally and of general psychopathic make-up'.[73]

Michael Roe has written at length about the criticism that Australia directed both at policy-makers and migrants between the wars.[74] At the root of the antagonism there lay the perennial tension between demand and supply. The empire settlement legislation had effectively reopened old wounds by demonstrating the basic incompatibility in the objectives of the British and Australian governments: while Britain wanted to use the funding to tackle domestic socio-economic problems, Australia's priority was to gain access to British development capital as a means of meeting its own labour needs and growing its own economy.

When in the mid-1920s the Ministry of Labour considered making an 'intensive effort' to recruit unemployed Scottish miners for farm work in Australia, the response was decidedly lukewarm. As a Ministry memorandum explained:

> The position is that the Australian authorities, while they are prepared here and there to take young single miners, insist on claiming that they are dangerous people to take for farm work because they gravitate to the mines. For this reason they will not listen at the moment to taking miners over in small groups from the same area, a point of substantial importance if migration is really to become popular with miners as they are gregarious people.[75]

From a different perspective, the Australian Miners' Federation was vehemently opposed to the idea for fear that the immigrants would exacerbate the already 'intense' unemployment in the Australian mining industry.[76]

The animosity that permeated the Australian Commonwealth and State governments, as well as trades unions, also soured relations between nominators or employers and migrants. On returning from a visit to Australia in 1922, the Conservative MP Sir Arthur Stanley commented that he had observed a 'dislike and hostility towards the new settler – almost a wish that he should not succeed',[77] while the yellow press delighted in reporting stories of dysfunction. Migrants were harried for repayment of passage loans by the Commonwealth and State authorities, police and employers, and were stigmatised as failures if they failed to settle down immediately. After-care was poor and, according to Roe, 'the more people needed help, generally the less they received it'. Australians were, he added, 'ready, even anxious, to exploit the newcomers', who were acceptable only if they were 'subordinates or supplicants'.[78] Self-funders, selected migrants and nominees alike were criticised, the first two on suspicion of aggravating job competition and swelling the ranks of the unemployed, and nominated migrants for incorporating too many individuals who were allegedly 'deficient in mind or body'.[79]

From the far right of the political spectrum, Governor General Lord Stonehaven, in the 1920s, lamented the class hatred with which he claimed migrants had infected Australia. Uppermost in his mind were probably his own countrymen, for Scottish radicals had a high profile in Australia as well as Canada between the wars. J.B. McLachlan's counterpart on the New South Wales coalfields was Charles Nelson from Broxburn, who had worked in the shale mines of West Lothian before emigrating to Australia in 1914. In 1925 he went to work at the Lithgow State Mine where he became active in union activities and also in the Communist Party of

Australia. Among those attracted to his Marxist study group was his fellow Scot, William Orr, originally from Bellshill, who also became a prominent Communist and union official. From 1933 to 1940, as general president of the Australasian Coal and Shale Employees' Federation, Orr succeeded – through industrial action and arbitration – in improving miners' pay and working conditions. Meanwhile, Jim Coull from Kincardineshire, who had cut his debating teeth by listening to Glasgow radical John Maclean, became involved with the Electrical Trade Union and the Victorian Socialist Party after emigrating in 1922. He was best known, however, for establishing his own speakers' corner in Melbourne, where his oratorical skills in denouncing the 'enemies of socialism' brought him notoriety and – in the 1940s – the scrutiny of the Australian Security Intelligence Organisation.[80]

After the war, when Australia, rather than Whitehall, was more firmly in the policy-making driving seat, official concern developed not around how best to exclude or expel undesirables, but how to retain expensively assisted migrants, who seemed to be leaving in droves. If 29 per cent of those admitted in 1959 had returned to Britain by 1966 – as one survey indicated – it represented, from the Australian perspective, a poor return on its heavy investment in assisted migration. Of course, as we saw in Chapter 4, some were simply taking advantage of the £10 passage to have a two-year holiday, since the heavily subsidised outward fare brought the cost of going home within reach. But there were enough returners who went back with a tale of woe to worry the Australian authorities that complaints about primitive hostel accommodation and homesickness were undermining its centrally steered white recruitment policy. Unadaptable 'whingeing Poms' became the focus of barbed attacks by the Australian media, producing a backlash from the British popular press, that – as in earlier generations – blamed failures and disappointments on misleading recruitment practices and unrealistic promises.[81]

The post-war period also saw a significant and growing polarisation between Britain and Australia over child migration, a practice that persisted until the 1960s. From the British perspective the Home Office – influenced by professionals who argued that child migration was unnecessary and potentially deleterious – wanted to ensure that the children would be given the same protection and prospects as had been afforded to their counterparts in British institutions under the Children Act of 1948. The Australian authorities, on the other hand, felt it was adequate to focus simply on material provision within the traditional institutional structure, ignoring problems of isolation and disregarding the recommendation that the natural family should be replicated as far as possible through fostering or adoption.[82] As in Canada at an earlier date, the children were also vilified as damaged – or inferior – goods, sometimes with 'nothing to recommend them'.[83]

From the late 19th century there was also concern in the Antipodes about the alleged importation of lunatics, or the negative effects of migration on migrants' mental health. Back in 1884 New Zealand's Inspector of Asylums had alleged that inmates from British institutions, or individuals who showed 'insane tendencies', were being shipped there in order to avoid 'the burden of their maintenance at home'.[84] Five years later factors such as homesickness, heat and intoxication were blamed for the insanity of migrants to Queensland who had been 'mentally sound enough on being landed'; while in 1913, the Inspector General for the Insane for Victoria ascribed the high proportion of immigrants in the State's asylums to their change of domicile, 'altered conditions' and loneliness. By the 1920s the temperature of the political and public debate had risen, reflected in restrictive legislation, as well as demands for stricter medical examinations and the deportation of those who had been consigned to hospitals or asylums.[85] Much more recently controversy was stirred up when Australia invoked the deportation weapon against a handful of UK migrants – mainly sex offenders – who had arrived as children, but were still legally deportable following conviction because they had never taken out Australian citizenship. They included triple murderer Archie 'Mad Dog' McCafferty, who in 1997, 39 years after arriving in Australia, on being released from prison on parole, was sent back to the Scottish homeland he had left as a small child.[86]

Disintegration, Dysfunction and Disappearance

Host countries' concerns about the damage that could be wrought by disgruntled migrants introduce us to the constituency for whom arguments about the pros and cons of migration had greatest relevance: the migrants themselves. While many personal narratives focus on successful adaptation or assimilation, there was, as we have seen in earlier chapters, a darker side to the story. In all locations where migrants settled or sojourned, adjustment could be difficult; occasionally the dislocation went beyond manageable disappointment or homesickness. Some migrants – as indicated earlier – found themselves in penitentiaries or hospitals, especially lunatic asylums, or were deported, especially from Canada, whose 'record in deporting immigrants was by far the worst in the entire British Commonwealth'.[87]

A few deportees reappeared in psychiatric institutions or prisons in their homeland, while others, eager to re-migrate, appealed against their deportation. Some migrants simply disappeared without trace.

Codification of health requirements generally preceded regulations on identity documents such as passports, and as immigration law evolved in various jurisdictions in the late 19th century, detailed health clauses were incorporated into the legislation. Screening was intended both to debar immigrants (through identification of hereditary, chronic or infectious disease) and admit them (through evidence of visible prophylaxis such as vaccination marks). But despite the detail, the criteria for exclusion or admission were racial and socio-economic, rather than based on epidemiological or microbiological science. Those priorities persisted well into the 20th century, exacerbated by eugenic arguments and economic depression.[88]

Within British imperial jurisdictions in particular, 19th-century immigration acts specified broadly defined mental or physical disease and criminality as the grounds for denial of entry or deportation. In the early years of the 20th century, the increasingly delineated vocabulary of illness (particularly insanity), immorality and impoverishment reflected a eugenics agenda, as well as the development of public health and welfare policies in the host countries. Lists of the excludable or deportable lengthened to include the promiscuous, the destitute (or potentially destitute) and the politically dangerous, as well as the diseased and disabled. In the USA, where the ethnicity of immigrants shaped the quota acts and other gate-keeping legislation, health clauses were used particularly against eastern and central Europeans, and mental illness tended to be judged according to cultural criteria. Across the border, the Canadian federal government, initially under pressure from British Columbia, discriminated against Chinese immigrants from 1885 to 1947.[89] Immigration of Japanese, East Indians, Blacks, Jews and – after 1917 – Communists and radicals was also discouraged by the Canadian authorities.[90]

While migrants from the British Isles may have been exempt from the politics of race and ethnicity embedded in discriminatory enactments, they were not immune from the penalties of generic legislation that aimed to control poverty, disease and dysfunction. Some new arrivals were turned back at the quayside following medical inspection. New Zealand's stringent immigration controls were designed to bar the door at source, but some slipped through and a snapshot from 1923 shows, for example, the rejection of an individual with tuberculosis and a would-be agricultural labourer, suffering from a double hernia.[91] Others were deported, usually within the three-year (or five-year) period between arriving and becoming a public charge on the state. Recent research into the deportation of lunatic migrants from Western Australia has identified over 100 such individuals who were deported from mental hospitals in the State between 1924 and 1939.[92] They included Robert M., aged 26, from Aberdeen, who was deported in 1938, three years after he had landed at Fremantle as an assisted immigrant. Having been diagnosed with 'dementia praecox' (schizophrenia), recovery was said to be 'very doubtful' and it was recommended that he be accompanied and kept under observation on the return voyage.[93]

The deportation weapon was wielded less regularly in Australia and New Zealand than in North America in the early part of the 20th century, partly because of distance, but mainly because antipodean migrants were screened rigorously before they left home. It was in 1906 that Canada first enshrined in law the practice of deporting immigrants, initially within two years of landing, though this was later increased to three, and then five years. Categories of prohibited immigrants were expanded, and the number of deportations increased significantly in the years before the war. Further amendments to the Immigration Act in 1919 added conditions such as 'constitutional psychopathic inferiority', chronic alcoholism and illiteracy to the grounds for exclusion or deportation, and also reflected concerns about unemployment and industrial unrest. In particular, a clause introduced in the wake of the Winnipeg General Strike made British-born immigrants subject to deportation on political grounds. This was a reaction to the prominence of British (not least Scottish) activists among the strike leaders, and although the controversial amendment was repealed in 1928, political deportation became federal policy in 1931, targeting immigrants who had organised or participated in strikes and labour activities, as well as members of the (now outlawed) Communist Party.[94]

Ever since 1922 a handful of migrants who had been assisted to Canada under the Empire Settlement Act had been returned whence they came, including 4.6 per cent of domestics recruited between 1926 and 1931. Most of those 689 women were sent back for moral and/or medical reasons, but by 1931 the fires of expulsion were being fuelled by the deepening depression. From 1930–34 'public charge' deportations increased more than sixfold from the previous five-year period, with expulsions on medical and criminal grounds also rising, to a total of 16,765.[95] Political deportation was sometimes disguised under economic, medical or criminal headings, and in 1940 a legal expert claimed that Canada's deportation policy was more arbitrary than in any of the other dominions. Its most notable feature was, he claimed, 'the apparent desire to get agitators of any sort out of the country at all costs' with 'a marked disregard for the niceties of procedure'.⁹⁶ It was driven, some scholars have claimed, by Canadian public resistance to paying for the social service infrastructure that would have been required to support dysfunctional and economically unproductive migrants, especially during the depression.⁹⁷

What did all this mean in practice? For individual migrants, paper arguments translated into a real fear that the increasingly restrictive legislation would mean denial or detention at entry ports, as well as the lingering threat of deportation if they fell foul of the regulations after gaining initial entry. A handful of individuals never got further than the quayside landing shed, and others were detained temporarily pending investigation into suspected physical or mental illness, or other perceived breach of immigration legislation. The traumas of the processing stations have been graphically relived in the first-hand accounts of those who passed through New York's famous Ellis Island, whose health screening, according to one study, prioritised civic concerns and the likely adaptability of the migrant to American culture.⁹⁸ While most Scots interviewed for the Ellis Island Oral History Project had been admitted without incident, it could still be an unpleasant experience. When 15-year-old Marge Glasgow from Motherwell arrived in 1922, she was already apprehensive because of her mother's warnings about the island's reputation for humiliating physical inspection.

> I remember they took all my clothes off and made me shower, and wrapped all my beautiful clothes in a duffel bag, which hurt me so much to see them being rolled up... I remember the Great Hall, and the desks there with me [sic]. I don't know if they were doctors, judges or what, questioning the people, you know. And that's when I was very scared, to be all alone in that big building being questioned. So I was really crying hysterically and sobbing so hard that the doctor came to me. They had doctors there examining everybody, and he put his arms around me and said, 'Please, please don't cry so hard. We're trying to help you. We only want to help you.'⁹⁹

At least Marge was offered a friendly shoulder on which to cry, unlike Mary Dunn, whom we also met in Chapter 2. Stirling-born Mary was 18 when she sailed to New York on the *Assyria* in 1923, to join two aunts in Pennsylvania. Unrelenting seasickness was a prelude to a whole day of medical examination and interrogation. 'Before I got off Ellis Island,' she recalled, 'I was wishing I was on the ship going back to Scotland because they asked you so many questions.' Unlike her dormitory-mate,

Ellis Island Federal Immigration Station

who was detained because of head lice, Mary had a clean bill of health, but resented the way in which some of the officials 'kind of pushed you around'. Despite going on to have 'a wonderful life' in the United States, her initial disillusionment still came to mind when she was interviewed in Florida at the age of 81.

> I cried many times, you know, wishing I had never come... We had heard so many things about the United States, come to America and the gold and money grows on the trees and all this kind of stuff. And the land of opportunity. And I'm saying to myself, 'If this is the land of opportunity, is this the way they treat everybody when they come in?' You know, they really treated you like they didn't want you.[100]

Infectious diseases meant detention. Tillicoultry boys Thomas and Willie Allan were 'terrified' when, aged nine and seven, they were quarantined for a week on Ellis Island after Willie had gone down with chickenpox while at sea. Forbidden from seeing their father, who had travelled from Nebraska to meet them, Thomas recalled 'screaming and hollering' as he was taken by four guards to the hospital ward, ensuring that 'My first impressions of Ellis Island were indeed the Island of Tears.'[101]

The Allans' experiences were mirrored in immigration sheds at many ports of landing. Across the border in Canada, for instance, 997 newly arrived immigrants were detained at the port of Quebec in 1923. Most were subsequently admitted, but 35 were deported, primarily for insanity or 'feeble-mindedness' but also for venereal disease, epilepsy, trachoma and, in just one case, tuberculosis. The majority of detainees (41.8 per cent) were English, followed by Scots (24.4 per cent) and Irish (8.4 per cent) and the key triggers for temporary detention were infectious illnesses, physical deformities, and defective hearing or eyesight. Three decades later, among the much smaller number – 335 immigrants – detained at Canadian ports and airports in 1956–57 were 62 Scots (along with 212 English, 36 Irish and eight Welsh). The main concern was still to detect infectious diseases, but the priority was to spot those with (usually inactive) pulmonary tuberculosis. By now mental health was rarely mentioned, and only three individuals were declared to be insane.[102]

Mental illness might be more likely to manifest itself some time after arrival, and in some cases resulted in the committal of the unfortunate migrant to an overseas asylum. The meticulous records of many of those institutions – as well as recent scholarship based on their records – allow us to track the experiences of a number of migrants who found themselves detained in this way, but only from the 1850s to the first decade of the 20th century. Privacy legislation prevents scrutiny of nominal records for the last hundred years, but we can dip into material from most of the decade before the First World War to explore contemporary perceptions of the relationship between migration, ethnicity and mental illness, and draw on anecdotal evidence from other sources to speculate about whether these attitudes and responses continued into a later period.

We have already seen that host countries sometimes complained they were being saddled with migrants who were already known – or suspected – to have a history of mental illness. Medical records also cited predisposition and heredity as factors in migrants' maladies. Annie, a native of Caithness, was committed to Dunedin's public asylum in 1901. Aged 53, it was her second attack, and second incarceration. Case notes record that her sister was an inmate of the Sunnyside Asylum at Montrose, while her brother, who had been born an imbecile, was boarded out. Annie had been in New Zealand for ten years, preceded by two years in Tasmania. Ten years into her second hospitalisation, she suggested that she would not have suffered such a fate had she been in Scotland. In a semi-accusatory letter to her brother, she wrote: 'had I been at Home the doctors would not have dared to as this upon me (sic) but here, advantage has been taken of me as I have nobody in the colony but yourself that knows anything about me'.[103] Three years later she was discharged and returned to Britain, where by 1924 she was living in Glasgow.

As the Australian commentaries quoted earlier suggested, a change of environment could trigger a breakdown. Perhaps the risk was greatest among those whose very restlessness – manifested in the pulling up of their roots – may itself have been a symptom of mental instability. The actual journey, even the long voyage to the Antipodes, was much less traumatic than in the days of sail, but the pain of parting was not always easily assuaged. Nor was the shock of finding that the land of promise had sometimes turned into a land of disappointment. The consequences might emerge in alcohol abuse (regarded as both a cause and a consequence of mental illness), domestic or public violence, anxiety, depression and self harm.

Scots – evenly divided between men and women – made up almost 5 per cent of patients admitted to the Queen Street Hospital for the Insane in Toronto between September 1904 and January 1906.[104] In four cases one or more relatives were said to have been insane. Robert, a 56-year-old book-keeper, had spent six months in an asylum in Scotland 36 years earlier, and three months in the Toronto Asylum in 1887. 'Business worries' had triggered his most recent attack, which manifested itself in delusions – he 'thought he was king of Scotland' – and 'profane language'. He recovered, and was discharged after 15 months.[105] Business worries were blamed for four other admissions, including Andrew, a farmer from Huron County, who 'talks in melancholy manner and suggested suicide to his wife'.[106] In these cases, and some others, the diagnosis was melancholia – depression – which in the case of another patient, Jean, led to suicide. And it was, of course, the suicides of three home boys in Canada in 1923 that led to the appointment of the Bondfield delegation and more rigorous regulation of child migration.

Some individuals, like Annie in Dunedin, returned to Scotland. So did the enigmatic Charles, a native of Forres, who in 1903 was admitted to Inverness District Asylum suffering from acute mania and melancholia, demonstrated in suicidal tendencies. Transferred almost immediately to Aberdeen, and subsequently to Elgin, he died in Elgin District Asylum four years later, aged 38. Although his condition was attributed to heredity, we might speculate about both the cause and effect of his change of occupation and location from coach builder in Forres to cowboy in southern Colorado.[107] In 1930, 29-year-old Bathia was admitted for a second time to the Aberdeen asylum, straight from the ss *Minnedosa* after it had docked in Glasgow. Although she had suffered her first attack of 'dementia praecox' seven years earlier, she had emigrated to Canada in 1928. Two years later, however, having fallen ill again, she was sent back to her homeland.[108] Also returned from Canada with the same illness and removed straight from ship to asylum in 1932 was Mary, a 34-year-old domestic servant. She was sent first to Stobhill hospital in Glasgow before being transferred to Kingseat Hospital, Aberdeenshire, where she died in 1949.[109]

Fast-forwarding to the 1960s, it was very clearly depression – and its likely consequences – that led John and Margaret Hardie to leave Australia after three years in the La Trobe Valley in Gippsland, Victoria. Interviewed by oral historian, Alastair Thomson in 2000, they recalled that, while John was happy in his work, Margaret's potentially pathological homesickness was the key trigger in his decision to bring the family back to Scotland. Stuck at home with a toddler, she had become

> very homesick, very homesick... Not just immediately I would say but I wouldnae like to say how long before it really started to hit home, I really was miserable an awful lot of the times and he said, he'd come in from work and I was preparing the meal, standing at the sink and I've got 'Green Green Grass of Home', Tom Jones, and the tears were flowing, just could not stop them. I was really sometimes very very unhappy... I missed my family, I missed my brother very very much, but then it could go for a while and I was all right again but it never really left me... It was with me *every* day, but some days were worse than others and other times you could forget it. I think maybe if, you know, if Gillian hadnae been so young and I had been out in the workplace, that might even have been better but as I wasn't that didn't work so.

When John Hardie encountered a group of female patients in a psychiatric hospital in Gippsland, Victoria, he was told by a staff member that they were all Scottish women who had become clinically depressed. The implications were not lost on him.

> I said, 'Nothing you can do?' He says 'The only thing we can do is put them on a train, or a plane or a boat back, that's the only cure', he says '90 percent of who you see here won't do it' because through medical situations, medical bills – touch wood we were never really bothered with that – you know they've got themselves into such a financial hole and owe so much money they would never ever get out of Australia unless someone from the UK could come forward and say there's your fare.[110]

The Hardies themselves made the decision to return. Others had no choice in the matter, for – as previously hinted – the deportation weapon was wielded regularly against the undesirable. But while Canada may have headed the league table of deporting dominions, it has not maintained a good paper trail of its practice, and – with a few anecdotal exceptions – deportees are extremely difficult to track down. Nominal deportation forms were not retained until the 1940s, and later records are embargoed. Published statistics give us just a basic skeleton, demonstrating that until the mid-1930s the majority of deportations were of British citizens. The largest numbers (4,218) were sent back in 1931, with Scots constituting 64 per cent of that year's deportees. Of the 13,828 British citizens deported between 1928 and 1945, 23.6 per cent were Scots.[111]

In order to clothe the statistical skeleton with some of the traumatic human experiences surrounding deportation, we are forced back on anecdotal evidence found in the immigration authorities' files, much of which revolves around disputed decisions, or the financing of compulsory repatriation. Albert Stott was an elderly Glaswegian who was deported in 1904, just over a year after arriving in Winnipeg. A dry goods salesman, he had failed to find employment in his own line, and had been working for a florist 'at wages simply sufficient to keep him alive' until he suffered a fall in which he had fractured two ribs and punctured a lung. Unable to work, and with little prospect of a full recovery, this 'eminently respectable' man was being supported temporarily by private charity, but was about to become a public charge, 'I would strongly recommend', the acting immigration physician advised the immigration commissioner in Winnipeg, 'that you get him to his friends in Glasgow; as his case is a thoroughly deserving one. He is too old and too feeble for this country; should never have left home'. The CPR passenger traffic manager was duly instructed to arrange for Stott's free transportation to Saint John, and thence across the Atlantic.[112]

At the other end of the age spectrum, the anguish of relatives in Scotland when a migrant fell ill was evident in the case of William, a young Scot who in autumn 1904 was committed to the Selkirk Asylum in Manitoba, 'full of delusions and mentally deranged'. As the authorities debated for a year the financial and logistical issues concerning his deportation to Liverpool and on to Glasgow – including the need for an attendant to accompany him across the Atlantic – William's parents in Kirkintilloch, who were 'almost frantic with grief and anxiety', pleaded repeatedly for his return to be expedited. By July 1905 his father was preparing to come to Winnipeg to bring him home, a proposal that was discouraged by federal emigration superintendent, J. Bruce Walker, in case William might already be on his way back while his father was travelling in the opposite direction.[113]

Around the same time, no one wanted to take financial responsibility for Hugh, a 30-year-old Scot who had arrived in Montreal in November 1904. 'It was quite evident from the beginning', according to the secretary of the city's Charity Organisation Society, 'that he was not in his right mind'. After initially entering the Protestant Insane Asylum at Verdun as a voluntary patient, his condition worsened, and in January 1906 he was formally committed, but although he had assets in Scotland, his solicitors refused to shoulder financial responsibility, claimed that Hugh had 'from the time of his schooldays indulged continuously in alcoholic excess' and argued that his repatriation would have a detrimental effect on his relatives, especially his sister. The Charity Organisation Society, which was holding the 800 dollars that had been in Hugh's possession, was unwilling to become liable for his maintenance and referred the case to the federal immigration authorities, which claimed it was yet another example of the way in which both England and Scotland frequently 'sent their ne'er-do-wells, and even their defectives to the colonies, first as we may hope with the idea that they may do better there, and second with the idea of getting rid of them'.[114] At the same time, however, it was judged that Hugh's assets and length of residence rendered him ineligible for deportation under current legislation.

Even before chronic alcoholism was added to the list of deportable conditions, inebriation and its consequences featured in a number of cases. In 1905 Alexander, from Kirkcaldy, attempted to commit suicide on board the train from Fort William (Thunder Bay) to Winnipeg, where his wife and baby were then lodging with a family friend. According to the city's immigration commissioner, Alexander was a

> habitual drinker, and was in the Hospital in Scotland for six months apparently being treated for inebriety or delirium tremens. He was released from the Hospital about six weeks before sailing for Canada and started drinking again on the steamer; so much so that he broke part of the ship's fittings and was threatened with irons by the Captain. It is my intention, when the man is recovered from his rash act, to have him specially examined, as he has not shown himself to be a very desirable immigrant up to the present time.[115]

Still in Winnipeg, three years later, 21 Scottish tradesmen who had come out under three-month contracts to work as strike-breakers for the CPR became public charges (and therefore deportable) after being dismissed from their employment when the strike was settled. Their ocean fares were deducted from their wages and some of them were allegedly 'obliged to walk the streets and go without food and shelter'.[116] When challenged, the CPR representative claimed that 'with three exceptions the men... proved to be so consistently intemperate it was impossible to keep them working, and they were dismissed on account of their drunken habits... I do not think these men have any desire to work at all.' Many of them, alleged another official, were 'purposely endeavouring to represent themselves as eligible for deportation, it meaning free transportation across the Atlantic to their homes'.[117]

`Not surprisingly, the migrants – most of whom had dependents in Glasgow – sang from a very different song sheet. William Robertson, for instance, strongly denied the charge against him, and claimed he was being deported for an act of which he was blameless. After working initially as a boilermaker in Brandon, he had been given a pass to Winnipeg, where his promised job did not materialise on the grounds that he had been dismissed – unfairly – for drunkenness. 'I do not wish to be deported', he wrote to the federal immigration authorities on 10 December, 'as I am in good health, and quite willing to work for myself and wife and family'. By that time he was in the Immigration Detention Hospital in Montreal awaiting deportation, a delay which was causing financial problems for his dependents in Glasgow. He continued, underlining some points for emphasis:

> I have been in this home here since Saturday and I came here thinking I was going home in the Empress of Ireland and I find now that I will not get away till the 25th of the month. <u>Sir, I wish to know if I cannot get away at once or get my liberty to go out and try to earn a dollar or 2 for the support of my wife and family who are in starvation at home</u> which I have letters in my pocket to prove. I only which [sic] for my liberty which is every Scotchman's right who is neither Criminal nor Lunatic.[118]

Finally, reverting to Scottish records, the fragmentary biographies of migrants who simply disappeared without trace also offer tantalising glimpses into the darker side of the story. It was in the 1880s that Westminster first legislated in respect of Scotland to create a procedure for issuing death certificates and winding up the estates of individuals who had gone missing and were presumed dead. The bulk of these individuals had disappeared overseas, and in most cases their relatives wanted to settle inheritance claims. When petitions were made under the Presumption of Life Limitation (Scotland) Act, the court papers often included a summary of the missing person's last known movements and – although the information is by its very nature incomplete – it is by reading between the lines of these statements that we find hints of disappointment or failure.

Some evidence is purely circumstantial. In 1929 David Tevendale petitioned in respect of his nephew, James Begg, who had disappeared in Canada three years after leaving Aberdeen in 1907. During that period he had written home irregularly, but 'the information about himself was very meagre' and advertisements placed by his parents in British and Canadian newspapers after his disappearance elicited no response. Before emigrating he had been, according to the petition, 'addicted to drink and... unable to keep his situation'. His mother (whose death had triggered the action) clearly feared that a change of environment had not brought a change of habit. 'She did not speak to me very much about James,' recalled her brother David, 'as she was rather disappointed about him seeing that he had not been doing very well.'[119]

Begg was not the only individual in whose presumed downfall drink seems to have played a part, although the reader is generally left to join the dots. A number of cases involved men who had disappeared in the highly hazardous and unstable environments of the Australian, New Zealand or Klondyke goldfields. A few petitions, however, give a slightly clearer indication that their subjects had fallen on hard times. The cases of William Wood and Alexander Henderson both came before the Court of Session in 1950. Wood had emigrated from Aberdeenshire to Toronto as a child in 1912, but disappeared from the family home in 1920. Shortly afterwards he returned, penniless, only to disappear again after a few weeks. On two subsequent occasions he telephoned asking for money, which his parents duly sent, but after the second call – made from New York in 1932 – all communication with his family ceased. Enquiries to the Salvation Army established that in 1935 he was still in New York but 'in bad health and impoverished'. By 1937 he was still in 'reduced circumstances' and had been in hospital. After that the trail went cold.[120] When Alexander Henderson went to the USA in 1927 he 'never acquired a settled residence' but drifted around, taking odd jobs. He occasionally saw his three brothers in Chicago and also wrote to them for money 'which they sent to him until they stopped doing so owing to the frequency with which they were asked'. When last seen by his brother John in 1932, 'he had no job and did not appear to have any means of support'. In 1950 his siblings petitioned to have him declared dead so that they could claim their shares of the estate of a late aunt.[121]

Conclusion

Through the ages there has clearly been no single, undisputed opinion about the impact of the Scottish diaspora: on its participants or on the donor and host societies. The 20th century was no exception, when for almost every upbeat assessment, we can flip the coin to reveal images of public and political acrimony and migrant disappointment. Exclusion, incarceration and expulsion, we have seen, were an undeniable and sombre part of the narrative. No destination or time period was exempt, although the vehemence of the antagonism tended to fluctuate in response to economic ups and downs. Throughout the century, as in earlier times, the accusations and accolades that suffused the whole process of migration coexisted in constant and complex tension. This chapter opened with a verse from 'Rocket to the Moon' by the Celtic folk-rock band Runrig. But its implication that reluctant migrants were fleeing from their moribund, workless homeland is countered in the same song by the positive portrayal of a Canadian nation that had been forged by the brawn and brain of enterprising Scots.

> You came, you trapped, you charted
> You laid the railroads and the schemes
> And you tamed this land by enterprise
> And by the power of your dreams.
>
> But you made this Clan great
> And you made this nation bloom
> And you rose
> With your people through the new world
> Like a rocket to the moon.[122]

That both stereotypes were misleading in equal measure is demonstrated in the final chapter, where, in their own words, a selection of Scottish migrants reflects on the triggers, tribulations and triumphs of their life-changing decisions.

CHAPTER 6

Emigrants' Voices

AT THE HEART of the Scottish diaspora is a multi-hued human story that is best told in the words of the men, women and children who experienced it. While the policies of governments, sponsors and employers may have formed the organisational backdrop against which decisions were reached and implemented, official records often track only numbers and procedures, not the real people who inhabited the statistics. And many individuals and families – whether they left, stayed behind, or moved on, around or back – were more acutely aware of the impact on their decision-making of an informal web of personal networks than they were of carefully planned but anonymous promotional strategies.

Most of the emigrants who have spoken so far have had only fleeting walk-on parts. With the exception of some of the fur traders who appear in Chapter 3, they have either emerged tangentially from written documents – mainly private and published letters – or their opinions have been culled from radio programmes and major oral history archives such as the Ellis Island collection or (in one case) the New South Wales bicentennial oral history project. This chapter – while not ignoring such sources – turns the spotlight explicitly on previously unheard emigrant testimony, giving free rein to a new collection of voices from the Scottish diaspora. Through their reflections we revisit some key themes: motives, recruitment practices, transitions, rhetoric and reality in a new environment, return migration, and issues surrounding identity. Most interviewees speak from personal experience of emigration, but for a handful the involvement was a vicarious one, drawing on the stories told by their parents, or – in one case – an emigration agent's observations of the life-changing decisions of clients.

'Voices from the Scottish Diaspora' is an ongoing oral history project that began in 2005 with the objective of recording, preserving and disseminating stories of migration and emigration from Scotland in the 20th century.[1] At time of writing it encompasses a databank of 64 life-history conversations with 70 participants who were interviewed mainly as individuals, occasionally as couples and in two cases as – respectively

– mother and son and three siblings. There were 30 male and 40 female interviewees, whose ages ranged from 26 to 100. Some people were interviewed twice, by telephone and then face-to-face. The two oldest participants – both women – had emigrated in 1923 and 1930, but the majority had left Scotland in the 1950s and 1960s and were in their 60s or 70s when interviewed. Canada and New Zealand featured most frequently among their destinations, followed by the United States and Australia, and they pursued a variety of occupations. Sixteen had returned to live in Scotland.

Interviewees were identified in several ways: through my own personal and professional contacts built up over many years of researching Scottish migration; via responses submitted to the interactive Scottish Emigration Database website;[2] and as a result of publicising the project in newspapers and genealogical magazines, as well as at evening classes, workshops and conferences. On rare occasions sheer serendipity also played a part.[3] The current selection clearly offers only a partial picture and makes no claim to be a representative sample of 20th-century Scottish emigrants. Although the identification of interviewees was not random, neither did it employ strictly scientific selection criteria to produce a balanced spectrum of origins, destinations, ages, occupations and time periods. The priority to date has been to capture recollections whenever the opportunity arose, particularly of elderly participants whose experiences covered the inter-war era, while the emphasis on Canada and New Zealand reflected my greater familiarity with those locations. Forty-one interviews from the collection have been used in this chapter, and supplementary material from published collections has been used to plug some of the gaps in coverage. In due course it is hoped that the 'voices' project will extend its reach to reflect more comprehensively the global nature of the modern Scottish diaspora.

As with all oral history evidence, we also have to be aware of the generic limitations of the medium, in particular the distorting effects of self-selection, filtered memories, the nostalgia (or occasionally bitterness) of hindsight, and the influence of the interviewer. Those who come forward for interview are generally individuals with stories of success which they are happy to recall and articulate: in only one case was an interviewee unequivocally negative – and that was about his father's experience, rather than his own. The reliability of memory as a historical source has been much debated, particularly in terms of interviewees' self-censorship and tendency – deliberately or subconsciously – to remember the past selectively and in ways shaped more by their circumstances when interviewed than their thoughts and actions at the time of their emigration.[4] But no source is flawless and complete, and oral life stories are most effective when interpreted in conjunction with a wide spectrum of documentary evidence. Weaknesses can also be strengths: the explicit subjectivity and variability of memory remind us that all sources are inherently unstable and incomplete, while the interaction of interviewer and informant creates a dynamic, evolving narrative that is never the same twice.[5]

Conducting the interviews was a delight, because through them I made so many new friends, was shown heart-warming hospitality, and was given privileged insight into a kaleidoscope of personal life experiences. Face-to-face meetings were held at a variety of venues in Scotland, England, Canada and New Zealand: private homes, university campuses, hotels and restaurants. They were semi-structured around a standard template that was based on themes and topics suggested by the documentary sources on which the rest of the book is based. These issues were addressed within a life-history approach that also encouraged interviewees to lead the discussion and explore any other avenues they wished. The early recordings, which were made using a cassette recorder, were subsequently digitised, while later interviews were recorded straight on to increasingly sophisticated and unobtrusive digital equipment. Almost three quarters of the interviews took place face-to-face, with the rest being conducted over the phone. Most conversations lasted for between one and two hours, although the enthralling interview with centenarian Agnes MacGilvray was spread over more than three hours.

Escape, Employment and Excitement

A handful of interviewees could look back to personal or parental recollections of the inter-war decades. Katherine Annie MacLeod was born in Winnipeg, into a well-established Hebridean community that was the product of considerable chain migration. When Katherine's mother Christina (1888–1972) left Portnaguran for Manitoba in 1921, she already had two sisters in Canada: Jessie, who had left Lewis with her husband around 1907 to settle in Fort William (Thunder Bay), Ontario; and Mary, who shortly afterwards went to Crandall, Manitoba, married Ontarion Charles Cartwright in 1912, and had three children. Christina, meantime, had worked in service in Lewis, but had also experienced seasonal migration, having followed the fishing to Lowestoft. It was following the birth of Mary's third child that Charles Cartwright paid Christina's passage to Crandall so that she could take care of her sister, but when Mary's health improved, she moved to Winnipeg, where she met her future husband, who had come from Bayble in Lewis some time before 1915, when he had enlisted in the Cameron Highlanders in Winnipeg. They married in 1925 and Katherine was born in 1928.[6]

Two years after Christina and Angus MacLeod were married, ten-year-old Morag MacLeod passed through Winnipeg, having crossed the Atlantic aboard the ss *Marloch* in Andrew MacDonell's pioneer party of emigrants from the southern Outer Hebrides. She was the youngest of seven children who were brought to the prairies by their parents, in a quest for better opportunities for the family. 'Oh, well there was nothing there in Benbecula for the family, for the boys, you know. I had four brothers and two sisters, and as you know, there's nothing in Benbecula.'[7] Morag's sentiments were echoed by Anne Morrison, whose uncle emigrated from Portvoller in Lewis to Ontario, probably on the *Canada* in 1924.

His father [who had been killed in the war] had been a fisherman, the fishing industry wasn't doing that well, there wasn't a lot of other work on the island, all the things that Lord Leverhulme had promised didn't come to fruition, and I think he felt that there would be better opportunities there than there would be if he came to the mainland.[8]

On the other side of the border, chain migration probably played a part in steering Sandy MacLeod's father from Coigach on the west coast of Sutherland to Montana as one of the last in a line of sojourning Highland sheep-herders in that State. 'Quite a lot of guys from the area had gone out before,' his son recalled, 'so I think from the 1890s onwards there had been a regular traffic of men from Scotland and certain areas seemed to get more emigrants than others, and I think this was probably due to word of mouth, and people writing letters home or actually sending money so that a brother or whoever could get passage out there and join them out in Montana.'[9] Sandy's speculation is corroborated and extended by John Maclennan, the Canadian government emigration agent for the north of Scotland, who complained in a written report in 1908 about the competition he was encountering slightly further south from agents who were recruiting sheep herders from Torridon for the 'gold and silver' state.[10] Sandy's father – one of many from Assynt who followed the Montana trail – told his son that the workforce on some ranches was 50 per cent Gaelic-speaking Scots and 50 per cent Native Americans. And Rob Gibson, in *Highland Cowboys*, tells of Coigach emigrant and songwriter Murdo MacLean, who during his Montana sojourn composed a Gaelic song – '*Mo Shoraidh Leis a'Coigich*' ('My Farewell to Coigach') – which was sung when the 'Celtic cowboys' gathered in Billings to relax in a hotel that was owned by Gaelic-speaking compatriots.[11] Meanwhile, among those who returned to the Highlands, silver dollars were allegedly used for many years as currency in the pubs of Achiltibuie.[12]

On the other side of Sutherland, 22-year-old Minnie Anne Fraser left her position in service with the bank manager at Dornoch to try her luck in Detroit in 1926, along with a friend from nearby Embo. 'I suppose just because I wanted to wander', Minnie Anne answered in response to her daughter's question about how she had become interested in America. A native of Halladale, in the north of the county, Minnie Anne 'wanted to see other countries, and then I knew that in my line of work, we would be much better paid out there, and that the work would... be in a way easier'.[13]

A similar sense of adventure inspired Agnes Lawrie, who was three weeks short of her 101st birthday when interviewed at her home in West Kilbride in 2009. Born on a farm near Whithorn in Wigtownshire, Agnes had gone to Liverpool in 1924 to work in domestic service before moving to London with her employers three years later. It was through her friend and workmate Gladys that she put her name down for the United States, sailing for New York on 28 May 1930.

By that time, you see, this friend Gladys had cousins home from Connecticut from the States and he was a farm manager there and

Agnes MacGilvray (née Lawrie)

they told her they didn't know why she was working for 7/6 a week or something like ten bob, I think, and she should go out there. And immediately I said, 'Oh, you put your name on the waiting list and I'll follow on,' and so that's what we did.[14]

The search for opportunity and excitement also suffused the recollections of the next generation of emigrants. Like Minnie Anne Fraser before her, Annie Matheson from the island of Lewis worked for the Studebaker family in Detroit, having been fascinated by tales of America told by neighbours as she grew up in the village of Coll.

In those homes I used to hear all about America, 'cos they had families who emigrated. And just hearing conversations in those homes about conditions in the US, that was what – it started to interest me and was something that never left my mind. I thought, when I grow up I'm going to go over there. Then, of course, I grew up, went to school, and then the war came, so I had no opportunity to go until after the war. And after the war when they were issuing visas to go to the States I applied and I just wanted to go over there and hopefully better myself because I knew conditions were better, wages were much higher, and I was just hoping I could do it, and I did.[15]

Annie contrasted her job in a Stornoway clothing store – where after eight years her starting pay of 30 shillings a week had risen to just £3 10s – with the apparently untold riches of the United States, where the perception was that earnings were 'ten times that much', and so in December 1952, at the age of 23, she sailed for New York. Romance also played a part in her decision, for her fiancé, Norman MacRitchie, had emigrated from Coll to Detroit a year earlier and, like many Lewismen, was working on the Great Lakes.

For many emigrants the anticipation of better opportunities was still harnessed to varying degrees of disillusionment with the country they were leaving. Although by the 1950s the acute economic hardships of the 1920s and '30s had receded, ration-book austerity and housing shortages had a dispiriting effect. In 1947 the Reverend Henry Thornton left the parish ministry in Newmachar, Aberdeenshire, having secured a lectureship in philosophical psychology at the University of Otago. According to his daughter Alison – who was 17 months old when the family emigrated – he not only 'really wanted to be in university teaching', but also 'thought that Britain was finished after the war'.[16] The new horizons opened up by enforced military service also provoked itchy feet. Brian Coutts' father – a coach painter for Edinburgh City Council – 'had seen a bit of the world' in India and Burma during the war and 'thought there were better opportunities for my brother and I... overseas'.[17] In 1955 he took his family to Dunedin, a year after Paddy McFarlane, an Edinburgh butcher and war veteran, 'decided to look for greener fields' in the same location.

Back then, after the Second World War, there was a lot of emigration to Australia, New Zealand, Canada, Southern Rhodesia. A lad that I worked with had a brother in Southern Rhodesia, and gave me glowing reports of living in Southern Rhodesia, which is now Zimbabwe. And it finished up, my papers arrived from New Zealand House before the Southern Rhodesian ones, and I had my medical and my interview and was accepted before the Rhodesian ones come to light, so I was probably very lucky in a way.[18]

Paddy's sentiments about Southern Rhodesia were echoed by Easton Vance from Rutherglen, who was galvanised by a combination of frustrated opportunities in Scotland and a wanderlust generated partly by national service. In 1956 he left his job as an engineer with Colville's steel works at Ravenscraig to settle in British Columbia.

> Disappointment [with a failed promotion] and the fact that I couldn't get decent housing encouraged me to look elsewhere. And at that time practically every country in the Commonwealth

Paddy and Mary Mcfarlane

and elsewhere were [sic] calling for emigrants. You didn't have to look too far, so I made a choice to come to Canada, having looked at quite a few of them. What I did was acquire all the newspapers of the countries in which I was interested, and then decided from what I could glean from that what the cost of living would be like relative to the earning power. And then I settled on Canada, but on this particular part of Canada. I didn't want to get into the extreme weather climates. New Zealand appealed to me, but it was economically in a pretty poor way, and so I decided that this was the place. Although, I have to tell you, I was tempted to look at Rhodesia, and I'm sure glad I didn't. The reason for Rhodesia was that they had – we had – training camps... the RAF had training camps in both Kenya and Rhodesia, and I met some of the fellows that had been there and had photographs of the places and they were really beautiful.[19]

Three years earlier Cathy Donald's father had taken his wife and daughter from Burntisland to New Zealand, partly out of a similar frustration at housing shortages and partly because he anticipated better educational opportunities – including a university place – for his ten-year-old daughter.[20] And in 1959, when Jim Wilson was only six, his parents emigrated from Edinburgh – 'I think it was a drab, dreary place' – to Dunedin, in order to give their two sons a better chance in life.[21]

Echoes of economic hardship and frustrated ambitions persisted into the 1960s, although their reverberations became less prominent. When schoolteacher, Katrine McLean, and her husband, both Aberdeen University graduates, went to join her sister-in-law in Auckland in 1961, Katrine recalled that they left because 'I was pregnant, and we couldn't afford to stay.'²² Four years later, Rob and Cathie Tulloch left Morayshire for Whangarei in New Zealand. Cathie had recently returned from training as a nursery nurse in Aberdeen to marry Rob, who was milking on a farm at Roseisle. Cathie's recollections encapsulate the coalescence of displacement and opportunity.

> I felt a little bit unsettled, having come back from Aberdeen feeling there must be a little bit more to life than just Roseisle – I felt Rob was not being valued – he was a very hard-working person, still is, and I felt he was not being valued or appreciated for anything he was doing. Then one Sunday the *Sunday Post* came in, the dear old *Sunday Post*, and here was a little advert for farm workers wanted in New Zealand, so that was the start of our journey – was to send away for the advert and we got lots and lots of information.²³

Advertisements also provided two Edinburgh University graduates, Roddy Campbell from South Uist and Alison Gibson from Dumfries, with the answer to their search for better career opportunities. Although he had recently become a Fellow of the Royal College of Surgeons, Roddy felt in 1966 that the outlook was limited.

> It was very hard to become a consultant surgeon. Eventually I would probably get a place, but it might be in the Black Country or somewhere like that, and I didn't fancy that, so I saw this advert in the *British Medical Journal* telling me that a place was available in Canada at Nakusp. I had never heard of Nakusp, but I had been to Canada before, working on a farm in Ontario, and I really liked the country very much.²⁴

A year after Roddy Campbell, with his wife and newborn son, headed for the remote interior of British Columbia, Alison Gibson and a friend arrived in Halifax to take up jobs as computer programmers with the provincial government of Nova Scotia. The press publicity generated by Canada's centenary and the Expo 67 exhibition had attracted their attention, so 'we went, thinking we'd have the adventure, but also, the salaries were double what we were earning in London'.²⁵

The upbeat, adventurous spirit of the 1960s generation persisted among later emigrants, although Anne Simpson's condemnation of Scotland in 1970 as a country where everything was depressingly monotone was more reminiscent of the sentiments of war-weary recruits from the 1950s. Returning briefly to her homeland after a year in Canada, she found that

> everything was grey. The houses were grey. The roofs were grey. The trees were grey. The ground was grey. The people wore grey, and their

Murdo MacPherson

faces were grey. And they whinged. They whine about everything, and they didn't seem to have any will to do anything. They didn't think that they would be able to change anything.[26]

The refrain of better workplace opportunities persisted, as did the flexibility of an increasingly global employment market. When Murdo MacPherson enrolled at the University of Toronto as a postgraduate student in 1977, he went 'basically just to see what Canada was like'.[27] His general desire to 'see somewhere else' was echoed by Graham McGregor, a linguistics lecturer who in 1989 – following encouragement from two antipodean colleagues – moved from Newcastle University to a post at the University of Waikato in New Zealand.[28]

The recollections of this cast of interviewees show how the decision to emigrate was rarely based on one criterion. Brian Coutts' father was influenced by Scotland's economic climate, but also by its cold, damp physical environment, which was endangering his wife's already delicate health and frustrating his own longing for the tropical sun. Both Jim Wilson and Rob Tulloch came from families with experience of migration, while the *Sunday Post* advertisement that sparked the Tullochs' interest reminds us of the long-standing significance of the press as a medium of communication and propaganda. That significance is confirmed in a recent study of New Zealand's Department of Labour, which observes that after the war the Immigration Division, having experimented with 'a wide range of advertising techniques', found the best method to be 'advertisements with cut-out coupons placed in popular Sunday newspapers'.[29]

Alison Gibson

For some, like the Tullochs, Roddy Campbell and Alison Gibson, the choice of destination was directly linked to promotional advertising, though Rob Tulloch had decided that he did not want to follow his brother to Canada. Brian Coutts' parents had been 'within a couple of weeks' of going to Canada in 1951 when they pulled out because of the enforced separation that would have ensued while his father went ahead to secure a job and a house. Their subsequent choice of a £10 passage to New Zealand was based on the promise of work and accommodation, while sponsorship was a key factor in directing the steps of others to the Antipodes. In the case of Murdo MacPherson, perceived familiarity, environmental conditions and distance all had a part to play in his decision to opt for Canada in 1977.

> I never considered any other places – I didn't consider Australia or New Zealand or anywhere like that, partly because I'd been to Canada, I suppose, and I *did* know people there. I liked the environment, I didn't want to go to a hot place like Australia. New Zealand was just a bit far off the beaten track.

Occasionally the destination appears to have been selected almost at random, steered by the impulse to leave Scotland rather than go anywhere in particular. When in 1958 Isobel Gillon was persuaded by a friend to emigrate with her to Australia, she was advised otherwise by a colleague at the Galashiels textile mill where she worked. Pointing to the world map pinned to his wall, he told her:

> You don't want to go to Australia, you want to go to that wee country down there, New Zealand. So I takes the message back to Margaret, and she says, 'I'm no fussy, as long as it's somewhere.'[30]

Recruitment

Personal contacts, community networks, and sometimes accidental encounters like Isobel's, dominated interviewees' perceptions of the decision-making process. Strikingly, formal recruitment mechanisms played almost no part in their remembered experiences, even though their decisions were often formulated within a framework of empire settlement policies or in response to employers' sponsorship strategies. Morag MacLeod had a vague impression that the *Marloch* emigrants were part of a Soldier Settlement Board plan 'to open up the prairies', but she was unaware (perhaps not surprisingly for a 10-year-old) of the imperial legislation that allowed Andrew MacDonell to turn his colonising dreams into reality. And while Agnes MacGilvray spoke of the constraints of the American quota system, its requirements and red tape did not loom large in her recollections.

Angus Macdonald, who in 1987 was interviewed for the New South Wales bicentennial oral history project, spoke of how, as a 21-year-old in North Uist, he was prompted to emigrate to Australia in 1926 after an agent from Australia House had visited Lochmaddy.[31] From the 'voices' collection, only Rob and Cathie Tulloch mentioned an encounter with an agent, although we know that recruitment meetings were well attended and promotional campaigns attracted comment, as well as sometimes consternation. For the Tullochs the agent's role was crucial, since they had almost given up hope, a year having elapsed between the submission of their application and their interview in Aberdeen. As Cathie recalled:

> By the time we got the interview Rob said to me, 'I don't think, I don't think we should carry on.' And I said, 'Well, let's go to the interview anyway, we haven't had a day off for a long time, let's go to the interview.' So we went. And the interviewer literally sold New Zealand to us. He was a lovely person... And he really told us more and more about New Zealand, just confirming everything we'd read and the books etc. Yeah, it was really, it really clinched the deal for us. I think he, he was the one that made it or broke it, you know. He certainly made it for us.

The damaging effects of the time-lag that often occurred between application and interview were highlighted by an interviewee who came from the other side of the desk. Gordon Ashley, an Australian businessman and politician, was sent to Glasgow as an emigration officer in 1969. He estimated that between 80 and 85 per cent of applicants were accepted, although not all subsequently emigrated, perhaps because they became discouraged by the delay of up to a year between interview and sailing date. The Tullochs were re-enthused by their interview, but that was not the experience of all.

For Gordon Ashley, the recruitment of migrants was just part of a varied career tapestry, which he summarised at the beginning of his interview.

> [I] grew up on a farm in South Gippsland in Victoria, studied theology in my early to mid 20s. With the need of something to do by sheer circumstance I ended up taking a position with the Department of Immigration in the late '60s and was promptly selected to go overseas to be involved in recruiting people to settle in Australia under the £10 scheme. And so I arrived in London in early '69 and found myself being sent up to Glasgow for three years, and then spent two years after that back in London doing the same kind of work. The position was very restricted in terms of movement around in Scotland because most of the people who were going to Australia were going from the west of Scotland, so most of the interviews were done in Glasgow. There would be an occasional trip across to Edinburgh, if the officers there were away or on holidays.

I did four trips to Northern Ireland, two before the Troubles started, two afterwards. And I'd do an occasional trip down to Carlisle in the three years that I was here. After that I went back to Australia, worked with the Productivity Council of Australia for three years before the Secretary was seconded from the public service and then came back – and I was five years – and came back to the UK in '78 as Professions Adviser at Australia House. Worked for three years doing that, more at the trade, at the sub-professional and professional end, engineers and sorting out those who were able to settle in Australia given that their qualifications were accepted, from those whose qualifications weren't. And then I went and established a small business in personnel consulting, concentrating on finding good positions with good Australian firms for people from all over the world, but principally the UK. And I did that for ten years before I entered the Victorian Parliament, of which I was then a member for another ten years, taking me up to the beginning of 2003. So that's the potted version.[32]

Sent to Glasgow at a time when assisted emigration was reaching its peak, Gordon ran the Jamaica Street office almost single-handedly. The work could be relentless, he recalled.

A typical day would be to interview between six and eight units. That may be a single or a couple or a family. More time was given to families, usually three quarters of an hour, singles and couples were generally half an hour, though sometimes it might be a little longer, and if all of them turned up to interview, then it was a really, really hard slog. This was repeat work where you were asking questions as to the motivation of people and also trying to give information at the same time, and trying to crowd that into that time slot. They also had other written information, but no one could be sure how much a person had actually read or not. So it was not an easy thing to do.

I remember once in Glasgow doing 44 interviews in a row, without anyone not turning up – and it was when people did not turn up that you had a break, could catch your breath, and could actually write some sort of reasonable report. Otherwise it could easily become slapdash. Most days, because I guess I was conscientious, I would end up being late. I would be finishing up an hour or more after everyone [else], after the office had closed, say at 5, I would be [working] on. And it was not easy sometimes to remember who the cases were, so you had to make little notes to ensure that you didn't make mistakes about this couple and that couple.

Local offices such as Glasgow had a considerable degree of autonomy. Only 'problem' cases were referred to the Chief Migration Officer in London, but in the dying days of the White Australia policy these, to Gordon's chagrin, included non-whites, as well as those with criminal convictions.

The interviewer's priority was to ensure that applicants – about a third of whom were young families – realised the challenges they might face.

> Did they understand the consequences of, for example, a baby arriving soon after arrival and what that might do in the woman's situation and how that would possibly simply isolate her from the real world around her. And remember, many of them to begin with were staying in migrant hostels, so this was going to be a big, big cultural shock to the system, not easy to cope with and especially if a girl went to Australia thinking that she was going to be out there as a secretary or whatever and suddenly ended up with a young baby.

Applicants – all of whom were seeking assisted passages – had been alerted to Australian opportunities either by films, Australia House advertisements or family stories. Political sensitivities meant that the days of disseminating information through labour exchanges had 'well and truly passed'. 'I think there was a concern that that would be seen politically to be aiding and abetting the flight of skilled people, and... the government wasn't prepared to go that far any more.' Applicants' motives, however, were still dominated by the economic concerns that had preoccupied previous generations. 'Most of it was "I cannae get a decent job here" or "We want a better life for our kids".' Their recurring questions were about climate, housing and health – and 'What about the creepy crawlies?'

Transitional Experiences

Most interviewees had clear memories of the journey to a new land and a new life, at least if it involved a sea voyage. Until the 1960s that was the universal experience, although even when flying became an option, some preferred to slow the pace of transition. Alison Gibson and her friend could have flown to Canada in 1967, but opted to take a six-day voyage on the *Empress of Canada* from Greenock to Montreal. 'It was such a huge change in our life,' she recalled, 'flying seemed too simple, just to leave one whole life behind and start fresh overnight'.

The dominant narrative was one of enjoyment, especially for children. The *Marloch* introduced Morag MacLeod to previously unknown conveniences.

> Oh, I remember quite a bit about the voyage, the icebergs, and it was foggy, and we had to anchor. It took us about, oh my goodness, close to two weeks to cross. We were stuck in the fog. The icebergs were huge... I remember the blasting of the fog horn for sure, I can still hear it... we

Morag Bennett (née MacLeod)

were put in the state rooms, you know, to sleep and that – and we never had running water in Benbecula... it was just a well, and we didn't know what the bowl and the taps and all this sort of things were...

Minnie Anne Fraser's memories of her second-class transatlantic trip to New York on the *Cameronia* in 1926 were of 'all American food, right away' and of lots of singing and dancing with the third-class passengers – 'a very cheery, happy lot of people' – in the bowels of the ship. Her daughter, Sandra Train, takes up the story:

The voyage she enjoyed tremendously. They went from Glasgow. The other girls said to her, they said amongst each other, 'Let's buy some outfits in Glasgow for America,' but my mother said, 'No, let's wait till we get to America, the fashions there might be different.' Far-seeing of her. They found that although they had quite good accommodation on the ship, they found that the best fun was to be had with the steerage passengers, which were mainly Irish, and they danced the same dances, sang more or less the same types of songs, and they had a fellow feeling for them[33]

When Agnes Lawrie sailed from Liverpool to New York four years later, she recalled paying £22 10s for a third-class passage and sharing a cabin with a girl from Dundee who was going to join relatives in Detroit. Like Minnie Anne, she found that the food was 'very good, really good, and plenty of it of course. And they were telling us all what we had to do and what to look out for when we got to New York.' Her memories of good food and shipboard lectures were echoed by emigrants from the immediate post-war generation, when the groaning tables made a vivid contrast with the restrictions of a ration-book diet.

Seasickness did not dampen Annie Matheson's enjoyment of her voyage from Southampton to New York on the *Queen Elizabeth* in 1952.

> It was just like being in a floating luxury hotel. You had your own waiter at the table, you were assigned a table and you had your own waiter, and white linen cloths and big linen napkins and huge fruit – oranges and apples that you never saw in your life yet. And we got excellent meals. Printed menu, I still have some of these menus that I saved... I shared my cabin with two or three war brides who were going across and another older woman, and it was interesting to talk to them.

Even in 1967, Alison Gibson's memory of the 'wonderful' shipboard food was influenced by having been brought up in the era of rationing. 'We loved the sailing across, and there were so many young people, all going to all over Canada, just emigrating at that time. We had a really fun time. It was like staying in a great hotel, which we had never done before.'

Some New Zealand-bound ships sailed through the Panama Canal, others went round the Cape of Good Hope. Gail Anderson was only a year old when in 1946 her mother took her to Dunedin to join her New Zealand-born husband, whom she had married in Glasgow four years earlier. The ship, the *Rangitiki,* was full of young women and children, and when it broke down in Panama, her mother was left to babysit the children of mothers who 'wanted to go out and party'. Some of them did not re-embark, so when the ship docked in Wellington 'there were men waiting for these fiancées or wives... and they just weren't there – they had decided to stay in Panama'.[34] For children such as Brian Coutts, the long voyage to the Antipodes was 'great fun', a sentiment echoed by Paddy McFarlane, who at the age of 22, particularly highlighted the experience of Panama as 'really terrific'. The *Northern Star,* the Shaw-Savill ship that on its maiden voyage brought Ian and Helen Campbell and their two young sons to New Zealand in 1963, came via the Cape, where the need for major repairs meant that the passengers were treated to a week's sightseeing in Cape Town and Durban respectively.[35] Two years later, when the *Oriana* brought Rob and Cathie Tulloch to Auckland, the voyage was characterised by fun and relaxation until journey's end was imminent. 'It wasn't until we left Australia to come to New Zealand,' Cathie recalled, 'that everybody started to get a bit tense because we then knew the next port was ours and we didn't know what was before us.'

Others had less happy voyage experiences. Shipboard mortality occasionally reared its ugly head, albeit less frequently than in the 19th century. When Cathy Donald's mother – who had already suffered several miscarriages – became pregnant while waiting for the sailing papers, the family's embarkation for New Zealand was accelerated.

But unfortunately a baby boy was born on the voyage, and they didn't tell me until it was over, but they had a little ceremony and buried him at sea... He lived, apparently he lived, and they said, had he been on land... but they couldn't... they didn't have all the equipment that they needed... I guess my mother landed and that was it, they had to just get on with life. Didn't have a lot of money and I quite admire my mother, because she didn't sit around and mope and so on. But she said to me years after that every time she heard the cry of a baby, that used to bring back the memory of it, you know, just that little newborn cry.

Cathy Timperley (née Donald)

The debarkation port was rarely the final destination and some interviewees recalled seemingly endless train rides before they reached journey's end. Dunedin-bound migrants faced the inter-island ferry trip to Lyttleton, followed by a train journey south. In 1946 Gail Anderson's mother

really thought she was coming to the end of the world, and very apprehensive and very homesick, extremely homesick, of course, six weeks at sea, you know. And coming to this man who, okay, she had... they'd been married for four years – three or four years... but he was still... in this land was a stranger to her really. They hadn't been together an awful lot of the time in that four years.

Those bound for western Canada, at least in the 1920s, faced an onward journey on an unfamiliar mode of transport, under conditions not dissimilar from the early days of the transcontinental railway. 'I remember that I saw a train when we got off the boat in New Brunswick, and I didn't know what it was. It looked like little houses,' recalled Morag MacLeod. During the journey passengers could cook their own food in kitchens at the end of the carriage and at night they made tiered bunks out of the seats. In 1923 the journey to Red Deer took 'a few days' but more than three decades later, after a ten-day voyage from Greenock to Montreal, Easton Vance still spent three days and four nights on the train to Vancouver.

Adjusting to a New Life

The young Morag MacLeod enjoyed both the journey and her new life on the prairies. She acknowledged, however, that her parents' sentiments were more negative, as they faced the challenges of pioneering in an unfamiliar environment where they remained for ten years until the family moved to Vancouver during the Depression.

> Oh well, you know, I was young, and I thought it was great, especially the winter. I loved the snow, you know, big drifts and playing in the snow, but you must remember, I was just ten years old, but my parents, my mother brought a few plants from Benbecula, and of course she didn't know that the winter was so cold and they all froze, the first frost in the winter.

She echoed the colonists' frequent – and much documented – complaints about the quality of the prefabricated accommodation.

> The houses were very small. Of course they all had big families, that was the idea, to bring out the big families and get the prairies settled. And the houses were just sort of like a square box and not insulated at all. So you can imagine... Boy, I tell you, it was a terrible time.

She also suggested that a crofting background was not a good preparation for successful prairie farming.

> Hebrideans didn't know how to farm properly. You know what I mean? The Russian ones, that had the good farms, they knew what they were doing, but from what I can think back on now, the Hebrideans didn't know.

Housing was an area in which Brian Coutts also found that the reality did not coincide with the rhetoric. He recalled that, when the 'guaranteed' house did not materialise on the family's arrival in Dunedin, they were given makeshift emergency accommodation for a month.

> That's when the family became unhappy about the arrival, having left the old stone atmosphere of Edinburgh to be (sic) a ramshackle wooden house with a rusty tin roof with water that you got from a tank – you know, drinking water and the water for cooking and the toilet all came from a large tank... My father was angry and he stayed angry till the day he died.

The dismay of £10 Poms with Australian hostel accommodation is well documented, but was only partially corroborated by interviewee Sandra Munro, who was seven when she emigrated with her parents from Paisley

Sandra Munro

in 1965 after her father got a job in the Port Kembla steel works. Although Sandra's mother disparaged the family's hut at Berkeley in New South Wales as 'a tin shack cut in half', she settled in quickly once she had invested in an electric frying pan so that the family could avoid eating the unpalatable canteen food. She was subsequently more perturbed by the 'dunny cans' that constituted the sanitary facilities in their newly built council house.[36]

Across the Tasman Sea, accommodation posed 'no problems' for Rob and Cathie Tulloch, who had a farm cottage waiting for them at Maromaku in the Bay of Islands. They were unequivocal in their praise for the way in which their employers and 'the whole community just absolutely adopted us when we arrived, and that was just amazing, it made settling down a lot easier'. They also relished the egalitarianism of New Zealand society. 'When we first arrived in New Zealand there was absolutely no class distinction. You were on equal par with the boss. And in Scotland we had bought tickets to go to a ball and because we had found out the boss was going we knew we couldn't go to that function, so we had to sell the tickets.'

The three women in the sample who were employed in domestic service were provided with live-in accommodation. For Agnes Lawrie the whole experience was a great adventure. She sailed from Liverpool to New York on the Cunard liner *Athenia* in May 1930, lodged initially with her friend Gladys and then – through Hutchison's employment agency in New York City – had a succession of positions with wealthy families. Work was a means to an end, for Agnes's main objective was to enjoy fun and freedom. When she took up her fourth job

> I went there and then I sent my brother the address right away. And he wrote back and said, 'What are you playing at? This is the fourth address you've had in two years. Why are you not staying in your jobs?' But that was me... One had to stay on duty until 10 o'clock and you could do as you liked after that because you got your key... Well, I went to more musicals and more theatre and more everything...

The seven years that Agnes spent in that post encompassed the Wall Street

Crash and the onset of the Depression, a crisis to which her employers, she recalled, made only a cosmetic concession:

> They had decided like everybody else that they were cutting down expenses, because they had to. They didn't have to, the Coreys didn't need... but a lot of other people like them who lost everything in the 1929 Crash... the Coreys thought they'd better look as though they had lost, and so they closed the country house...

Four years before Agnes arrived in New York, Minnie Anne Fraser had passed through the city on her way to Detroit, where she spent most of her six-year American sojourn in the service of the Studebaker family. Almost three decades later, when Annie Matheson spent a year in service with another Detroit automobile family, their business was merged with that of Studebaker-Packard. During that time Annie was not only able to save enough money for her wedding, she was also given an invaluable induction into American habits and customs, punctuated by occasional encounters with well-known figures on the international stage.

> It was a wonderful experience when I lived with an American family. I got used to the American cooking, the food they ate was different, and the way they served, you know, the servings, the way they set a table and all that. It was an opportunity for me to learn these things. It would have been harder if I wasn't living with an American family, to get into the way of life. So I was very happy to be there. And although they were very wealthy people they were so nice, they just treated me like I was one of themselves... [Roy Chapin's] father founded the Hudson Motor Car Company and then they joined with Studebaker Packard while I was working with them and they formed American Motors... They used to have Henry Ford at his home – I met him and his wife. They were there for dinner and I waited table and I thought she was like a china doll. I never saw a real person as dainty looking as she was. She was just immaculate and just like a painted doll... I met the ambassador to Belgium who was a guest at their house too.

The transatlantic gulf in living standards was particularly evident in the 1950s. Annie felt that she was 'living in luxury compared with conditions in post-war Britain, and the wages were so much higher in America. You could go to the store and buy care packages to send to Britain, you could buy butter in tins and sugar packaged specially for that purpose... I did it a few times.'

It was in an attempt to buy margarine rather than butter that Helen Campbell, newly arrived in Balclutha, unwittingly caused offence in a New Zealand dairy farming community.

Well, the first thing that really struck me was – I went to do shopping – the messages, and I asked for margarine, and that was an absolute no-no in those days. I thought I could get Stork margarine for baking, 'cause I had never baked with butter. And they just – they nearly ran me out of the shop. I really remember that, yeah... Everything was made with butter. Even two or three years after that, you couldn't buy margarine unless you had a doctor's line for it.

Helen Campbell

Helen also spoke of the miserable school experience of her elder son, who came home with weals on his legs, inflicted by a teacher who 'didn't understand what he was saying', just as Donald Campbell, for his part, did not understand the teacher's accent. Eight years earlier, Brian Coutts soon learned to adapt his accent to his surroundings.

> I got quite a hard time about having a Scottish accent, and so I lost that in public very quickly. I retained it for being at home, 'cause it was either being teased at home or being teased at school, so I decided I didn't like either, so I picked up a New Zealand accent as quickly as possible for school and I spoke to my parents with a Scottish accent.

On the other side of the world in the 1920s, Morag MacLeod spoke Gaelic at home but English at school, where 'we wanted to be like the other children, and we didn't think much of the Gaelic language at that particular stage'. In her mid-90s, however, and after a lifetime in Canada, she admitted that she still thought in Gaelic. From a later generation, 12-year-old Alan Blair was similarly determined 'to adapt and blend in as quickly as possible' when he emigrated to Sarnia, Ontario, with his parents and three younger siblings in July 1968. 'I didn't like being the centre of attention, and I was certainly the centre of attention for the first part of that first school year. So probably by Christmas of that year I was a proper little Canadian and indistinguishable from Canadians on either side of me.' His mother confirmed that 'he practised his accent in front of the mirror. You know, he really wanted to be Canadian, He did *not* want to stand out.' Almost four decades later, when Alan – by then on secondment to England as a colonel in the Royal Canadian Air Force – brought his family to Oxfordshire for three years, his elder daughter (also aged 12 when she arrived) adopted her father's childhood strategy of rapid assimilation, while her sister (aged ten) 'decided she was going to maintain her Canadian identity no matter what happened'.[37]

Coming and Going

Effortless adaptation was not a universal experience and some emigrants were hit by a homesickness so intense that they returned to Scotland. Gordon Ashley, aware that up to 35 per cent of recruits for Australia retraced their steps, was concerned that applicants for assisted passages looked at the country through rose-tinted spectacles. He felt that the lack of feedback given to recruitment agents such as himself contributed to the high return rate.

> That was one of the things I disliked intensely about the process. You did not know outcomes. You did not know how people fared. You did not know, there was nothing that you could work back from, and say well, I must learn a lesson from that, that that person had said to me something, I'd made a note of it, I in the end in the end accepted them for a passage for Australia but I should have taken more notice of that, there was more of a… there was more of a hesitancy in that than I recognised.

Gordon's illustration of the plight of lonely young mothers was borne out in the relatively recent experience of John and Margaret Hardie, described in Chapter 5.[38] And in the 1960s it was persistent and crushing homesickness that contributed to the break-up of Ena Macdonald's marriage, as well as her temporary and then permanent return from Australia to her parents' croft in North Uist. It was not the family's first experience of unhappy emigration. Ena's mother, Morag Miller from Mull, had moved reluctantly to Canada in 1925, in response to parental 'nagging' that she should go and keep an eye on an older sister who in the event relocated to the United States shortly after Morag arrived in Toronto. While working in service, she met Archie Macdonald from North Uist and was 'delighted' when in 1932 her husband – who feared redundancy from his job on the railway – responded to an opportunity to take up the tenancy of a croft back in the Hebrides. Almost three decades later, in 1961, their newly wed daughter emigrated to Sydney with her husband, a fitter-engineer from Clydebank whom she had met while working in Glasgow. Ena's memories of her anguish as she took the boat train from London to Southampton were still acute more than forty years later. 'And I was absolutely breaking my heart crying, absolutely – I was just torn apart. It was a horrible feeling.' The passage of time did little to restore her spirits, especially when an encounter in New South Wales gave her a poignant linguistic reminder of the Hebridean roots from which she had been severed.

> When I was working in that store in Sydney, I met lots of Scotch people, and this couple took us to a Scottish ball, and she said, it's a Lewisman that's playing. This was where I met Tommy Darkie, as they call him here, but Johnny Macleod. So he was playing, and we were dancing, and then there was an interval. So he came down off the platform and came down to speak to me... We were talking, that was the first Gaelic I'd spoken, you know. And anyway, he says, 'I'll have to go up and start playing again.' And he played a waltz. And he played all the Gaelic songs, and I had to get off the floor, I was just breaking my heart crying. I was forever homesick, homesick.

Ena hoped that a visit to North Uist might be the answer.

> I thought maybe if I go home I might settle, you know, go home for a little while, see my parents, and that was in '64, and I might settle... And it was when I was on my way home I realised I was pregnant... Anyway, I came home here. When I was on the ship, well, I don't think I had in my mind that I was coming home for good, I was just coming home just to try and feel better, you know. I thought, maybe if I see my parents, and maybe when we're apart for a wee while, I'll be happier going back again and all the rest of it. And then I came back here, oh it was great to be here.

Ena Macdonald

The second parting, a month after the birth of her son, was even more traumatic, and she continued to pine throughout the voyage.

Then it came to the time of going back, and I was dreading going back, absolutely dreading it, and I can still remember, I think everybody in the village came down to say cheerio to me. And they were standing out there, I think there was snow on the ground... When he [a neighbour who took her to the airport] drove away I can still remember, just going out the

gate there, and I looked behind, and my father was running after the car.
Oh, I nearly just said, 'Stop, I'm not going.' Sometimes I wish I had...
I remember when I went on board and oh, my appetite just disappeared,
I couldn't eat. I lost a stone in about ten days. And the stewards were so
nice and they said, 'Oh, is there nothing I can give you? You must eat,
you must eat.' And I says, 'I'm not hungry.'... Oh, I was just miserable.
Oh, I was just wishing I was back, you know, I didn't want to go. I was
seeing my father run after that car. Oh, I was just, it was just awful.

Ena's second sojourn in Australia – this time in Queensland, where her
husband had been relocated – was not successful, and after ten months she
decided to return permanently to North Uist. She and her husband had
drifted apart. 'He never missed anybody. He just, he didn't seem to have
any sympathy. He didn't... he wasn't nasty to me or anything like that, but
he just didn't understand what I was going through... I just kept thinking
of home, kept thinking of my sisters and my mother and my father.'.[39]

Ena's homesickness was is not unique. For Isobel Gillon in Dunedin,
dance music was also a trigger, although she planned in due course to
invoke the option to return home.

I'd been here, oh, probably two or three months, and then I started
getting homesick... You'd hear the tunes on the radio, which were the
dance tunes that I knew, and all of a sudden I'd be back home in the
living room and I'd cry. And I thought, well, I've got two years. Can't
tell my Mum and Dad I'm upset, because they'd get upset knowing that
if I wasn't happy. So, I thought, you'll just have to save hard and go
back after two years.

In the event, Isobel's plans were changed by Cupid's arrow, when she
met and married Dutch immigrant Willie Bouman, although waves of
homesickness returned periodically, especially (but not uncommonly)
when she underwent life-changing experiences, such as the birth of their
children.

In Canada, as we have seen, 28 per cent of a sample of post-war British
migrants returned on account of homesickness, with women being most
acutely affected.[40] The 'thousand dollar cure' which was common among
war brides in both the USA and Canada was still deployed in the 1960s,
though, according to Janet Blair – who has only made one visit back to
Scotland – it was not always effective.

Oh yes, quite a number, particularly women, who would go home on
their own or with their kids every year, and they would find that they
did not want to stay here. Their husbands used to call it the thousand-
dollar cure at one time, in the '60s. You know, send them back and they

would come back and decide to stay here, but a lot of them didn't, a lot of them went back home.

While Dr Roddy Campbell's Inverness-born wife was not desperately homesick, she 'was never really that happy in Canada', so after 11 years in British Columbia, first in the interior and then on Vancouver Island, the Campbells returned to Scotland with their two sons in 1977. Although he thoroughly enjoyed his work and had – just a few weeks before leaving – taken out Canadian

Isobel and Willie Bouman

citizenship as an insurance to facilitate possible remigration, Roddy was quite willing to leave Canada, since 'I think we concluded after a while that it wasn't really home for us... we didn't want to grow old there.'

Others returned to Scotland – sometimes unwillingly – to shoulder family responsibilities. After more than six years in Detroit, Minnie Anne Fraser arrived back in Halladale in 1932 with an American accent and idiom, as well as a ticket to return. But three brothers had died in 1927, followed by her father in 1930, and her mother told her that 'home is where you are to be'.[41] When she alighted from the train at Forsinard, she was greeted by Donald Macdonald – who three years later was to become her husband – just as casually as if she had been on a day trip away. Her daughter explains:

> That was very much a Highland or a strath thing, you know, not to be too fazed by the return of a native who had been away for six and a half years in America. My father was the post, he saw her coming off the train, and he just said, as he would say if she'd been coming from Dornoch, 'Hello Minnie, how are you?' And she said, 'Mighty fine, Donald.'

During her time in New York Agnes Lawrie returned twice to the UK: in 1935 to recuperate after an appendectomy, and in 1938 with the intention of working in London. But she changed her mind, and it was on the voyage back to the USA that she met her fiancé, Norman MacGilvray from Glasgow, a chief electrician with the Anchor Line. They married in

New York in August 1939, with the intention that Agnes would remain in service there for a year while her husband continued to criss-cross the Atlantic. But the outbreak of war put paid to their plans and by October 1939 they were both back in Glasgow.

Interviewees who became serial migrants or returned to Scotland had often never intended to put down permanent roots in one place overseas. They were itinerant adventurers and career emigrants, some footloose, others following the opportunities opened up to them by their trade or profession. After more than 20 years in Montana, Sandy MacLeod's father returned to Coigach in the 1930s, by which time he was in his 40s and had amassed enough money to buy most of Tanera Mòr, largest of the Summer Isles. A generation later, Angus Pelham Burn, who in the 1950s spent seven years in the employment of the Hudson's Bay Company before returning to Scotland to pursue a career as a farmer, banker, company director and Vice Lord Lieutenant of Kincardineshire, felt the Canadian North suited his bachelor lifestyle, but not the responsibilities of marriage.

> I decided that if I was going to stay, I couldn't stay on my own. You know, if I was going to get married, and I had no idea who I was going to marry, or anything like that, I just thought, I can't do this for the rest of my life, and I can't really have a wife from the UK or southern Canada up here, I mean, it's really not a life for a woman in that sense. I had very mixed feelings about it, but I came home and that's that.[42]

Others returned for vocational reasons. The Reverend Murdo Mac-Ritchie, having completed postgraduate studies at Westminster Theological Seminary in Philadelphia and served the Free Church of Scotland congregation in Detroit since 1952, was called back to a charge in Stornoway in 1966, bringing with him his Detroit-born wife, Marilyn. When she had first visited the island on honeymoon in 1957, her initial impressions had been of the striking lack of trees and the penetratingly cold climate, though she also recalled being met at the quayside by reporters, keen to interview the minister's exotic bride. When Marilyn returned to Stornoway nine years later, she found that 'coming from a big city, and coming to a small town, it was a bit difficult, because I felt I was in a fish bowl, everybody watching me swim around'.[43]

Some interviewees were perennial rolling stones. Wanderlust was built into the DNA of the Murray family from Shader in the Isle of Lewis. In 1927 Calum and Cathie Murray first went to Canada with their mother and three siblings, to join their father, who had left three years earlier for Prince Rupert. His experience of Canada predated the war, when he had worked on grain elevators in the strongly Hebridean community at Fort William (now Thunder Bay) in Ontario, but had returned to his native island, where he joined the naval reserve, resumed fishing and also married in 1917. After he was killed in a workplace accident in 1932, aged 51, his widow relocated near to her two sisters and three brothers in Calgary, but she could not tolerate the summer heat and a year later brought the children back to Lewis.

The next generation had, however, inherited their father's itchy feet. In 1947 Cathie, who was then working with her sister at the NAAFI in Germany, was actively seeking an opportunity to go back to Canada when she had a fortuitous encounter with a New Zealander.

> But meanwhile, I thought, I was aiming for Canada all he time, and I wrote Canada House, got no answer, so this Betty, she says to me, 'You go to New Zealand, you see what they're doing there.' So, to cut a long story short, they answered right off, and all I had to do was fill the forms and you could go over there for TEN POUNDS. And – of course – you had to work with them for two years. [That] was the best ten pounds – I ever spent.[44]

After two years in Wellington, Cathie moved north to Auckland. She would have settled in New Zealand permanently, had she not been obliged to return to Lewis after 16 years to look after her elderly mother.

> Oh, I wanted a job where I'd be free to roam, and I worked in the, first of all I worked in the hostel I lived in, in the cafeteria there. That's while I was in Wellington. I did my two years there, that was where they sent me… I'd met up with Australian girls and they had gone up to Auckland. 'Oh, why don't you come up here?' They'd started working in hospitals, and here I get another job up there, in a cafeteria in the nurses' home. Well, I was there for nearly 12 years, and that's when I started the [life of a] rolling stone. I went back, working my way back, got a permit, and worked in the States for two years, Canada two years, back home.

Calum, meanwhile, had followed in his father's footsteps. In 1954 he returned to Canada where, with the help of his uncle, he soon found a job freighting grain on the Great Lakes. For the next 30 years he was a transatlantic commuter, spending his summers on the Lakes and all but one winter with his wife and children back in Lewis, eventually retiring to his native island in the mid-1980s.

Calum Murray's work pattern was by no means uncommon. Norman Macrae, whose Lewis-born parents met and married in Detroit, recalled that in 1947 (when he was six) his mother returned to Lewis with her children to look after her parents-in-law, while her husband continued to work seasonally on the Great Lakes until he retired to the island in the 1960s.

> Of course, the Lakes froze over in the winter-time and he used to come
> home to Lewis round about the beginning of December and would be
> home until March when he would get a telegram that the lakes were
> de-icing and off he would go again for another nine months, leaving my
> mother to look after my grandfather.[45]

Some people resettled in Scotland almost by accident. When Sandra
Munro came back from Australia for a working holiday in 1980, she found
Ullapool too remote and had every intention of returning to Australia –
until she met her husband.

The remoteness of Kinlochbervie, 40 miles north of Ullapool, was
an asset rather than a deterrent to Murdo MacPherson, who did not
necessarily intend to resettle in Scotland when in 1996 he returned for a
year's leave of absence. Having spent 19 years in Toronto, he was looking
to relocate with his Canadian wife and family in a less populated area –
possibly the North-West Territories or the Yukon, but instead ended up
applying for a job as geography teacher in the newly opened high school
at Kinlochbervie.

> When this came up here, this actually filled that gap, because by
> Canadian standards Kinlochbervie's not in the least bit remote.
> I mean, we're two hours to Inverness. I mean, two hours barely gets
> you anywhere in Canada. You'd all the services, everything's there, but
> you're in a fairly wild area... This satisfied a lot of the desires to be in a
> wilder place, and that's why we came and stayed here.

Most of those who did not return permanently have been back to
Scotland to visit. In some cases their impressions have vindicated their
own – or their parents' – decisions. Alan Blair, like Anne Simpson, was
struck by the monotone greyness of North Lanarkshire in the 1970s. 'Very
grey and drab and dull and industrial, graffiti and lots of garbage, you
know, like a place that had lost its self-respect.' In 2009, however, Graham
McGregor felt that post-devolution Scotland had acquired a new vibrancy.

> When we got to Jedburgh I was astounded by the number of saltires that
> were flying. I was really, really surprised, I had never seen St Andrew's
> flags being displayed publicly in quite that way before. I was also struck
> by the conversations that I had with some English people south of the
> border who felt that life and things that were happening in Scotland were
> much better than they had because of access to EU funding and initiatives
> and a little bit of a green eye. Now, that had always been the reverse for
> me – we always looked to the south to say, 'Oh, it's better down there.'

Others were brought face to face with communities that had moved on or a homeland that did not match their memories and expectations. When Cathie Tulloch was about to visit Morayshire after six years in New Zealand, she was advised by a longer-term Scottish settler that she should 'be prepared to listen but don't expect to be listened to'. She was therefore not entirely surprised when former acquaintances were not particularly interested in her experiences. And Jim Russell, a classicist and archaeologist who in 1959 took up a post at the University of Manitoba, before moving to Vancouver seven years later, highlighted the tendency of emigrants to fossilise their native land in a time warp.

> Your mindset is still that of the time when you left... That is, I think, my experience, that when I go back I do have to shake myself and realise that the city of Edinburgh has changed, it's a whole different thing. Society has changed, and although I can come to terms with it intellectually, emotionally, you know, or sentimentally, I don't really come to terms with it. What I look back to is the time of my emigration. Even the literature that I read... the poets that I admire most are those... Scots poets that were in action, you know, in the middle of the century rather than the more recent ones. I do read modern poets... novels and so forth, [but] I don't warm to them the way that I did to Eric Linklater and people like that, and other poets you know – I don't mean just McDiarmid but Sydney Goodsir Smith and Robert Garioch and MacCaig and the rest of them. And of course I knew some of these people, you see, I met them, I mean, I didn't know them well, because I was just a student, but my teachers knew them and I did meet them on occasions, some of them. And so I was steeped in that – you know, the culture of Scotland at that time.[46]

Attitudes and Identities

Jim Russell has 'never felt a stranger in Canada', not least because the country's explicitly Scottish heritage has made him much more 'part of the warp and the woof' than in the United States, where he has also lived. Although he has been a member and office-bearer in Vancouver's Caledonian and St Andrew's Society, he feels that the organisation is now largely moribund, having failed to attract new infusions of young, professional immigrants since as far back as the 1950s. He also casts a slightly ironic and detached eye over celebrations of 'tartan Scottishness'.

> Well, I do Burns' addresses galore during the season, and you know, I play up to it, I enjoy doing it... my tongue is a little bit in my cheek

when I do it, but I play up the kind of sentimental Scot abroad and play up Burns as a part of the cult... I'm also a member of a Scotch club – we drink Scotch whisky, you know, once a month. But again, that's an interesting club because there are not many Scots in it... I mean, it's part of an act, and of course it's all looked on with bemusement, I think, by Scots in Scotland.

From a later generation, Murdo MacPherson highlighted the practical advantages of ethnic networking.

You could exploit the fact that you were a Scot. It would help you get a job, because Scots were regarded as reliable, hard-working, trustworthy. That still hangs on there... They had disproportionate influence for their numbers... They did manage to get themselves into positions of power in Ontario, I mean, municipal and provincial government, banking system. I don't think they were any harder working than the English or others, who greatly outnumbered them. So did the Irish, the Irish outnumbered the Scots. But I think they adapted quite well. They adapted quite quickly and readily to different circumstances. The English didn't do that. They tended to stay as they were.

In locations with a legacy of immigration, ethnic associations and networks have therefore provided a formal mechanism for socialising, as well as sometimes offering practical support. Some interviewees wanted to break out of the ethnic cocoon, while others embraced it. Agnes Lawrie did not join any Scottish clubs in New York in the 1930s, but was persuaded by the Glaswegian butler at the Corey household to go to the British Overseas League dances in the Grand Central Palace building. Across the border, in the 1960s, Joe and Janet Blair patronised the overseas club when they first arrived in Sarnia, but soon decided to differ from their fellow immigrants by enlarging their social circle and cultivating a variety of Canadian and other friends. In the 1970s Murdo MacPherson preferred to frequent Toronto's TRANZAC Club[47] than to cultivate Scottish connections, although he admits that he never celebrated Burns night until he went to Canada.

I didn't go to any of these Scottish societies at all... There's a couple of Scottish pubs which I avoided like the plague, because I didn't want to end up with a sort of, you know, the usual tartanism that people end up with, more Scottish than they ever were before.

Two decades earlier Easton Vance had expressed similar sentiments when he arrived in Vancouver.

Well, one of the first things that occurred when we got here is, we were invited to the Scottish Society, and Maggie and I went there, and we

Easton Vance

thought everybody there was in a time warp, so we decided not to continue, we decided we'd left that cultural background and were looking for new things, so we didn't want to continue in the way that we saw was happening here. Well, for one thing, they were a couple of generations removed from us, so that didn't help... we didn't want to continue... we didn't like it, so we decided we'll cultivate the people that are Canadian. Not that we discarded the Scots, but the younger people, people of my age, or our age at the time, were of a similar mind, we were seeking new places.

He declared emphatically that he had 'never been interested' in joining the Vancouver Burns Club, which he described as 'maudlin', adding that 'the Scots tend to bask in reflected glory, you know, and I don't, I don't go for that'.

But such sentiments were by no means universal. The Scots of Corby did not feel the need to defend their identity in the face of the eastern European influx after the war, and indeed continued to live in an ethnic bubble until the 1970s. 'It seemed to me that they just carried on living their own lives,' observed Corby-born Margaret McPherson, whose mother and husband had come to the town from Airdrie and Glasgow respectively in the 1930s. In Margaret's childhood (during the 1950s) as many as 14 coachloads of Scots would leave Corby every Friday night to spend the weekend with their families in and around Glasgow, returning on Sunday afternoon. It was a tradition that continued – albeit with diminishing numbers – until the late 1970s.[48]

Although Murdo MacIver has lived in Vancouver since 1953, he sounds as if he has just stepped off the plane from Stornoway. But while Easton Vance has a distinct Canadian twang, it is more than their accents that differentiates these two Scots, who arrived in the city only three years apart. Born at Arnol in the isle of Lewis in 1932, Murdo, like many islanders, joined the merchant navy. At the age of 17, he embarked on four years of worldwide travel that included voyages to Australia and New Zealand with cargoes of emigrants. He had considered settling in New Zealand, 'absolutely a fabulous country' with 'an awful lot of Lewis people on the coast... that had jumped ship, you know, after the war'. In June 1953, however, he found himself beached in Vancouver literally by accident, when an old back injury flared up and he came under the surgeon's knife. By the time he recovered his ship was long gone, but he had fallen in love with Vancouver and wanted to stay in a city which, according to the *Stornoway Gazette*, offered 'unusual opportunities for many types of Lewismen' and where it was 'just as easy to get a copy of the *Gazette*... as in Stornoway'.[49] That Murdo was able to fulfil his wish was thanks to the good offices of Angus Chisholm, an emigration officer who had come originally from Inverness, and Oban-born Iain MacTavish, personnel manager of a Vancouver shipping company, who had once worked on the *Clydesdale*, a MacBrayne boat. When

Murdo MacIver

Murdo revealed that he too had served on the *Clydesdale,* it proved better than any written reference, and helped him get his first job.

> Anyway the day I went up to see the emigration man, 'Oh,' he said, 'oh, you've been here since the 1st of August,' he says. 'What were you up to?' 'Oh,' I says, 'I was in the hospital and I just got clearance on Friday.' So this was Monday, I believe. 'Oh,' and he said 'Oh, and you're doing okay now?' 'Yeah, I'm doing great.' 'Well,' he said, 'Would you like to stay here?' Hah! 'Well,' I says, 'I was going to ask you exactly that same question. I would love to stay here.'... 'Well,' he says, 'it's people like you that we'd like to get here. By the way,' he says, 'my name is Angus Chisholm and originally I'm from Inverness in Scotland.' Oh, so I was in good hands there.[50]

Alongside a 35-year career with the Vancouver harbour fire service that saw him rise through the ranks to the post of battalion chief, Murdo has for more than five decades maintained strong connections with the Gaelic Society of Vancouver. His late wife, Mary, also came from Lewis, and each of them at different times served as Chief of the Society. Finding a home-from-home in the Pacific North-West was clearly important to him and he returned to Arnol regularly to visit his sister until her death in 2011. His recollections of learning about western Canada as he grew up echo Annie Matheson's memories of tales of the USA told in Coll. Murdo continued:

Now I was going to say when I first came here I was really surprised at how many people that was here from the Outer Hebrides. There was 11 people from that little village of Arnol staying in Vancouver at that time and myself being number 12. And I went up to visit – the second year I was here, in '54, I went up to Trail to visit a first cousin of mine that was living in Trail that had come out in 1929, and there was I think 14 people from Arnol between Trail and Procter... It was really, really nice to meet all those people and hear their stories. But I had heard some of the stories while I was growing up because quite a few of the people that used to come to our house and talk about their experiences in the army and in the navy and in South America and Canada and Australia. And a lot of them had gone home after being out here, sometimes before the First World War, and they went home in the early '30s at the beginning of the Depression because there was no jobs and stuff, and they went back home. And I heard about the Kootenay Lakes and the coast of British Columbia when I was 5, 6, 7, 8, 9, 10 years old, so I was – felt – quite at home here from the first day I landed here, and I have not regretted even for two minutes that I came here.[51]

Hamish and Isla Robertson from Banffshire initially joined the Gaelic Society of Vancouver in 1974 and also attended functions at the Scottish Centre – aka 'Haggis Hall' – but soon they heard about the Moray, Nairn and Banff Society, of which Isla in due course became president. She emphasised the practical functions of such organisations.

I'd never heard – even when we lived in Glasgow and Edinburgh, there was always a *Highland* Society, but there was never a Moray, Nairn and Banff Society... It just made you feel at home to walk in there and hear your own tongue, and it's useful, especially when you have children. When you're single and you're an immigrant, you'll get by, but when you've children, you don't really, you don't really understand the education system, and you know, how everything works, and so it's a big help if you have someone who has done it before you and knows how to point the way for you.[52]

Practical support was also a feature of the Lewis Society of Detroit. Between the wars it was a lifeline to the wave of migrants who had to struggle with the impact of the Depression, as well as a dating agency and social club, although by the time Annie Matheson arrived in 1953 it was on the wane. After more than five decades in Detroit, Annie still thinks of Lewis as home, and returns to the island for at least a month each year.[53] Until the advent of cheap telephone calls, she maintained her links with her family in the time-honoured way, as a faithful correspondent, and eagerly anticipated the receipt of news from home. She still treasures the letters that made their way in both directions across the Atlantic.

Every day I wrote and every day I got plenty mail from my parents, my sisters and brother – all my relatives and all my friends. Every day it was, my treat was looking forward to the mail man.

The institution that has been of greatest and most enduring influence in Annie's life, however, is the Detroit congregation of the Free Church of Scotland, which has provided spiritual support, social networks and a tangible link with her homeland. Her fiancé's older brother, Murdo MacRitchie, had just been called as minister to the Detroit congregation in 1952, and by the time Annie arrived a building had been constructed. 'The church that I belonged to in Lewis', she explained, 'they opened a church in Detroit and that kept, I think, a lot of the Lewis people together. You know, the church was a centre where we all met and worshipped and they were very, very wonderful people. They helped each other out, they were very close to each other'.

For Highland emigrants, the Gaelic language was another mechanism through which identity could be nurtured and displayed. Sandy MacLeod's father told him that 'if they [the Coigach sheep herders in Montana] met up in Billings on a Saturday night to have a drink, they would all be conversing in Gaelic, 'cos it was, it was their first language'. Perhaps their presence bestowed on the ranch hands and citizens of Billings the dubious legacy of an ability to swear in Gaelic, since, according to Sandy, his father returned to Coigach with a new vocabulary of colourful American profanities, to the horror of his strict Free Presbyterian mother-in-law. Gaelic was the everyday language of Morag MacLeod and her fellow Hebridean settlers at Ohaton in northern Alberta, while Marilyn MacRitchie tells of how, in the absence of a minister in the post-war years, 'the Lewis folk in Detroit kept their Gaelic worship services in meeting in homes', sending their children to Sunday school in English-speaking churches, with the result that 'they were more or less lost to our church'. As a result, although Gaelic was initially maintained in formal church services after Murdo MacRitchie's arrival, it eventually petered out as the older generation died. Along with their language, Marilyn also remembers that islanders from Ness maintained the tradition of eating guga (young gannets), which were salted and despatched for 'a big feast every year', at which her husband was guest of honour. She also mused on

how difficult it must have been to adjust to the American way of life for those ladies from Lewis, especially in a large city, because many of them had come from rural backgrounds in Lewis, and isolated places, and Detroit was a city of crime, and I'm sure they were surprised when they realised the police were armed with guns, and it must have been frightening at times for them. They had also to learn to handle the currency, a very different decimal system and learning Americanisms – although they spoke English, there were a lot of strange idiomatic expressions.

Spoken testimony gives us an extra insight into issues of identity: that of orality. The voices of the emigrants who have populated this chapter range across the linguistic spectrum, from those who, after half a century, still sound as if they have been freshly plucked from Scottish soil, to those whose accents are indistinguishable from those of their host societies. What determines whether individuals diverge or converge linguistically? Jim Russell, unlike his wife, has retained his Scottish accent, just like Rob Tulloch, whose wife Cathie attributes her own development of a Kiwi twang to the need to make herself understood as a public speaker. Jim Russell traces the difference partly to schoolroom influences, but also believes that 'women generally are more adaptable, more flexible'. Both observations are confirmed by linguistics lecturer Graham McGregor, who explains that women are sometimes categorised as 'linguistic innovators', who modify their accents with the deliberate aim of expanding their networks. The conscious – or subconscious – deployment of a Scottish accent to gain approval or advancement was also hinted at by Murdo MacPherson, who found in Canada that

> in the sort of day-to-day way of looking at things, somebody with an English accent in a workplace would be potentially a target for criticism, whereas somebody with a Scottish accent wouldn't, 'cause the English person would appear to a Canadian often to be superior. They may not have been doing, this may not have been their mindset, or what they were trying to do, but there's certain English accents, particularly, which would give that impression, whereas there are no Scottish accents that give that impression.

Graham McGregor's professional assessment is that convergence or divergence is a deliberate choice, which 'has to do with whether you see yourself as being linked to others or whether you distinguish yourself maximally from others'. School children (such as Alan Blair and Brian Coutts in the 1950s and 1960s) made every effort to converge, in order to avoid being teased, whereas adults were more likely to take pride in their linguistic distinctiveness. Before leaving the UK for New Zealand, Graham McGregor recalled being advised, in the course of a job interview, to jettison his Scottish accent in favour of received pronunciation.

So what I did in that situation was not convergence as it's called in linguistics, but divergence. And I found myself getting further and further away from that particular way of speaking to a much more Scottish voice, to say maximally, 'Hey mate, I'm not actually like you, I'm different. I have a different history, I have a different culture, I have a different ethnicity, I have a different musicology, I have a different sense of education, I have a different religious upbringing, I have a different past. I have a different history, and I remember it, and we're not the same.'

Graham's retention of his Scottish accent during more than two decades in Dunedin is interwoven with a nationalism which has deterred him from taking out New Zealand citizenship because of the requirement to swear allegiance to the 'English crown'. While he recognises that he may spend the rest of his life in New Zealand, he wants his ashes to be scattered in Scotland, and has 'made the choice that my identity is going to be marked and known through the way that I speak. And that's a conscious choice'. It is an attitude that he also ascribes to many of his fellow countrymen.

For many many Scots that's the way you are, this is who I am, this is the way I speak, and that's, I suppose, the linguistic equivalent of wearing a tartan scarf or listening to the bagpipes or whatever the other stereotypes are, or having haggis for breakfast, you know, whatever it is we're supposed to do... it's a statement. And it's one way too that I think we retain the connect with Scotland and with other Scots, even although we're not in their company because you're never quite sure where one's going to turn up.

Interviewees' attitudes to the significance of their origins varied considerably. Some clearly wanted to retain or cultivate a Scottish ethnicity once it was no longer their default culture, while others were happy to shed it. The adoption of multiple and malleable identities was easy for some, while others felt displaced. After more than four decades in Canada, Alison Gibson (McNair) still finds – not unusually – that

whichever country I'm in, I will talk about home as the other. Because I have actually been able and chosen to come back quite often, I have much more interest in being a Scot now than I had when I was growing up, and felt confined.

In Elvira Gonnella's opinion, however, the process of emigration brings in its train a loss of identity. Elvira, a music professor at Dalhousie University, was a professional singer when she emigrated from Dundee to Moosejaw in Canada with her five-month old baby in 1960 to join her English-

Elvira Gonnella

born husband, a newly qualified doctor who had chosen to do his national service with the RCAF. They subsequently spent five years in Baltimore, and some time back in Scotland, before settling in Halifax, Nova Scotia. 'You are never really part of either country,'[54] she reflected. And even Alan Blair, who from the age of 12 wanted to 'blend in as quickly as possible', felt that neither his Canadian citizenship nor his service in the RCAF had made him '100 per cent Canadian' – perhaps, he reflected, because 'there is still that draw of the motherland'.

Conclusion

'The memories of men are too frail a thread to hang history from.'[55] Perhaps the assertion has some validity if those memories remain isolated and uncorroborated. But history has always hung from a multitude of frail threads, gaining its strength when the individual strands are woven into a multicoloured tapestry of theory, narrative and evaluation. The oral testimony of Scottish migrants clothes the diaspora's formal, collective history with personal and individual reflections, highlighting the ebb and flow of encouragement, and the complexity of expectations, experiences and outcomes. It reminds us that most migrants were characterised by ambition – and a few by reluctance – as they grasped opportunities and tackled obstacles in unfamiliar environments.

Throughout a century of multifaceted upheaval, there were some changes of emphasis, particularly in the cultural sphere. The significance of the church to the migrants' identity, which would have taken centre stage in previous centuries, was mentioned by only two interviewees, and in the post-war period the waning popularity of secular ethnic societies was reflected in falling membership numbers. That in turn was connected to a shift in perceptions of migration as a public, corporate phenomenon to a more atomistic and private process. On the whole, however, the interviewees' priorities and practices display a remarkable continuity, as different generations of migrants strove to improve their own or their children's prospects, deployed a combination of personal connections and official mechanisms to effect their relocation, and tapped into a variety of ethnic networks to facilitate their integration into new arenas of work and leisure.

It is fitting that the last word should be given to those who have a personal tale to tell. Their testimony brings us back to the recurring theme of this study: that the story of the Scottish diaspora is at its heart much more than a quantifiable but dry demographic narrative of strategy-driven social engineering. It is a part of a timeless human drama of mobility, centred on individuals and families whose experiences enliven the statistics, put flesh on the dry bones of policies and propaganda and draw the reader into the complex orbit of their dreams, dilemmas, delights and disappointments.

Endnotes

Introduction: Wandering Scots

1   N.H. Carrier and J.R. Jeffery, *External Migration. A Study of the Available Statistics* (London, 1953).

2   'Migration is one of the most difficult areas to obtain accurate information on' (email from David Shelton, General Register Office, to author, 8 February 2012); 'There is no comprehensive system which registers migration in the UK, either moves to or from the rest of the world, or moves within the UK'. (*Scotland's Population 2001 – The Registrar General's Annual Review of Demographic Trends* (Edinburgh, 2002), 38; http://www.gro-scotland.gov.uk/files1/stats/ scotlands-population-2001-the-register-generals-annual-review-147stedition/ scotlands-population-2001-the-register-generals-annual-review-147stedition.pdf; There is a peculiar lacuna in data on emigration' (Allan M. Findlay, *A Migration Research Agenda for Scotland* (Edinburgh, 2004), http://www.scotland.gov. uk/Resource/Doc/930/0034804.doc. Census returns, the annual reports of the Oversea Migration Board (1952–66) and the published annual reports of the Office of National Statistics have all been used in trying to quantify migration.

3   Richard J. Finlay, *Modern Scotland 1914–2000* (London, 2004), 101-2.

4   Carrier and Jeffery, *External Migration*, 96-7. The Scots constituted just over 22 per cent of the inward movement to Britain and Ireland from these locations.

5   GRO Scotland, Population and Migration. http://www.gro-scotland.gov.uk/files2/ stats/high-level-summary/j11198/hlss-updated-19-may-2011.pdf.

6   Spirit of the West, 'The Old Sod', on album *Save This House* (Warner Music Canada 1990). Print licence reference L120727-9008.

7   http://news.bbc.co.uk/1/hi/uk/3770071.stm (accessed 20 February 2007).

8   http://news.bbc.co.uk/1/hi/scotland/3672971.stm (accessed 1 September 2005); Duncan Sim, *American Scots. The Scottish Diaspora and the USA* (Edinburgh, 2011), 190-3.

9   Sim, *American Scots*, 190, 193.

10 Gordon Donaldson, *The Scots Overseas* (London, 1966).

11 The most recent publication is T.M. Devine, *To the Ends of the Earth: Scotland's Global Diaspora, 1750–2010* (London, 2011).

Chapter One: The Road to England

1   James Boswell, *Life of Johnson*, edited by R. Chapman (Oxford, 1953), 302.

2   Michael Flinn (ed.), *Scottish Population History from the Seventeenth Century to the 1930s* (Cambridge, 1977), 441.

3   Angela McCarthy, 'The Scots' Society of St Andrew, Hull, 1910–2001: Immigrant, Ethnic and Transnational Association', *Immigrants & Minorities*, 25: 3 (2007), 209-33.

4   J.A. Galloway and I. Murray, 'Scottish Migration to England 1400–1560',

Scottish Geographical Magazine, 112:1 (1996), 29-38.

5 *Census of England and Wales*, 1951, 1981, Birthplace and Nationality of the People; Isobel Lindsay, 'Migration and Motivation: a Twentieth-Century Perspective', in T.M. Devine (ed.), *Scottish Emigration and Scottish Society* (Edinburgh, 1992). 156; Richard J. Finlay, *Modern Scotland 1914–2000* (London, 2004), 302.

6 Census of England and Wales, 1911, Birthplaces, vol. IX, p. iv, Online Historical Population Reports http://www.histpop.org/ohpr/servlet/ See also Jeanette Brock, *The Mobile Scot. A Study of Emigration and Migration 1861–1911* (Edinburgh, 1999), 25, 42.

7 *Census of England and Wales 1901, vol. 6, Summary tables* (1903), table XLV, 258; *Census of England and Wales 1911, vol. IX, Birthplaces* (1913), table 1, 1, 2; *Census of England and Wales 1921, vol. 1, General Tables* (1921), table 45, 178; *Census of England and Wales 1931, Preliminary Report* (1931), table 1, 1, and HISTPOP.ORG, General Report, 1931, 170; *Census of England and Wales 1951, General tables* (1956), table 32, 114; *Census 1961 England and Wales: Birthplace and Nationality Tables* (1964), table 1, 1; *Census 1971, Great Britain, Country of Birth Tables* (1974), table 3, 26; *Office of Population Censuses and Surveys, Registrar General Scotland, Census 1981, Country of Birth* (1983), table 1, 6; *1991 Census Report for England, Regional Health Authorities (Part 1)*, volume 1 of 2 (1993), table 6, 107. The 1981 and 1991 statistics relate to Scots-born in *England*, not England and Wales.

8 Susan Telford, '*In a World a Wir Ane': a Shetland Herring Girl's Story* (Lerwick, 1998), 1.

9 Telford, *In a World a Wir Ane*, 1; Paul Thompson, 'Women in the fishing: the roots of power between the sexes', *Comparative Studies in Society and History*, 27: 1 (January 1985), 9.

10 Christina Jackman, nee Leask, quoted in Telford, *In a World a Wir Ane*, 25.

11 *Yarmouth Independent*, 10 October 1936, 11a.

12 Ibid., 28 November 1936, 9d.

13 David Butcher, *Following the Fishing* (Newton Abbott, 1987), 111. See also ibid., 12, and Telford, *In a World a Wir Ane*, 21.

14 *Yarmouth Mercury*, 31 October 1936, 4a-g. See also *Yarmouth Independent*, 31 October 1936, 10a-c.

15 *Yarmouth Mercury*, 31 October 1936, 4a-g.

16 John Dunbar, head of Messrs I&J Dunbar, Fraserburgh curers, quoted in *Yarmouth Mercury*, 5 December 1936, 10e.

17 Telford, *In a World a Wir Ane*, 30, 31; Thompson, 'Women in the fishing', 11.

18 *Yarmouth Independent*, 28 November 1936, 9d.

19 Telford, *In a World a Wir Ane*, 25.

20 Butcher, *Following the fishing*, 15; Telford, *In a World a Wir Ane*, 29.

21 Church of Scotland, *Reports to the General Assembly with the Legislative Acts* (Edinburgh, 1931), Women's Home Mission Report, Work among the Fisherfolk, 329.

22 *Yarmouth Independent*, 21 November 1936, 11a-b.

23 J.F. Clarke, *Building Ships on the North East Coast, Part I, c. 1640-1914. A Labour of Love, Risk, and Pain* (Whitley Bay, 1997), 288-9; John A. Burnet,

'"Hail Brither Scots O' Coaly Tyne"? Networking and identity among Scottish migrants in the north-east of England, ca. 1860–2000', *Immigrants and Minorities*, 25: 1, March 2007, 5.

24   J.G. Duff to Lord Lansdowne, Secretary of State for War, quoted in Graham Stewart and John Sheen, *Tyneside Scottish. A history of the Tyneside Scottish Brigade raised in the North East in World War One* (np, 1999), 12.

25   Donald M. MacRaild, *Culture, Conflict and Migration. The Irish in Victorian Cumbria* (Liverpool, 1998), 53.

26   Cumbria Record Office (Barrow), 1881 census enumeration; 1911 Census of England and Wales. Birthplaces of the Population.

27   Bryn Trescatheric, *Vickerstown: A Marine Garden City* (Barrow-in-Furness, 1983), 23.

28   Bryn Trescatheric, *How Barrow was Built* (Barrow-in-Furness, 1985), 80.

29   *Bellshill Speaker*, 1 May 1936, 4d.

30   Ibid., 15 May 1936, 3d.

31   *Corby Works. A Town in Action* (Corby, 1989). See also Marjory Harper, '"Come to Corby": A Scottish Steel Town in the Heart of England', *Immigrants and Minorities*, forthcoming, 2013.

32   Frederick Scopes, *The Development of Corby Works* (Stewarts & Lloyds Ltd, 1968), 178-9; *Kettering Leader and Guardian and Northamptonshire Advertiser* [hereafter *Kettering Leader*], 9 March 1934, 6e-f; *Bellshill Speaker*, 5 January 1934, 1b.

33   *Kettering Leader*, 19 January 1934, 13a-b; 8 June 1934, 20e.

34   Ibid., 8 June 1934, 20e.

35   British Library Sound Archive, 'Lives in Steel', F2642-3, A/C, Brian Saunders, tape 1, side 1.

36   Ian Addis and Robert Mercer, *Corby Remembers, a Century of Memories: 100 Years of Change*, Kettering, 2000, 41, 42.

37   G.M. Boumphrey, 'Industry comes to Corby', *The Listener*, vol. XIII, no, 322, 13 March 1935, 430-4.

38   *Kettering Leader*, 15 March 1935, 6d,, 8d; *Northamptonshire Evening Telegraph*, 20 March 1935, 8b-c.

39   *Kettering Leader*, 9 February 1935, 6b; 28 September 1934, 13a-d.

40   *Bellshill Speaker*, 18 October 1935m 2a-b.

41   *Kettering Leader*, 9 March 1934, 6e-f.; ibid., 29 March 1934, 3d.

42   Addis and Mercer (compilers), *Corby Remembers*. 26-7.

43   Addis and Mercer, *Corby Remembers*, 48, 91, 97.

44   *Kettering Leader*, 2 March 1935, 7a-b, Nessie Phillips, quoted in Addis and Mercer, *Corby Remembers*, 40.

45   See, for instance, 19 January 1934, 5b; 2 February 1934, 5a; 23 February 1934, 5a; 6 April 1934, 5a; 11 January 1935, 5b; 15 March 1935, 5a.

46   Quoted in Addis and Mercer, *Corby Remembers*, 31.

47   Quoted in Addis and Mercer, *Corby Remembers*, 36-8. See also British Library Sound Archive, 'Lives in Steel', F2642-3 A/C, Brian Saunders, tape 1, side 1.

48   British Library Sound Archive, 'Lives in Steel', F2632-3 A/C, William Gibson Cockin, tape 1, side 1.

49   Quoted in Addis and Mercer, *Corby Remembers*, 40

50 Quoted in ibid., 43. See also below, pp. 141 and 248n73
51 *Bellshill Speaker*, 12 April 1935, 5a; 26 April 1935, 7c; *Kettering Leader*, 7 June 1935, 6d.
52 *Kettering Leader*, 21 December 1934, 8f-g.
53 *Bellshill Speaker*, 20 May 1935, 5f.
54 Memorandum by Corby Borough Council (NT 50) to the Select Committee on Transport, Local Government and the Regions, Appendices to Minutes of Evidence, Appendix 32, 23 August 2002. http://www.parliament.the-stationery-office.co.uk/pa/cm200102/cmselect/cmtlgr/603/603ap33.htm
55 Addis and Mercer, *Corby Remembers*, 139.
56 Ibid., 137.
57 Ibid., 158.
58 Ibid., 148.
59 Justine Taylor, *A Cup of Kindness: The History of the Royal Scottish Corporation, a London Charity, 1603–2003* (East Linton, 2003), 134.
60 David Stenhouse, *On the Make. How the Scots took over London* (Edinburgh, 2006), 19.
61 Ibid., 27, 46-9.
62 J.C.W. Reith, *Into the Wind* (London, 1949), 13.
63 Ian McIntyre, *The Expense of Glory. A Life of John Reith* (London, 1993), 114.
64 H.V. Morton, *In Search of Scotland* (London, 1929), 145, 146.
65 Penny Junor, *Home Truths: Life Around My Father* (London, 2002), 15, 16.
66 David Stenhouse, *On the Make*, 57. See also Peregrine Worsthorne's review of Penny Junor's biography in 'Sympathy for the devil', *New Statesman*, 12 August 2002 http://www.newstatesman.com/200208120026
67 William Lindsay, *A Scottish Input into the Metropolitan Police: Service Details of all Scotsmen who joined... between 1889 and 1909* (London, c.1985), iii-iv. Of the 893 Scottish-born recruits, 426 went on to full pension, 65 were dismissed, 49 died in service and 36 left on health grounds. The service records can be consulted in The National Archives, MEP 04/361 – MEP 04/477.
68 Taylor, *A Cup of Kindness*, 138, quoting Doug Cameron, *New Statesman*, July 2002.
69 Stenhouse, *On the Make*, 134.
70 Geoffrey Randall, *No Way Home. Homeless Young People in Central London* (London, 1988).
71 Suzanne Fitzpatrick, Robina Goodlad and Emily Lynch, *Homeless Scots in London. Experiences, Needs and Aspirations* (London, 2000), 1, 28.
72 Kathleen Caskie, *Living on the Borderline: Homeless Young Scots in London* (London, 1991), np.
73 Ibid.
74 Fitzpatrick et al, *Homeless Scots in London*, 13, 17.
75 Ibid., 15.
76 Ibid., 21, 9, 14.
77 Ibid., 31.
78 John Burgess, *The Scottish in Cumbria: The Religious History of Nineteenth Century Migrants* (Carlisle, 1987), 123; Cumbria Record Office (Barrow), BDFC/P/W/12, Presbyterian Church of England, Disjunction Certificate Book

1931–1956, St Andrew's Presbyterian Church, Walney.

79   *Bellshill Speaker*, 26 January 1934, 6e.

80   *Bellshill Speaker*, 4 May 1934, 1c; *Kettering Leader*, 2 November 1934, 3d.

81   *Kettering Leader*, 5 January 1934, 15f; 30 March 1934, 12e; 12 October 1934, 13c; 9 November 1934, 7d; 28 June 1935, 10d.

82   *Bellshill Speaker*, 26 June 1936, 3e.

83   Ibid., 20 December 1935, 3c.

84   Addis and Mercer, *Corby Remembers*, 41; *Kettering Leader*, 2 March 1934, 4g.

85   George G. Cameron, *The Scots Kirk in London* (Oxford, 1979), 208, 222.

86   Cameron, *The Scots Kirk*, 179-80, quoting from *St Columba's Magazine*, November 1909.

87   Cameron, *The Scots Kirk*, 181, 215; Taylor, *A Cup of Kindness*: 184.

88   Stenhouse, *On the Make*, 123.

89   *The London Scotsman*, 1888, quoted in Stenhouse, *On the Make*, 112.

90   Quoted in Taylor, *A Cup of Kindness*, 148, 149.

91   Quoted in ibid., 149. At time of writing, membership of the Caledonian Society is still limited to men.

92   Stenhouse, *On the Make*, 112-13.

93   http://www.rampantscotland.com/features/societies.htm

94   The Reverend A.H. Boyd, Rector of Slaugham, *Mid Sussex Times*, 12 January 1926, 1c.

95   The Darlington Club was wound up in 1984, and the Sunderland Club in the late 1990s. The Whitley Bay and District St Andrew's Society folded in 2001, when some members steadfastly refused to accept a non-Scottish president. (Burnet, 'Hail Brither Scots o' Coaly Tyne', 16-17).

96   Burnet, 'Hail Brither Scots o' Coaly Tyne', 8; *Sunderland Daily Echo*, 12 May 1910, 3e.

97   Mrs Alice Adam, 'Looking Back', *The Hull Scot* (1974), 26, quoted in McCarthy, 'The Scots' Society of St Andrew', 214.

98   McCarthy, 'The Scots' Society of St Andrew', 219. The charge was made in the columns of the *Hull Scot* (1981), 11.

99   By May 1935 almost 200 copies of the *Bellshill Speaker* were being sold weekly in Corby (*Bellshill Speaker*, 24 May 1935, 5a).

100 Frederick Scopes, *The Development of Corby Works*, appendix xx, 237, 258.

101 Addis and Mercer, *Corby Remembers*, 145, 148-9.

102 *Kettering Leader*, 2 February 1934, 5f; *Bellshill Speaker*, 9 February 1934, 6c.

103 *Kettering Leader*, 30 March 1934, 12e.

104 Ibid., 7 March 1935, 7a-b.

105 Addis and Mercer, *Corby Remembers*, 46, 122-3.

106 British Library Sound Archive, Millennium Memory Bank, Ann Dean, interviewed by Willy Gilder, BBC Radio Northampton, 15 December 1999.

107 *Northamptonshire News*, 20 July 2002, accessed on http://www.bbc.co.uk/northamptonshire/news/2002/07/20/highland.shtml.

108 British Library Sound Archive, BBC 'Voices' recordings, Graham Martindale, interviewed by Willy Gilder, Radio Northampton, 14 April 2005.

109 Taylor, *A Cup of Kindness*, 138, quoting Doug Cameron, *New Statesman*, July 2002.

110 James McTurk (pseud.), 'Scotsmen in London' in *London*, vol 3, edited by Charles Knight (London, 1844), 322.
111 *Kettering Leader*, 24 August 1934, 1c; ibid., 31 May 1935, 6d; British Library Sound Archive, 'Lives in Steel', William Gibson Cockin.
112 *Kettering Leader*, 16 November 1934, 16d.
113 Ibid., 21 June 1935, 5d.
114 Both quoted in Stewart and Sheen, *Tyneside Scottish*, 26, 27.
115 T.W.H. Crosland, *The Unspeakable Scot* (London, 1902), 57-8, 190.
116 Ibid., 194.
117 Ibid., 197.
118 *The Unspeakable Crosland: A Scots Reply to 'The Unspeakable Scot'* (London, 1902); *The Egregious English* (London, 1903).
119 Taylor, *A Cup of Kindness*, 136, quoting from *Daily Telegraph*, 1961 (nd).
120 Edward Heathcote-Amery, 'The insidious rise of the McMafia', quoted in Stenhouse, *On the Make*, 28. See also Stenhouse, 'Time to heed those English rumblings', *The Sunday Times*, 9 May 2004.
121 *Daily Telegraph*, 14 March 2005. See also Jeremy Paxman, *The English: A Portrait of a People* (London, 1999), 43-8. Wheatcroft's comments are quoted in Bryan Curtis, 'Who rules London?' http://www.slate.com/id/2151854/ The Scottish Invasion, 19 October 2006.
122 Simon Heffer, 'Cronies and Sleaze: why do we pander to the Scot?', *Daily Mail*, 10 November 2001, 15; Simon Heffer, 'Now, more than ever, she is the Queen of England', *Sunday Telegraph*, 2 June 2002, np. See also Heffer, *Nor Shall My Sword. The Reinvention of England* (London, 1999).
123 Boris Johnston, 'Diary', *The Spectator*, 9 April 2005.
124 BBC online, http://www.bbc.co.uk/communicate/archive/ken_livingstone/page2.shtml, quoted in Stenhouse, *On the Make*, 198.
125 Ian Hay, *The Oppressed English* (Garden City, New York, 1917), 9, 30, 87.
126 Lord Barnett himself said in 2004 that his formula, devised in the 1970s, was outdated and only retained because of the power of the 'Scottish mafia' (Stenhouse, *On the Make*, 53).
127 http://www.gro-scotland.gov.uk/press/news2005/migration-statistics-from-census-2001.html
128 Paul Thompson with Tony Wailey and Trevor Lummis, *Living the Fishing* (London, 1983), 205.
129 See below, pp. 158-81, particularly Douglas Henderson's criticism of the activities of New Zealand recruitment agents on pp 165-66.
130 Stenhouse, *On the Make*, 225; Cal McCrystal, 'The "Little England" over the water: "White settlers" make up 15% of Skye's population', *The Independent on Sunday*, 25 September 1994, 4.
131 Murray Watson, *Being English in Scotland* (Edinburgh, 2003), 16-17, 126-45; Murray Watson, 'The English Diaspora: Discovering Scotland's Invisible Migrants – 1945 to 2000', *Journal of Scottish Historical Studies*, 22: 1 (May 2002), 23-49.
132 http://www.gro-scotland.gov.uk/statistics/theme/migration/census2001-migration-stats/index.html

Chapter 2: Legacies of War and New Dawns

1 E. Richards, *Britannia's Children. Emigration from England, Scotland, Wales and Ireland since 1600* (London and New York, 2004), 236; N.H. Carrier and J.R. Jeffery, *External Migration: A Study of the Available Statistics 1815–1950* (London, 1953), 93, 96-7, 100. There was a slightly greater divergence between Scotland and the British Isles in the statistics of inward movement in the 1930s. Within the four recorded destinations, Canada accounted for 37.6 per cent of inward movement, Australia for 25.5 per cent, the United States for 24.3 per cent and South Africa for 12.6 per cent, and inward movement from South Africa exceeded the outflow by 1,361.

2 For a full account of the *Iolaire* disaster, see John MacLeod, *When I Heard the Bell: The Loss of the* Iolaire (Edinburgh, 2010).

3 *Press and Journal*, 14 November 1923, 3c.

4 *Press and Journal*, 28 September 1923, 8f; 14 November 1923, 3c; Stornoway Town Council Minutes, 24 December 1923, vol. 12, p. 676.

5 Marjory Harper, *Emigration from Scotland Between the Wars: Opportunity or Exile?* (Manchester, 1998, pbk 2009), 93.

6 *Stornoway Gazette*, 11 February 1926, 4d.

7 Ibid., 5 April (5c), 26 July (5b), 30 August 1923 (4d).

8 New South Wales Bicentennial Oral History Project, National Library of Australia, Oral TRC 2301/137, interview with Angus Macdonald by Paula Hamilton, 1 September 1987.

9 *Hawkesbury Herald*, 24 July 1924, 3. Thanks to Angus Johnson for alerting me to this reference.

10 *Highland News*, 8 April 1911.

11 Library and Archives Canada [hereafter LAC], RG76, vol. 5, file 41, part 3 (C-4660); D.J. Murphy to J.O. Smith, 25 January 1923.

12 LAC, RG76,, vol. 632, part 1 (C-10446), D. J. Murphy to J.O. Smith, 19 December, 1923.

13 Iain MacLeòid, 'Bàs Baile' ('The Death of a Township'), in *An Tuil. Anthology of 20th-centutry Scottish Gaelic Verse*, edited by Ronald Black (Edinburgh, 1999), 412-17, 779. See also below, p. 173. I am grateful to Margaret MacIver for drawing this poem to my attention.

14 *Press and Journal*, 16 April 1923, 7g.

15 *Press and Journal*, 23 April 1923, 7g; *Glasgow Herald*, 23 April 1923, 11e; *Highland News*, 28 April 1923, 3b-c.

16 Harper, *Emigration from Scotland Between the Wars*, 98.

17 Ibid., 99.

18 LAC, RG76, vol. 248, file 179046, part 1 (C-10446), undated memorandum from Anne MacDonald to the Department of Immigration and Colonisation, October or November 1924.

19 The Canadian government began to appoint female officers in the 1920s, mainly to oversee female migration. (R. Mancuso, 'For Purity or Prosperity: Competing Nationalist Visions and Canadian Immigration Policy, 1919–30', *British Journal of Canadian Studies*, 23: 1(2010), 1-23.The reference is on page 3.)

20 *Scottish Farm Servant*, August 1927, 305, quoting statistics from the *Scottish Journal of Agriculture*.

21 The National Archives [hereafter TNA], LAB 2/1233/EDO289/1926, W. Eady to Mr Price, 18 June 1926.

22 For further details of dominion land schemes funded under the Empire Settlement Act, see S. Constantine (ed.), *Emigrants and Empire: British Settlement in the Dominions Between the Wars* (Manchester, 1990) and R. Mancuso, 'Three Thousand Families: English Canada's Colonizing Vision and British Family Settlement, 1919-39', *Journal of Canadian Studies*, 45, 3 (Fall 2011), 5-33.

23 LAC, RG76, vol. 49, file 1945, part 3, J. Obed Smith, Assistant Superintendent of Immigration, to W.D. Scott, Superintendent of Immigration, 22 April 1914, quoted in Ellen Scheinberg and Melissa K. Rombout, 'Projecting Images of the Nation: The Immigration Program and Its Use of Lantern Slides', *The Archivist*, no. 111 (1996), 13-24.

24 Author's interview with the late Annie Noble and Gilbert Buchan, Inverallochy, 16 September 1985.

25 H.D. Watson, *Kilrenny and Cellardyke: 800 Years of History* (Edinburgh, 1986), 192.

26 A. Slaven, *The Development of the West of Scotland, 1750-1960* (London, 1975), 185; C.H. Lee, 'Scotland, 1860-1939: growth and poverty', in R. Floud and P.A. Johnson (eds), *The Cambridge Economic History of Modern Britain, Volume 2: Economic Maturity, 1860-1939* (Cambridge, 2004), 428-55.

27 R.J. Finlay, 'National identity in crisis: politicians, intellectuals and the "end of Scotland", 1920-1939', *History*, 79 (1994), 244.

28 G.M. Thomson, *Scotland That Distressed Area* (Edinburgh, 1935), 5.

29 New South Wales Bicentennial Oral History Project, TRC/2301/54, interview with Jim Comerford, 15 May 1987, quoted in A. McCarthy, 'Personal Accounts of Leaving Scotland, 1921–1954', *Scottish Historical Review*, LXXXIII, 2, 216 (October 2004), 196-215. The quotation is on pages 203-4.

30 N. Gray, *The Worst of Times: An Oral History of the Great Depression in Britain* (London, 1985), 160.

31 C. Greig, *Not Forgotten: Memorials in Granite* (Moruya, privately published, 1993, revised 1998); A.V. Colefax, *Moruya's Golden Years* (Moruya, 1997).

32 Ellis Island Oral History Project, interview EI-547.

33 www.abdn.ac.uk/emigration. This figure excludes the 595 passengers who joined the *Marloch* and the *Metagama* in Lochboisdale and Stornoway. For an analysis of the database, see M. Harper and N.J. Evans, 'Socio-economic dislocation and inter-war emigration to Canada and the United States: a Scottish snapshot', *Journal of Imperial and Commonwealth History*, 34, 4, December 2006, 529-52.

34 Peter Morton Coan, *Ellis Island Interviews. In Their Own Words* (New York, 1997), 131.

35 www.ellisisland.org/

36 Of the 6,322 women in the Scottish Emigration Database, 37.5 per cent were wives accompanying their husbands. Domestic servants, cooks and housekeepers accounted for 47 per cent of the sample of employed women and factory workers for 12 per cent, including 69 individuals from Dundee. There were 70

shop assistants and 65 typists.

37 The pros and cons of using personal testimony are discussed in greater detail in Chapter 6, pp. 194-96

38 Ellis Island Oral History Project, interviews EI-435 (Cook); DP-46 (Hansen); EI-442 (Pedersen); NPS-146 (Quinn); EI-823 (Rohan).

39 Ibid,. interview EI-172.

40 Ibid., interview AKRF-127.

41 Ibid., interview EI-440.

42 Interview with Marge Glasgow, quoted in Coan, *Ellis Island Interviews*, 135.

43 LAC, RG76, vol. 435, file 652806, part 3 (C-10315), D.J. Murphy to M.V. Burnham, Canadian Government Superintendent of Female Immigration, 24 May 1923.

44 LAC, RG76, C-4661, vol. 5, file 41, part 3; *Scottish Farmer*, 25 July 1925, 983; 17 March 1928, 346.

45 *Scottish Farmer*, 2 October 1920, 1115.

46 South Australia State Records, South Australia Immigration Department, GRG 7/8/793, file 793.D.

47 *House of Commons Parliamentary Debates* [hereafter HCPD], vo. 264, col. 967, 14 April 1932.

48 LAC, RG76, vol. 230, file 127825, part 1, Justine Calderwood to matron of Canadian Women's Hostel, Toronto, 28 September 1925.

49 *Winning Through: Stories of Life on Canadian Farms, told by New British Settlers* (Ottawa, 1929), William Wilson, 25 March 1929.

50 *Stornoway Gazette*, 10 January 1924, 7b-c; 28 February 1924, 2f.

51 M.E. Campbell, *In Yesterday's Footsteps* (np, 1986), 147-8. For settlers' commendations of New Brunswick, see *Scottish Farmer*, 26 September 1925, 1244; 9 January 1926, 33; 24 October 1931, 1453.

52 Private collection, James Young Lind to mother, 17 October 1928.

53 Ibid., 13, 26 December, 14 November 1928, 19 March, 14 April 1929.

54 Ibid., 13 January 1929.

55 Ibid., 25 January, 25 February 1929.

56 In his letter of 19 March, James Young Lind had hinted at the possibility of return, when he 'thought maybe Father might be wanting me Home'. Some time after William Lind's death in 1934, James Young Lind was appointed Chairman and Managing Director of the Company, which grew into a large concern and was taken over by Tarmac in 1970. (Family information supplied by James Young Lind's son, the Reverend Michael Lind).

57 See, for instance, a passing comment about return migration 'on account of trade depression' in D. Mackinnon, 'Among the Gaelic-speaking Highlanders in Canada', *The Monthly Record of the Free Church of Scotland* [hereafter *Monthly Record*], November 1935, 280.

58 The lodges of the Daughters of Scotia (the Order's female counterpart) had 14,000 members and the ladies' auxiliaries numbered 7,000, making a total of 45,000 individuals connected with the movement in 1926. (*The Scotsman*, 3 August 1926, 5). 10 July 1932, 10; 17 July 1934, 7a.

59 *The Scotsman*, 5 August 1924, 7.

60 Ibid., 19 July 1932, 9.

61 Ibid., 25 May 1936, 8.
62 LAC, RG76, vol. 6, file 41, part 2 (C-4661), Noxon to W.J. Egan, Deputy Minister of Immigration, 7 February 1925; Harper, *Emigration from Scotland Between the Wars*, 100.
63 J. Wilkie, *Metagama. A Journey from Lewis to the New World* (Edinburgh, 2nd edition, 2001).
64 *Saturday Night* (Toronto), 21 July 1923.
65 *Stornoway Gazette*, June 1923, 4c; 28 June 1923, 5e.
66 *Saturday Night*, 21 July 1923.
67 LAC, RG76, file 968592, part 3 (C-10446), H. Roy to F.C. Blair, 20 August 1924.
68 Provincial Archives of British Columbia, Reynoldston Research and Studies Collection. T0238:0001, George Bowman Anderson interviewed by Marlene Karnouk, 26 November 1973.
69 James Young Lind to mother, 17 October, 14 November 1928.
70 Ibid., 1924, p 156.
71 R. McLeod, Free Church Manse, Dunoon, 'Our congregations in Canada', *Monthly Record*, November 1930, 280-1.
72 *Acts and Reports of the General Assembly of the Free Church of Scotland, Report of the Foreign Missions, Colonial, Continental and Jewish Missions Committee*, 1925, p. 121.
73 G.N.M. Collins, 'A visit to Canada', *Monthly Record*, August 1931, 207.
74 D. Mackinnon, 'Among the Gaelic-speaking Highlanders in Canada', *Monthly Record*, November 1935, 280.
75 Norman Campbell, 'A tour among Free Churchmen in Canada', *Monthly Record*, December 1932, 303.
76 Neil Macleod, 'The claims of Canada', *Monthly Record*, February 1929, 42.
77 *Acts and Reports of the General Assembly of the Free Church of Scotland, Report of the Foreign Missions Committee*, in *Monthly Record*, June 1936, 143.
78 *Acts and Reports of the General Assembly of the Free Church of Scotland, Report of the Foreign Missions, Colonial and Continental and Jewish Missions Committee*, 1926, 352.
79 R.J. Macleod, 'A trip to Canada', *Monthly Record*, December 1924, 198.
80 Stornoway Public Library, Minute books of the Lewis Society of Detroit, vol. 1, 28 June 1924; January 1933; 22 April, 27 May 1933.
81 Ibid., 23 February 1924, 27 March 1926.
82 James Young Lind to mother, 14 April 1929.
83 Ellis Island Oral History Project, interview EI-440, Margaret Jack Kirk.

Chapter 3: Sponsored Emigration and Settlement

1 *House of Commons Parliamentary Debates* [hereafter *HCPD*], vol. 174, col. 570, 28 May 1924.
2 *Aberdeen Journal*, 24 August 1911, 3b; *All the World* (October 1922), 427.
3 *HCPD*, vol. 153, col. 582, 26 April 1922.
4 *Press and Journal*, 30 January 1924, 6d; *Stornoway Gazette*, 23 September 1927, 5e.
5 www.abdn.ac.uk/emigration. There was a total of twelve sailings. The *Metagama*

ENDNOTES

made three trips and the *Marburn* two.

6   Alexina Grewer, interviewed by Marilyn Barber on 3 March 1985 for 'Domestic servant interviews' (private collection).

7   Letter from F.H. Mather, Winnipeg, published in *Workers' Weekly*, 31 July 1925, 6.

8   *Scottish Manhood*, September 1928, 16; March 1929, 17.

9   The magazine changed its name to *Scottish Manhood* in October 1926, having previously been entitled *The Scottish Red Triangle News*.

10 *Scottish Manhood*, May 1929, 17.

11 Marjory Harper, *Emigration from Scotland Between the Wars: Opportunity or Exile?* (Manchester, 1998, pbk. 2009), 169-73. See also below, Chapter 5.

12 A.G. Scholes, *Education for Empire Settlement: A Study of Juvenile Migration* (London, 1932), 71-90.

13 For an expanded description and analysis of Quarrier's emigration schemes, see Marjory Harper, 'Halfway to Heaven or Hell on Earth? Canada's Scottish Child Immigrants' in C. Kerrigan (ed.), *The Immigrant Experience* (Guelph, 1992), 165-83; Harper, *Emigration from Scotland Between the Wars*, 185-9; Marjory Harper, *Adventurers and Exiles: The Great Scottish Exodus* (London, 2003), 160-96; Marjorie Kohli, *The Golden Bridge: Young Immigrants to Canada, 1833–1939* (Toronto, 2003). The emigration dimension is incorporated within a wider history of Quarrier's in Anna Magnusson, *The Quarriers Story: A History of Quarriers* (Edinburgh, 2006, revised edition).

14 Quarrier's Orphan Homes of Scotland, Bridge of Weir, uncatalogued case files. Two other siblings – Murdo and Malcolmina – had also been taken into Quarrier's.

15 Case files, Thomas, Robert, James, William and Alexander. The five brothers had all been admitted together after their father and mother had died of tuberculosis in 1916 and 1918 respectively.

16 Quarrier's Orphan Homes of Scotland, *A Narrative of Facts Relative to Work done for Christ in Connection with the Orphan and Destitute Children's Emigration Home, Glasgow* [hereafter *Narrative of Facts*], 1920, p. 29; 1921, p. 28.

17 *Narrative of Facts*, 1930.

18 The reunions were organised by David Lorente of Renfrew, Ontario, son of a Quarrier boy and founder of 'Home Children Canada'. See http://www.bytown.net/homekids.htm

19 *Narrative of Facts*, 1919, 29.

20 Reports by Claude Winters, 5 August 1931, 6 January 1932, 15 July 1932 in William's case file.

21 Claude Winters to W. Douglas, 5 January 1932 in Frederick's case file.

22 Frank Ogden to Claude Winters, 20 October 1932 in ibid.

23 Case files, Margaret H and Jessie H. Winters suspected there was an illicit relationship between Jessie and her employer.

24 Case file, Norman R.

25 Letter from Alexander McP. to his son, 16 March 1930, quoted in John's case file.

26 Claude Winters to William Douglas, 19 August 1932, quoted in Jeanie's case file.

27 Letter from Travellers' Aid to Winters, 3 December 1929, quoted in Norah's

case file; case file, Robert A.

28 David Lorente, *The Little Emigrants*, BBC Radio Scotland, 25 December 1994.

29 Ibid.

30 Pamela Power, CBC news feature, 1994.

31 *Narrative of Facts*, 1929, 44.

32 Library and Archives Canada [hereafter LAC], RG76, file 234636 (C-78221),
    annual report of the Cossar Boys' Training Farm Inc., 1927-8, by Duncan
    Watson; Harper, *Emigration from Scotland Between the Wars*, 176, 185.

33 *Press and Journal*, 15 April 1924, 5f.

34 National Records of Scotland [hereafter NRS], AF51/171, annual report of the
    Cossar Boys' Training Farms Inc., 21 December 1923.

35 Undated letter from 'JW' in annual report of the Cossar Boys' Training Farms
    Inc., 1927-8. For further examples of letters from emigrants and employers,
    see Harper, *Emigration from Scotland Between the Wars*, 176-7; Marjory
    Harper, 'Cossar's Colonists: juvenile migration to New Brunswick in the 1920s',
    Acadiensis, XXVIII, 1 (Autumn 1998), 47-65.

36 LAC, RG76, vol. 567, file 811910, part 2 (C-10646-7), Hugh Paterson to his
    mother, 'Sunday 6th' [September 1924].

37 LAC, RG76, vol. 568, file 811910, part 1 (C-10647), G. Bogue Smart, department of
    Immigration and Colonisation, Chief Inspector of British Immigrant Children and
    Receiving Homes, to John Jackson, superintendent of Gagetown farm, 17 August
    1928.

38 LAC, RG76, vol. 568, file 811910, part 1 (C-10647), Margaret Waugh to G.G.
    Melvin, Chief Medical Officer, Fredericton, New Brunswick, 14 November
    1924.

39 LAC, RG76, C-10646-7, vol. 567, file 811910, part 3, D.J. Murphy to G. Bogue
    Smart, 4 July 1930.

40 LAC, RG76, vol. 568, file 811910, part 1 (C-10647), Rev. William Smith,
    Gagetown, to Department of the Interior, 14 October 1913; ibid., vol. 282, file
    234636 (C-7821), F.C. Blair to J.A. Murray, 24 June 1931.

41 *Glasgow Herald*, 14 April 1923, 7; 6 April 1923, 5.

42 See above, p. 97.

43 For amplification of post-war policy, see Stephen Constantine, 'The British
    Government, Child Welfare, and Child Migration to Australia after 1945', *The
    Journal of Imperial and Commonwealth History*, 30: 1 (January 2002), 99-132.
    In 2010 the film, *Oranges and Sunshine*, directed by Jim Loach, told the story
    of the campaign waged by Nottingham social worker, Margaret Humphreys, to
    expose scandals and reunite children and parents.

44 The National Archives [hereafter TNA], MH 102/1995, Emigration of Children
    under the Big Brother Scheme, undated memorandum by Australia House, ref.
    942.834/2; *The Star*, 8 December 1953.

45 *Press and Journal*, 3 January 2007, 7.

46 For a full account of the scheme, see V.C. Goodall, *Flockhouse: A History of the
    New Zealand Sheepowners' Acknowledgement of Debt to British Seamen Fund*
    (Palmerston North, 1962).

47 *Evening Post*, vol. CX, issue 110, 6 November 1930, p. 17.

48 TNA, MH 102/1565, Emigration of Deprived Children to New Zealand,

Reopening of Flock House, undated description of the scheme.

49 *Press and Journal*, 3 January 2007, 7.

50 In one case, the sister, C.L. Stewart from Bellshill, went first, in 1927 and was followed by her brother three years later.

51 *Press and Journal*, 11 November 1925, 8.

52 Flock House, http://genebug.net/flock.html

53 *Press and Journal*, 28 July 1925, 5f.

54 *Evening Post*, vol. CXIII, issue 58, 9 March 1932, 8. Papers Past.

55 TNA, MH 102/1565.Emigration of Deprived Children to New Zealand, Reopening of Flock House, undated description of the scheme.

56 TNA, MH 102/1565, memorandum by J.M.W. Maxwell, 23 June 1948; D.M. Rosling to M.C. Smith, 1 July 1948; C. Knowles to D.M. Rosling, 24 August 1948.

57 *Press and Journal*, 3 January 2007, 7.

58 Michael Fethney, *The Absurd and the Brave. CORB – The true account of the British Government's World War II Evacuation of Children Overseas* (Lewes, Sussex, 2000), 235, 246.

59 Jean Lorimer, *Pilgrim Children* (London, 1942), 6-7.

60 Fethney, *The Absurd and the Brave*, 47-51.

61 The ships were the *Ruahine* for New Zealand, the *Llandaff Castle* for South Africa and the *Bayano* and *City of Paris* to Canada. (Fethney, *The Absurd and the Brave*, 121. See also TNA, DO 131/5, CORB (Scot.), Scottish Advisory Council, Minutes of Meetings).

62 Geoffrey Shakespeare, *Let Candles Be Brought In* (London, 1949), 251.

63 Fethney, *The Absurd and the Brave*, 64-5.

64 Imperial War Museum [hereafter IWM], 1446 87/23/1, Private Papers of S. Mackay, manuscript account by Shiela Mackay.

65 Letter from Finlayson to Michael Fethney, quoted in Fethney, *The Absurd and the Brave*, 81.

66 TNA, DO 131/74, Confidential Report to CORB on U2 Party submitted by Roland Cartwright, 28 September 1940.

67 IWM, manuscript account by Shiela Mackay.

68 TNA, 1446 87/23/1, private papers of S. Mackay, clipping from unnamed Grangemouth newspaper, 4 September 1940.

69 IWM, 107 89/6/1, Private papers of E.F.M. Sowerbutts, 'Days of Empire', vol. III, 'Hire and Fire', unpublished typescript memoir by Sowerbutts.

70 Fethney, *The Absurd and the Brave*, 177.

71 Ibid., 253, 194.

72 TNA, DO 131/109, CORB, Canada 3, pp 803, 885.

73 Archives of Ontario, A01-V01-03-021-02-03-03, RG 9-7-8, b387078, Ontario House, General files sent down by Colonel Young, 'B', 1944 to 1946, Mrs James Bruce, 26 Landsdowne Crescent, Glasgow to George Drew, Premier of Ontario, 18 June 1944.

74 Ibid., E.J. Young, Executive Assistant, Ontario House, Toronto, to Margaret Bruce, 11 July 1945.

75 Fethney, *The Absurd and the Brave*, 21, 64-5, 70.

76 TNA, DO 131/109.

77 Ibid.

78 TNA, DO 131/104, CORB to the Edinburgh Council for Social Service, nd
79 *Glasgow Herald*, 26 July 1945, 4d-3.
80 'The Bay Boys', BBC Scotland, 4 December 2011. http://www.bbc.co.uk/
    programmes/b017ptsn
81 For the early history of Scottish involvement, see Suzanne Rigg, *Men of Spirit
    and Enterprise. Scots and Orkneymen in the Hudson's Bay Company 1780-1821*
    (Edinburgh, 2011).
82 Saskatchewan Archives Board, MS 1162/28. File of correspondence relating to
    HBC mainly concerning applications for various posts in the Company, 1913-
    14; MS 1162/29/1 – accounts, testimonials and associated papers relating to the
    HBC, 1913-14. F.C. Ingrams to Ranald Macdonald, 30 October 1913. See also
    Ingrams to Macdonald, 10 March 1914.
83 Department of Anthropology, University of Aberdeen, 'Material Histories: Scots
    and Aboriginal Peoples in the Canadian Fur Trade', http://www.abdn.ac.uk/
    materialhistories/stories.php
84 *Press and Journal*, 6 March 1925, 2b.
85 Jock Gibb, *Tales from a Fur Trader*, (Rosetta Projects, np, nd), 5.
86 Author's interview with Nellie Wallace, Portlethen, Aberdeen, 24 April 2010.
87 Jock Gibb, *Tales from a Fur Trader*, 24.
88 Email to author, 18 February 2010.
89 Email from Alistair McGregor, Vernon, BC, to author, 18 February 2010.
    Rothesay-born Alistair was recruited in 1964.
90 Interview with John Wallace, Portlethen, Aberdeen, 24 April 2010.
91 Department of Anthropology, University of Aberdeen, 'Material Histories',
    Angus Pelham Burn, 20 July 2007, http://www.abdn.ac.uk/~wad023/people.
    php?id=1 and interviewed by author, 6 April 2010.

Chapter 4: Post-war Impulses, Initiatives and Identities

1 Rev. Arthur Morris Russell, interviewed by Dr Steven Schwinghamer, 16 May
   2006, *Our Canadian Stories*, catalogue no. 06.05.16, Canadian Museum of
   Immigration, Pier 21, Halifax, Nova Scotia.
2 J.M. Bumsted, 'Scots', *The Canadian Encyclopedia* (Historical Foundation of
   Canada, 2008, http://www.thecanadianencyclopedia.com/articles/scots. Russell
   subsequently moved to Newfoundland, Toronto and the Bahamas.
3 *House of Commons Parliamentary Papers* [hereafter *HCPP*] 1961-62, Cmnd.
   1586. Commonwealth Relations Office, *Seventh Report of the Oversea
   Migration Board*, December 1961. Chapter II, Migration in 1960, p. 11.
4 *Annual Abstract of Statistics*, 1952-73 ('Movement direct by sea of immigrants
   and emigrants between the United Kingdom and non-European countries',
   1952-63; 'Migration into and out from the United Kingdom, by nationality and
   country of last permanent or intended future residence', 1964-72). This is a gross
   figure.
5 *Scotland's Population 2001. The Registrar General's Annual Review of
   Demographic Trends* (Edinburgh, 2002), Chapter 5, 'Migration', p. 32. A paper
   of the Scottish Economic Planning Council states that migration peaked in 1964,
   with a post-war record figure of 41,000. National Records of Scotland [hereafter

NRS], AF70/611, SEPC 65(1), 'Basic Problems of the Scottish Economy', 10 March 1965.

6 *Census 1961, Scotland, volume 3 – Age, Martial Condition and General Tables* (Edinburgh, 1965), xx; Office of National Statistics, *Registrar General's Annual Report, 1992*, Section 0, Natural Change and Migration, 01.1. Intercensal and annual changes in births, deaths and migration and their effect on population, Scotland, 1861 to 1991 and 1981 to 1991.

7 NRS, AF70/611, SEPC (65)1, 'Basic Problems of the Scottish Economy; 65(10), The National Plan and Industrial Growth'.

8 NRS, AF70/609, SEPB 69/24, Working Group on Population: Summary of Interim Report, Papers attached to meeting of the SEPB, 24 April 1969.

9 HCPP 1961-62, Cmnd. 1586, Commonwealth Relations Office, *Seventh Report of the Oversea Migration Board*, December 1961, Chapter 2, Migration in 1960, p. 11.

10 HCPP 1965-66, Cmnd. 2861, *Commonwealth Relations Office. Oversea Migration Board. Statistics for 1964*, UK passport holders leaving the UK by all routes, table based on the International Passenger Survey; Janet Dobson and Gail McLaughlan, 'International Migration to and from the UK 1975-99: consistency, change and implications for the labour market', *Population Trends* 106 (Winter 2001), 29-38, http://www.geog.ucl.ac.uk/research/mobility-identity-and-security/migration-research-unit/pdfs/pop_trends.pdf.

11 Jenel Virden, *Good-Bye, Piccadilly: British War Brides in America* (Urbana and Chicago, 1996), 4; HCPP 1953-54 [Cmd. 9261], *First Annual Report of the Oversea Migration Board*, July 1954; HCPP 1955–56 [Cmd. 9835], *Second Report of the Oversea Migration Board*, August 1956; Eric Richards, 'Australia and Scotland: the Evolution of a Long-Distance Relationship', *Australian Journal of Politics and History,* 56: 4 (2010), 485-502; Richard Finlay, *Modern Scotland 1914-2000* (London, 2004), 307. Returns for South Africa and Southern Rhodesia (later the Federation of Rhodesia and Nyasaland) in the 1940s and 1950s simply record British-born immigrants.

12 Duncan Sim, *American Scots. The Scottish Diaspora and the USA* (Edinburgh, 2011), 21, 36; T.M. Devine, *To the Ends of the Earth. Scotland's Global Diaspora, 1750–2010* (London, 2011), 274.

13 Devine, *To the Ends of the Earth*, 276; Sim, *American Scots*, 21.

14 Richard Finlay, *Modern Scotland*, 307.

15 Sim, *American Scots*, 36, 38. By 2000, the figure had fallen to 5,406,421 (1.7 per cent) of the population, and the Scots had dropped one place in the league table.

16 N.H. Carrier and J.R. Jeffery, *External Migration: A Study of the Available Statistics 1815-1950* (London, 1955), 39-40.

17 *Overseas War Brides: Stories from the Women who Followed their Hearts to Australia* (East Roseville, NSW, 2001), 4.

18 Good Housekeeping, *A War Bride's Guide to the USA* (London, 2006, repr. from June 1945), 13, 14.

19 Pier 21, Online story collection, war brides, May Ella Comrie, 2. http://www.pier21.ca/research/collections/the-story-collection/online-story-collection/war-brides

20 *Overseas War Brides*, 13.

21 Ibid, Stella Higgins, 1; Jenny Matheson Zorn, née McGill, 3.
22 Ibid., Eleanore Coburn, 2.
23 Susanna Moodie, *Roughing it in the Bush, or Forest Life in Canada*, edited by Carl Ballstadt (Ottawa, 1988), 83.
24 Val Wood, *War Brides. They Followed their Hearts to New Zealand* (Auckland, 1991), 139, 173.
25 Ibid., Isabella Ross Horvath, nee Wilcox. At the behest of the Canadian Wives' Bureau, 32 such clubs were established across England and Scotland.
26 Ibid., Christina Sharpe; Dorothy Blaikie, née Shipley, 1.
27 Barbara Ladouceur and Phyllis Spence (eds), *Blackouts to Bright Lights. Canadian War Bride Stories* (Vancouver, 1996), 234.
28 Quoted in Barry Broadfoot, *The Immigrant Years. From Britain and Europe to Canada 1945-1967* (Vancouver, 1986), 44.
29 *Echoes*, 174 (February 1944), 2, quoted in Katie Pickles, *Female Imperialism and National Identity. Imperial Order Daughters of the Empire* (Manchester, 2002), 104.
30 'Sally' (pseudo.) quoted in Meylnda Jarratt, 'The War Brides of New Brunswick' (MA thesis, University of New Brunswick, 1988?) consulted online at http://www.canadianwarbrides.com/thesis.asp. The couple eventually divorced after the children had grown up. See also Jarratt, *Captured Hearts: New Brunswick's War Brides* (Fredericton, NB, 2008).
31 Barbara B. Barrett *et. al.* (eds), *We Came from over the Sea. British War Brides in Newfoundland* (Portugal Cove, Nfld, 1996), 108.
32 Sometimes referred to as a '$5,000 cure', depending on the time of return. (A. James Hammerton, 'Epic stories and the mobility of modernity: narratives of British migration to Canada and Australia since 1945', *Australian-Canadian Studies*, 19: 1 (2001), 48.
33 W.S. Cruickshank, 'Emigration from Scotland', *The Scotsman*, 4 May 1950, 6.
34 Harold Macmillan, speech to a Conservative rally in Bedford, 20 July 1957. http://news.bbc.co.uk/onthisday/hi/dates/stories/july/20/newsid_3728000/3728225.stm
35 F.G. Brownell, *British Immigration to South Africa* (Pretoria, 1985), 46, from *The Economist*, CLXXXII, 5920, 9 February 1957, 456.
36 Angus Maude, 'Flight from Britain', *The Spectator*, 1 February 1957, 137. Sauce for the goose was not sauce for the gander, since Maude himself was to leave for Australia in 1958 to become editor of the *Sydney Morning Herald*.
37 E.M. Johnston, Beattock, 'Fuller life in rural areas', letter to *The Scotsman*, 23 May 1950, 6. See also below, p. 168.
38 Finlay, *Modern Scotland*, 304. Finlay specifies the car, electrical and chemical industries.
39 Ibid., 303-4.
40 *Inquiry into the Scottish Economy 1960–1961: Report of a Committee appointed by the Scottish Council (Development and Industry) under the chairmanship of J. N. Toothill* (Edinburgh, 1961), 20, 108-9.
41 Finlay, *Modern Scotland*, 104.
42 Ibid., 20.
43 Ibid., 183.

44 NRS, AF70/611, SEPC (65)1, Scottish Economic Planning Council, 'Basic Problems of the Scottish Economy', March 1965; SEPC (65)10, SEPC, 'The National Plan and Industrial Growth', nd.

45 NRS, AF70/606, SEPB50/65, Minutes of Meeting of Scottish Economic Planning Board, 29 July 1965; ibid., AF70/606, SEPB59/65, 'Supply of Skilled Craftsmen in Engineering Industries in Scotland, c. 1963-8'; AF70/607, Inter-regional migration, note by Ministry of Labour, 30 September 1965. The 208 companies contacted for the Ministry of Labour survey each employed 580 or more workers. Forms were returned by 160 companies, which employed a total workforce of 258,846. The SEPB acknowledged flaws in the sample, including the short period covered and the reliance on the judgement of a third person rather than on the direct answers of the migrants themselves.

46 Geoffrey Goodman, 'Harold Wilson: Leading Labour Beyond Pipe Dreams', *The Guardian*, 25 May 1995

47 NRS, AF70/607, SEPB 69/65, 'Inter-regional migration, note by Ministry of Labour, 30 September 1965. The survey reported a total of 564 migrants among their salaried professional, scientific and technical staff, all but three of them male. The discrepancy between the totals of 429 and 564 mentioned - somewhat confusingly – in different parts of the report is probably because the smaller figure referred to those who had left their job as well as their country, while the latter included those who had been transferred by their employer.

48 *The Monthly Record of the Free Church of Scotland* [hereafter *Monthly Record*], February 1951, 28.

49 John Stobbs, 'The Highlander's Last Chance?', *Picture Post*, 21 November 1953

50 *Monthly Record*, December 1953, 240.

51 Ibid., April 1965, 65.

52 NRS, AF70/606, SEPB45/65, Draft Final Report of the Advisory Panel on the Highlands and Islands, 1965.

53 STUC Archive, Glasgow Caledonian University, GB1847 STUC, STUC Bulletin, September/October 1964, 375, p. 6, contained in loose leaf folder in Annual Reports of the Scottish Trades Union Congress, Highlands Conference, Inverness, 26 February 1965.

54 NRS, AF70/610, SEPB (69)54, South West Development Study, Note by Scottish Office, September 1969.

55 Maxwell Gaskin, *North East Scotland: A Survey and Proposals* (Edinburgh, 1969). See also AF70/610, SEPB69(44), summary of Gaskin Report.

56 Stephen Constantine, 'Waving Goodbye? Australia, Assisted Passages, and the Empire and Commonwealth Settlement Acts, 1945-72', *The Journal of Imperial and Commonwealth History*, 26: 2 (1998), 176-195. The reference to the legislation is on page 176.

57 *HCPP*, vol. XVIII, Cmd 9621, 1953-4. *First Annual Report of the Oversea Migration Board, July 1954*, 7.

58 Constantine, 'Waving Goodbye?', 176.

59 Reg Appleyard et al, *The Ten Pound Immigrants* (London, 1988); 2; Freda Hawkins, *Critical Years in Immigration: Australia and Canada Compared* (Kingston and Montreal, 1989), 35; Marjory Harper and Stephen Constantine, *Migration and Empire* (Oxford, 2010), 59.

60 *The Scotsman*, 30 August 1950, 5.

61 Harry Martin, *Angels and Arrogant Gods: Migration Officers and Migrants Reminisce, 1945-85* (Canberra, 1989), 54-5.

62 http://www.nzhistory.net.nz/culture/assisted-immigration/leaving-the-grey-uk from *New Zealand Official Year Book*.

63 Megan Hutching, *Long Journey for Sevenpence: An Oral History of Assisted Immigration to New Zealand from the United Kingdom, 1947–1975* (Wellington, 1999), 62, 64; John E. Martin, *Holding the Balance. A History of New Zealand's Department of Labour 1891-1995* (Christchurch, 1996), 272.

64 Archives New Zealand [hereafter ANZ], L1 22/1/37, pt. 3, Monthly Report from Chief Migration Officer, London, as at 31 December1955, p. 2 (report dated 24 January 1956).

65 Alan Lennox-Boyd, MP for Mid-Bedfordshire, *HCPD*, quoted in *The Scotsman*, 2 May 1950, 4. Previously they had been allowed to transfer £5,000; Jean Bruce, *After the War* (Don Mills, Ont., 92.

66 Quoted in Broadfoot, *The Immigrant Years*, 89.

67 *The Times*, 19 January 1950, 10b, advertised single transatlantic fares on the Cunard liner *Stratheden* as £57 tourist class and £107 first class.

68 Quoted in Bruce, *After the War*, 93.

69 Hugh Keenleyside, quoted in Bruce, *After the War*, 91.

70 *Canada, House of Commons, Debates*, 1955, p. 1254, quoted in Anthony H. Richmond, *Post-War Immigrants in Canada* (Toronto, 1967), 3.

71 BBC Written Archives Centre [hereafter BBC WAC], Home Service [hereafter HS] *Enterprise and Achievement. Lands in Search of People*. Programme 2, 22 November 1948.

72 *The Scotsman*, 7 January 2012, 33. See also http://www.emigrate2.co.uk/.

73 John M. MacKenzie, *Propaganda and Empire. The Manipulation of British Public Opinion, 1880-1960* (*Manchester*, 1984), 88; 'Scotland on screen', http://scotlandonscreen.org.uk/database/record.php?usi=007-000-000-428-C. In 1929 there were 113 cinemas in Glasgow.

74 MacKenzie, *Propaganda and Empire*, 130, 137-9.

75 J. Richards, 'Imperial heroes for a post-imperial age: films and the end of empire' in S. Ward (ed.), *British Culture and the End of Empire* (Manchester, 2001), 132.

76 *The Manchester Guardian*, 6 March 1950, p6, c5. Other titles included *High Country Muster, High Country Farm, Meet New Zealand, Golden Boy, Exotic Forests* and *Beautiful New Zealand*. See Alistair Fox, Barry Keith Grant and Hilary Radner, *New Zealand Cinema: Interpreting the Past* (Bristol, 2011), 169-71.

77 Martin, *Holding the Balance*, 275.

78 Archives of Ontario [hereafter AO], RG 9-7-7, B236007, Ontario House promotional files, 'Articles and Speeches 1961–64', 1 MM/HGD/HFW, unattributed report dated 29 August 1962.

79 Ibid.

80 Ibid., folder labelled 'Advertising, 1963-67', Hamish Ogilvy, advertisement manager, *Montrose Review*, to Ontario Immigration Branch, 28 July 1967; P.R. Bliss, Assistant Public Relations Officer, Ontario House, to Miss Gibson, Thames Advertising Service Ltd, London, 7 August 1967. The other newspapers were

the *Kincardineshire Observer* and the *Mearns Leader*. UK nurses' salary statistics were kindly supplied by Dr Anne Cameron, Royal College of Nursing Archives, Edinburgh, from an untitled internal document prepared by the Labour Relations Department of the RCN in c. 1984 (RCN/28/11AB). Email from Anne Cameron to author, 3 February 2012.

81 AO, RG 9-7-7-, B236007, container 146K, Trans EDEV-00003, Employment for visiting Canadians to Attorney General – Papers and Miscellaneous, Folder labelled 'Immi Film Show Glasgow No. 28/68'. The films were also shown at the Highlanders' Institute in Glasgow. The Dundee venue was the YMCA Auditorium, with a seating capacity of 500, and in Edinburgh the film was shown at the Music Hall Assembly Rooms, with a seating capacity of 1,000.

82 MacKenzie, *Propaganda and Empire*, 141.

83 Quoted in Hutching, *Long Journey for Sevenpence*, 91.

84 ANZ, LI 22/1/37 pt. 3, Monthly Report from Chief Migration Officer, London, as at January 1955, p. 1 (report dated 15 February 1955); *Manchester Guardian*, 29 January 1955. 'Teleclub', broadcast fortnightly, was the BBC's first dedicated series for teenagers.

85 I am grateful to Jeff Walden of the BBC Written Archives for guiding me through the complexities of card indexes and other finding aids.

86 Information supplied by Dr Simon Potter, from his forthcoming book, *Broadcasting Empire: the BBC and the British World, 1922–1970* (Oxford, 2012).

87 BBC WAC, HS, *Enterprise and Achievement, Lands in Search of People*, Programme 1, 15 November 1948.

88 Ibid., Programme 2, 22 November 1948.

89 Ibid., Programme 5, 13 December 1948.

90 Ibid., Programme 4, 6 December 1948.

91 Ibid., Programme 7, 3 January 1949.

92 BBC WAC, HS, *New Lands for Old: A Report to the People on Commonwealth Emigration*, narrated by Iven Senson, 13 June 1952.

93 Ibid.

94 BBC WAC, HS, Radio Talks Scripts pre-1970, Maurice Whitbread, *One Who Came Back*, 26 March 1957.

95 BBC WAC, HS, *A Land Beyond the Sea*, 6 June 1963.

96 BBC WAC, Light Programme [hereafter LP], *Woman's Hour*, Marian Cutler, 'Do you want to emigrate?', 30 January 1947.

97 BBC WAC, LP, *Woman's Hour*, Christine Cook, 'Women and Emigration', 21, 28 October, 4 November 1947.

98 BBC WAC, LP, *Woman's Hour*, Joyce Thom, 'Letter from New Zealand – Emigration', 6 March 1957.

99 BBC WAC, LP, *Woman's Hour*, 'Emigrating to Canada' by Mrs O'Higgins, 19 March 1957; ibid., Radio 2 [R2], Anne Howells interviewing Brenda Green, 'Going to Australia', 21 May 1968.

100 BBC WAC, HS, *Enterprise and Achievement. Lands in Search of People*, programme 2, 22 November 1948.

101 Dudley Illingworth, 'Emigrants to Canada', *The Spectator*, 15 April 1949, 514-16.

102 *The Times*, 7 November 1957, 7.

103 Hutching, *Long Journey for Sevenpence*, 126, 47.

104 See above, p 73.

105 A. James Hammerton, 'Postwar British emigrants and the "transnational moment": exemplars of a "mobility of modernity"?' in *Connected Worlds: History in Transnational Perspective*, edited by Ann Curthoys and Marilyn Lake (Canberra, 2005), 132.

106 Harper and Constantine, *Migration and Empire*, 334. See also above, pp. 77-8.

107 Broadfoot, *The Immigrant Years*, 64-6. The interviewee is unnamed, and the date of her emigration is not given.

108 A. James Hammerton and Alistair Thomson, *Ten Pound Poms. Australia's Invisible Migrants* (Manchester, 2005), 127-32, 167-88.

109 BBC WAC, LP, *Woman's Hour*, Ida Jenkins interviewed on British migrants, 26 June 1967.

110 Martin, *Angels and Arrogant Gods*, 25.

111 Richmond, *Post-War Immigrants in Canada*, 244-5; Committee on Social Patterns, Commonwealth Immigration Advisory Council, *The Departure of Settlers from Australia, Final Report* (Canberra, 1967), 12; *Inquiry into the Departure of Settlers from Australia, Final Report, July 1973* (Canberra, 1973), 8.

112 Henry G. Dalton, *The History of British Guiana*, 2 vols (London, 1855), I, 307.

113 Stornoway Public Library, Minute Books of the Lewis Society of Detroit, vol. 3, 1954–72, 23 February 1963.

114 Ibid., 25 March 1967; Accounts Book 1926-45.

115 BBC WAC, HS, *Enterprise and Achievement. Lands in Search of People*, Programmes 1 and 5, 15 November, 13 December 1948.

116 BBC WAC, Radio Talks Scripts, pre-1970, Oliver Duff, *The Scots of Otago*, 24 June 1948.

117 *Monthly Record*, April 1950, 69.

118 Ibid., February 1955, 33.

119 See above, p. 84.

120 For reflections on the Detroit congregation, see below, pp. 218, 226.

121 *Acts and Reports of the General Assembly of the Free Church of Scotland, Report of the Colonial Missions Committee 1953*, 149-50 (Professor D. MacKenzie).

122 Ibid., 1971, 118; 1973, 112; 1974, 127.

123 Sim, *American Scots*, 1, 12; Devine, *To the Ends of the Earth*, 277, 284.

124 Sim, *American Scots*, 93.

125 Ibid., 126-7, 197-9.

126 Paul Basu, *Highland Homecomings: Genealogy and Heritage Tourism in the Scottish Diaspora* (London, 2007).

127 Hammerton, 'Postwar British emigrants', 127.

Chapter 5: The Dysfunctional Diaspora

1 Runrig, 'Rocket to the Moon', verse 4, from *The Cutter and the Clan* (1998).

2 *House of Commons Parliamentary Papers* [hereafter HCPP], 1802-3 (45) IV 1, Thomas Telford, *A Survey and Report of the Coasts and Central Highlands of*

Scotland (1802).

3   Marjory Harper, 'Adventure or exile? The Scottish emigrant in fiction', *Scottish Literary Journal*, 23: 1 (May 1996), 21-32.

4   *Chambers' Edinburgh Journal*, I (9 June 1832), 149; *Aberdeen Herald*, 20 September 1845.

5   Charlotte Erickson, 'The encouragement of emigration by British trade unions, 1850–1900', *Population* Studies, 3: 3 (December 1949), 248-73; Marjory Harper and Stephen Constantine, *Migration and Empire* (Oxford, 2010), 283.

6   Library and Archives Canada [hereafter LAC], RG76, vol. 405, file 590687, part 1 (C-10294), Maclennan's report for week ending 22 February 1908; ibid., report for week ending 4 October 1910.

7   'Acres of Dreams: Settling the Canadian Prairies', exhibition at the Canadian Museum of Civilisation, 2005-6. Information from Dr Steven Schwinghamer, curator of the Canadian Museum of Immigration at Pier 21.

8   Marjory Harper, *Emigration from North-East Scotland*, vol. 1, *Willing Exiles* (Aberdeen, 1988), 259-68.

9   *Otago Daily Times*, 20 August 1872, anonymous letter to the editor.

10   *Aberdeen Journal*, 25 June 1873.

11   University of Cape Town Library, Department of Manuscripts and Archives, BC 1038, Laburn Collection, A4.4, Mr McNaughton to John Walker, 13 December 1881. See also John M. MacKenzie with Nigel R. Dalziel, *The Scots in South Africa. Ethnicity, Identity, Gender and Race, 1772–1914* (Manchester, 2007).

12   LAC, RG76, vol. 633, file 968592, part 3 (C-10446), Report on trip to Britain, Andrew MacDonell to W.J. Egan, 16 July 1925.

13   LAC, RG76, vol. 5, file 41, part 3, Egan to Walker, 28 August 1926. See also Walker to Egan, 30 July, 19 October 1926.

14   *Scottish Farmer*, 28 February 1925, 265, letter from J.L. Anderson.

15   *John O'Groat Journal*, 3 August 1930.

16   *Scottish Farmer*, 27 February; 6, 20, 27 March 1926, pp. 271, 299, 374, 413.

17   *The Scots Independent*, II: 2 (December 1927), 20.

18   National Records of Scotland [hereafter NRS], AF51/178, Lewis Spence to Sir John Gilmour, 2 July 1927.

19   Angus Clark, 'Must the Scot emigrate?', *Weekly Herald*, 25 April 1936, cutting in Dr Lachlan Grant's scrapbooks, National Library of Scotland [hereafter NLS], Acc. 12187/9.

20   *Stornoway Gazette*, 13 April 1956, 7d, letter to the editor.

21   *Scots Independent*, 7 January 1956, 1a-c; 10 March 1956, 2b-c.

22   Ibid., 18 February 1956, 3b. See also 25 February 2b; 3 March 1a-c; 19 May 1d-e; 2 June 3b-c; 11 August 3b-c; 25 August 1d-e; 22 December 2b-c.

23   For intimidation of agents in Ireland, see Marjory Harper, 'Enticing the emigrant: Canadian agents in Ireland and Scotland, c. 1870–c. 1920', *Scottish Historical Review*, LXXXIII, 1: no 215 (April 2004), 41-58.

24   Bob Purdie, '"Crossing swords with W.B. Yeats": twentieth century Scottish Nationalist encounters with Ireland', *Journal of Irish Scottish Studies*, 1: 1 (September 2007), 191-201. The reference is on page 204.

25   *The Times*, 13 January 1956, 12b; ibid., 14 January 1956, 6c. The incident does not seem to have been reported in *The Scotsman*.

26 Harry Martin, *Angels and Arrogant Gods: Migration Officers and Migrants Reminisce, 1945-85* (Canberra, 1989), 53.

27 Archives New Zealand [hereafter ANZ], LI, 22/1/28, Suggestions and Criticisms, Pt 2, Douglas Henderson, National Secretary, The Nationalist Party of Scotland [sic], to Sidney Holland, 18 December 1956.

28 R. Croucher, *We Refuse to Starve in Silence. A History of the National Unemployed Workers' Movement, 1920–46* (London, 1987), 66.

29 *Forward*, 7 April 1923, 3c-d. See also ibid., 5 May 1923, 5e-f; 30 June 1923, 5a-b.

30 Ibid., 10 January 1925, 11e; 17 January 1925, 3b-d.

31 *House of Commons Parliamentary Debates* [hereafter HCPD], 213, 7 February 1928; Marjory Harper, *Emigration from Scotland Between the Wars: Opportunity or Exile?* (Manchester, 1998, pbk 2009), 209.

32 HCPD, 155, 21 April 1952, ibid., 1565, 1 March 1962.

33 *The Times*, 12 February 1957, 6.

34 Interim report of the inquiry, published in *The Times*, 10 September 1957, 5.

35 Annual Reports of the Scottish Trades Union Congress, Special Convention Conference on the Highlands and Islands, Inverness, 26 February 1965, undated paper on population changes in the seven crofter counties since the 1951 census.

36 St John Ervine, 'The exodus from Britain', *The Spectator*, 24 January 1947, 111. See also Neil M. Jordan, 'Emigration' in ibid., 12 September 1947, 335-6; and 'Emigration policy', editorial in ibid., 30 July 1948, 130.

37 'Migration from Scotland: A Pressing Problem', *The Scotsman*, 15 April 1950, 9.

38 Letters to the editor in ibid., 4 May 1950, 6; 6 May 1950, 6.

39 The National Archives [hereafter TNA], LAB 8/3204, Report of the Working Party on the effect on the British economy by increased emigration to Canada, Australia and New Zealand. Notes and Papers, 1965–1967.

40 D.I. Mackay, *Geographical Mobility and the Brain Drain: A Case Study of Aberdeen University Graduates, 1860-1960* (London, 1969), 24.

41 *The Times*, 29 September 1966, 11.

42 G.N.M. Collins, seconding the adoption of the Deliverance from the Highlands and Islands Committee to the General Assembly, *Monthly Record of the Free Church of Scotland* [hereafter *Monthly Record*], June 1935, 162-3.

43 *Monthly Record*, June 1947, 122, Report of the Highlands and Islands Committee to the General Assembly. See also ibid., May 1951, 124 when the same committee's report wished for 'a development that would attract back the sons and daughters of the Highlands rather than the incoming of an alien population'.

44 *Acts and Reports of the General Assembly of the Free Church of Scotland, Report of the Committee on Public Questions, Religion and Morals*, IX, 1972, 163-4.

45 *Monthly Record*, September 1906, 148; ibid., June 1920, 108.

46 Ibid., June 1924, 96; January 1938, 7.

47 Ibid., June 1946, 102; December 1953, 240-1.

48 Lachlan Grant, copy of letter to J. Ramsay Macdonald, 3 March 1934; Grant, 'Lunacy and Population', *Caledonian Medical Journal*, XVI: 3, July 1937, 35. All references to Grant's writings are taken from copy letters or press cuttings in his

scrapbooks in the NLS, Acc. 12187/8-13, 1935-40.

49 Lachlan Grant, 'Churches and Emigration. A vicious and soulless propaganda', *Northern Times*, 4 July 1935.

50 Iain MacLeòid, 'Bàs Baile' ('The Death of a Township'), in *An Tuil. Anthology of 20th-century Scottish Gaelic Verse*, edited by Ronald Black (Edinburgh, 1999), 416-17.

51 Ralph Connor, *The Man from Glengarry: A Tale of Western Canada* (London, 1901), 5; Hugh MacLennan, *Each Man's Son* (Toronto, 1951), vii-viii; Alistair MacLeod, *No Great Mischief* (London, 2001).

52 Edwin Muir, *Scottish Journey* (London, 1935), 3-4, 248.

53 For a recent study of migration and mental illness, see Angela McCarthy and Catherine Coleborne (eds), *Migration, Ethnicity and Mental Health: International Perspectives, 1840–2010* (New York, 2012).

54 LAC, RG76, vol. 505, file 590006 (C-10294), Jeannie Caldwell, undesirable immigrant. Police Department, Hamilton to Immigration Department, Ottawa, 14 December 1906.

55 C.K. Clarke, 'The defective and insane immigrant', *University Monthly* (University of Toronto), 8 (1907-8), 273-8.

56 See above, pp. 97-9.

57 *Montreal Gazette*, 30 April 1923.

58 LAC, RG76, vol. 633, file 964675, part 2 (C-10446), 'People of Hebrides suited to Canada', William James interviewed by *Toronto Globe*, n.d.; R. Law, Toronto, to the Department of Immigration and Colonisation, 22 February 1923.

59 Public Archives of Nova Scotia [hereafter PANS], Nova Scotia Hospital Fonds, RG 25, MRM 9631 and 9633, Admission Records, 1892 and 1900; *Census of Canada, 1891; Fourth Census of Canada, 1901*.

60 LAC, RG76, vol. 632, file 968592, part 1 (C-10447), W.R. Little, Immigration Commissioner, Ottawa, to J.V. Lantalum, 18 April 1923.

61 William Kenefick, *Red Scotland! The Rise and Fall of the Radical Left, c. 1872 to 1932* (Edinburgh, 2007), 210; Jonathan Hyslop, 'The British and Australian Leaders of the South African Labour Movement, 1902–1914: A Group Biography', in *Britishness Abroad: Transnational Movements and Imperial Cultures*, edited by Kate Darian-Smith, Patricia Grimshaw and Stuart Macintyre (Melbourne, 2007), 91, 95. See also Hyslop, *The Notorious Syndicalist J.T. Bain: A Scottish Rebel in Colonial South Africa* (Johannesburg, 2004).

62 *Forward*, 28 February 1913, 7d.

63 See above, pp. 81-2.

64 Provincial Archives of British Columbia, Reynoldston Research and Studies Collection. T0238:0001, George Bowman Anderson interviewed by Marlene Karnouk, 26 November 1973. Anderson did comment that antagonism against newcomers was directed primarily at the English.

65 Clifford Sifton, 'The immigrants Canada wants', *Maclean's Magazine*, 1 April 1922, 16.

66 David Frank, 'McLachlan, James Bryson', in *The Canadian Encyclopaedia*, http://www.thecanadianencyclopedia.com/index.cfm?PgNm=TCE&Params=A1ARTA0004962 See also Frank, *J.B. McLachlan: A Biography. The Story of a Legendary Labour Leader and the Cape Breton Coalminers* (Toronto, 1999).

67 Kenefick, *Red Scotland!*, 210.
68 Ibid., 209, 211.
69 *The Scotsman*, 17 September 1928, 7; 11 October 1928, 10.
70 TNA, LAB 2/1237/9 (Pres. No. A73/1926). Ministry of Labour, Employment and Insurance Department, EDO 985/1929. W. Taylor to J.M. Cairncross, Divisional Office, Edinburgh, 25 October 1929.
71 Jim Wilkie, *Metagama. A Voyage from Lewis to the New World* (Edinburgh, 2001, originally published 1987), 89, 105, 146-7.
72 Jane Perry Clark, *Deportation of Aliens from the United States to Europe* (New York, 1962), 493-518.
73 Ibid., 99-100.
74 Michael Roe, *Australia, Britain, and Migration 1915–1940. A Study of Desperate Hopes* (Cambridge, 1995). See also Roe, '"We can die just as easy out here": Australia and British migration, 1916–1939' in Stephen Constantine (ed.), *Emigrants and Empire: British Settlement in the Dominions Between the Wars* (Manchester, 1990), 96-120.
75 TNA, LAB 2/1233/EDO385/1925, Emigration. Suggestion that efforts be made to induce emigration in Scottish mining industry, especially to Australia, 1925, undated memorandum from W. Eady to Mr Barlow.
76 Ibid., LAB 2/1233/EDO289/1926, cutting from the *Daily Herald*, 30 July 1926.
77 Quoted in Roe, *Australia, Britain and Migration*, 150 from TNA, CO 721/67, Commonwealth Parliamentary Papers, 1923-4, vol. 2, p. 12, Sir Arthur Stanley, report of conversations, 7 February 1923.
78 Roe, *Australia, Britain and Migration*, 246, 249.
79 Quoted in ibid., 235.
80 References to Nelson, Orr and Coull are all taken from the online *Australian Dictionary of Biography*, http://adb.anu.edu.au/biographies/search/?sortBy=search.
81 Harper and Constantine, *Migration and Empire*, 320; Alistair Thomson, '"My wayward heart": Homesickness, longing and the return of British post-war immigrants from Australia', in Marjory Harper (ed.), *Emigrant Homecomings: The Return Movement of Emigrants, 1600–2000* (Manchester, 2005), 106-8.
82 Stephen Constantine, 'The British Government, Child Welfare, and Child Migration to Australia after 1945', *Journal of Imperial and Commonwealth History*, 30 (2002), 99-132.
83 Report by a Fairbridge Society representative to the Society's headquarters about a party of children which arrived in Australia on 19 May 1950, quoted in Philip Bean and Joy Melville, *Lost Children of the Empire. The Untold Story of Britain's Child Migrants* (London, 1990), 113.
84 *Appendices to the Journals of the House of Representatives* [hereafter AJHR], 1884, H-7, p1.
85 Quoted in Philippa Martyr, 'Having a Clean Up? Deporting Lunatic Migrants from Western Australia, 1924-1939', *History Compass*, 9/3 (2011), 171-99.The quotations are found on page 174. The first is from 'Our Immigration System', *The Queenslander*, 12 January 1889, 58-9; the second is from 'Lunacy Amongst Immigrants', *The Mercury*, 24 February 1913,4h.
86 Harper and Constantine, *Migration and Empire*, 322.

87 Irving Abella, foreword in Barbara Roberts, *Whence They Came: Deportation from Canada, 1900-1935* (Ottawa, 1988), ix.
88 These issues are discussed in detail in Alison Bashford, *Imperial Hygiene: A Critical History of Colonialism, Nationalism and Public Health* (London, 2004). See also Bashford (ed.), *Medicine at the Border. Disease, Globalisation and Security, 1850 to the Present* (Basingstoke, 2006), 6-10.
89 Harper and Constantine, *Migration and Empire*, 31, 170-6.
90 Ninette Kelley and Michael Trebilcock, *The Making of the Mosaic. A History of Canadian Immigration Policy* (Toronto, 1998), especially 143-6, 178, 219-20, 441-2.
91 ANZ, L1, Box 125, Nosworthy to High Commissioner, Imm no. 386, 12 November 1923; Imm no. 419, 27 Nov. 1923.
92 Martyr, 'Having a Clean Up?', 171.
93 File of Robert Morrice, PP6/1 33/H511, 4309364, National Archives of Australia, quoted in Martyr, 'Having a Clean Up?', 180.
94 Details of Canadian immigration legislation are taken from Canadian Council for Refugees, 'A hundred years of immigration to Canada, 1900-1999', http://ccrweb.ca/en/hundred-years-immigration-canada-1900-1999.
95 Barbara Roberts, 'Shovelling out the "Mutinous": Political deportation from Canada before 1936', *Labour/Le Travail*, 18 (Fall 1986), 77-110. The statistics quoted are found on page 81.
96 C.F. Fraser, quoted in Roberts, 'Shovelling out the "Mutinous"', 108.
97 Barbara Roberts, 'Shovelling out the "Mutinous", 103; R. Menzies, 'Governing Mentalities: The Deportation of "Insane" and "Feebleminded" immigrants out of British Columbia from Confederation to World War II', *Canadian Journal of Law and Society*, 13 (1998), 135-73.
98 A.L. Fairchild, *Science at the Borders: Immigrant Medical Inspection and the Shaping of the Modern Industrial Labor Force* (Baltimore, 2003), 9-14, 68.
99 Peter Morton Coan, *Ellis Island Interviews. In Their Own Words* (New York, 1997), 136-7. See also above, pp. 69-70, 72, 75.
100 Ellis Island Oral History Project, interview KECK-127, Mary Dunn, interviewed by Dana Gumb, 23 January 1986. See also above, pp. 71, 72.
101 Ibid., interview NPS-149, Thomas Allan, interviewed by Jean Kolva, 16 July 1984.
102 LAC, RG 29, vol. 762 (T-12591), Record of Detentions at Canadian Ports kept 1921-35 by Immigration Medical Services of the Department of Pensions and National Health; RG 29, vol. 754A (T-12589), Record of Detentions 1936-57. The records for the 1950s do not indicate the disposition of the cases.
103 Quoted in Angela McCarthy, 'A difficult voyage', *History Scotland*, 10: 4 (July/August 2010), 29.
104 Archives of Ontario, RG10, Ontario Ministry of Health, Queen Street, General Register, vol. 7, 21 September 1904-4 January 1906.
105 Ibid., no. 9049, p. 18.
106 Ibid., no. 8866, p. 8.
107 Highland Health Board, HHB 3/3/2, Inverness District Asylum, Register of Lunatics, 1889–1904, no. 4533; Grampian Regional Health Board [hereafter GRHB] 2/4/30, case book, 22 May 1903 – 26 August 1904, p. 176.

108 GRHB 2/3/19, Aberdeen Royal Asylum Register of Lunatics, 2 January 1929 to 20 January 1935. Bathia's first admission had been on 22 July 1921.Her departure for Canada can be found in findmypast.co.uk and her return in ancestry.co.uk. Thanks to Fiona Watson, Northern Health Services Archivist, for this supplementary information.

109 GRHB 8/2/6, Kingseat Mental Hospital Register of Patients, volume 4, 14 February 1927 to 10 November 1936.

110 John and Margaret Hardie, interviewed by Alistair Thomson, 9 September 2000, quoted in Thomson, 'My wayward heart', 119-20.

111 LAC, RG26, vol. 16, Deportation, annual statistics 1928-45. There are no statistics for 1932.

112 LAC, RG76, vol. 827, part 1 (C-4697); Dr James Patterson to J. Obed Smith, Commissioner of Immigration, Winnipeg, 21 January 1904; Smith to W.D. Scott, Superintendent of Immigration, Ottawa, 21 January 1904; Scott to Robert Kerr, Passenger Traffic Manager, CPR Company, 27 January 1904.

113 LAC, RG76, vol. 827, part 1 (C-4697), Paupers (insane, criminal or otherwise) to be returned 1893-1896.

114 Ibid., G. Bryce, Chief Medical Inspector, Department of Immigration, to W.W. Cory, Deputy Minister, Department of the Interior, 4 February 1905.

115 Ibid., J. Obed Smith, Commissioner of Immigration, Winnipeg, to W.D. Scott, Superintendent of Immigration, Ottawa, 12 July 1905.

116 Ibid., J. Bruce Walker, Commissioner of Immigration, Winnipeg, to Grant Hall, Superintendent of Motive Power, CPR, 27 November 1908.

117 Ibid., Grant Hall to J. Bruce Walker, 28 November 1908; M. McNicoll, CPR Vice-President, to W.D. Scott, 21 December 1908.

118 Ibid., William Robertson to Immigration Department, 10 December 1908.

119 NRS, SC1/13/1929/9, Aberdeen Sheriff Court. I am grateful to Jane Brown for drawing these records to my attention.

120 NRS, CS46/1950/1/61, Court of Session.

121 Ibid., CS46/1950/2/96. Alexander Henderson had last been seen by two other brothers in Chicago in August 1934.

122 Runrig, 'Rocket to the Moon', verse 2 and refrain.

Chapter 6: Voices from the Scottish Diaspora

1 The recordings, along with the interview summaries, will in due course be deposited in the University of Aberdeen Special Libraries and Archives, and will be subject to full archival referencing.

2 The Scottish Emigration Database. www.abdn.ac.uk/emigration, 'Your input'.

3 Gordon Ashley, whom a colleague and I had met at his own request to discuss the historical context of the Highland clearances for a novel he was writing, mentioned in passing that he had worked as an Australian emigration agent in the 1970s.

4 See in particular A. James Hammerton and Alistair Thomson, *Ten Pound Poms: Australia's Invisible Migrants* (Manchester, 2005), 18.

5 Alessandro Portelli, 'What makes oral history different?' in Robert Perks and Alistair Thomson (eds), *The Oral History Reader*, 2nd edition (London, 2006),

32-42.

6   Telephone interview with Katherine Annie MacLeod, Winnipeg, 8 February 2011.

7   Telephone interview with the late Morag Bennett (née MacLeod), Sechelt, 21 February 2005.

8   Interview with Anne Morrison, Cumbernauld, 2 July 2009.

9   Interview with Sandy ('Boots') MacLeod, Ullapool, 27 March 2009.

10 Library and Archives Canada [hereafter LAC], RG76, vol. 405, file 590687 (C-10294-5), correspondence and weekly reports of John MacLennan, week ending 14 March 1908.

11 Rob Gibson *Highland Cowboys* (Edinburgh, 2003), 154.

12 Tom Bryan, 'Tracking the Rocky Mountain men of Coigach', *West Highland Free Press*, 28 January 1994.

13 The late Minnie Anne Macdonald (née Fraser) interviewed by Sandra Train at Bayview House, Thurso, 17 July 1996.

14 Interview with the late Agnes MacGilvray (née Lawrie), West Kilbride, 18 July 2009.

15 Telephone interview with Annie MacRitchie, Stornoway, 19 October 2009.

16 Interview with Alison Thornton, Dunedin, 30 November 2010.

17 Interview with Brian Coutts, Dunedin, 30 November 2010.

18 Interview with Paddy McFarlane, Dunedin, 28 November 2010.

19   Telephone interview with Easton Vance, Thetis Island, British Columbia, 9 July 2008.

20 Interview with Cathy Timperley, Dunedin, 30 November 2010.

21 Interview with Jim and Jane Wilson, Dunedin, 26 November 2010.

22 Telephone interview with Katrine McLean, New Zealand, 3 November 2010.

23 Telephone interview with Rob and Cathie Tulloch, Whangarei, New Zealand, 2 November 2010.

24 Interview with Roddy Campbell, Inverness, 8 October 2010.

25 Interview with Alison McNair (née Gibson), Aberdeen, 12 September 2005. Alison had moved to London after graduating from Edinburgh University in 1964.

26 Interview with Anne Simpson, Dunedin, 29 November 2010. After qualifying as a doctor, Anne spent three years in Canada before moving to New Zealand with her two children.

27 Interview with Murdo MacPherson, Kinlochbervie, 24 February 2005.

28 Interview with Graham McGregor, Dunedin, 26 November 2010.

29 John E. Martin, *Holding the Balance. A History of New Zealand's Department of Labour 1891–1995* (Christchurch, 1996), 269. See also Duncan Sim, *American Scots. The Scottish Diaspora and the USA* (Edinburgh, 2011), 145.

30 Interview with Isobel and Willie Bouman, Dunedin, 29 November 2010.

31 New South Wales Bicentennial Oral History Project, 1987, MLOH 48, the late Angus Macdonald interviewed by Paula Hamilton, 5 September 1987. http://acms.sl.nsw.gov.au/item/itemDetailPaged.aspx?itemID=414230

32 Interview with Gordon Ashley, Carnoustie, 10 July 2008.

33 Interview with Sandra Train, Dalhalvaig, Halladale, 5 November 2010.

34 Interview with Gail Gilmour, Dunedin, 26 November 2010.

35 Interview with Helen Campbell, Dunedin, 1 December 2010.
36 Interview with Sandra Munro, Ullapool, 26 March 2009.
37 Telephone interview with Alan Blair, Halifax, Nova Scotia, 12 January 2006; telephone interview with Janet and Joe Blair, Sarnia, Ontario, 10 February 2006.
38 See above, p. 188.
39 Interview with Ena Macdonald, Kyles, Bayhead, North Uist, 7 September 2011.
40 Anthony Richmond, *Post-war Immigrants in Canada* (Toronto, 1967), 244-5. See above, pp. 129-30.
41 Interview with Sandra Train.
42 Interview with Angus Pelham Burn, Kincardine O'Neil, 6 April 2010.
43 Interview with Marilyn MacRitchie, Stornoway, 6 September 2011. See also 'Stornoway minister inducted', *Stornoway Gazette* [hereafter *SG*], 19 March 1966, 1d-e; ibid., 26 March 1966, 1b-c.
44 Interview with Cathie and Calum Murray, Shader, Lewis, 25 February 2005.
45 Interview with Norman Macrae, Back, Lewis, 17 November 2010.
46 Telephone interview with Jim Russell, Vancouver, 8 December 2007.
47 The Toronto Australia New Zealand Club.
48 Interview with Margaret McPherson, Corby, 15 March 2012.
49 *SG*, 8 May 1956, 3d-e.
50 Telephone interview with Murdo MacIver, Vancouver, 7 December 2007.
51 Murdo's recollection of encountering people from Arnol in the interior of British Columbia is corroborated by the *Stornoway Gazette*, which on 27 January 1956 (p6, e-f) reported on the retirement of Captain John Macleod of Procter, a native of Arnol, after a 44-year career on the British Columbia interior lake boats. McLeod's brother, Norman, was captain of the ss *Moyie*, the last sternwheeler in western Canada, based at Kaslo on Arrow Lake.
52 Interview with Isla and Hamish Robertson, Vancouver, 7 December 2007.
53 The *Stornoway Gazette* sometimes noted the arrival or departure of visitors from Detroit. See, for instance, 'Six from Stornoway to Detroit', *SG*, 4 September 1956, 1c. Some of the married women in the party had returned to work for a couple of years to finance the trip 'home', and among the souvenirs being taken back across the Atlantic were 'sprigs of heather, lengths of tweed, home baked shortbread, salt fish, and a tape recording of a Lewis wedding service'.
54 Telephone interview with Elvira Gonnella, Halifax, Nova Scotia, February 2006.
55 John Still, *The Jungle Tide* (Edinburgh, 1955), 117.

Scottish Diaspora: Some Useful Sources

IN RECENT YEARS Scottish emigration and the Scottish diaspora have been subjected to considerable scholarly scrutiny, but the twentieth-century story has remained something of a Cinderella. General textbooks make passing mention of the phenomenon. It is discussed very briefly in Catriona M.M. Macdonald, *Whaur Extremes Meet. Scotland's Twentieth Century* (Edinburgh, 2009) and in slightly more detail in Richard J. Finlay, *Modern Scotland, 1914–2000* (London, 2004). T.M. Devine's textbook, *The Scottish Nation, 1700–2000* (London, 2006, originally published 1999) highlights the significance of three centuries of demographic upheaval, a subject to which he returns with a specific focus in *Scotland's Empire, 1600–1815* (London, 2004) and *To the Ends of the Earth: Scotland's Global Diaspora 1750–2010* (London, 2011). Marjory Harper, *Adventurers and Exiles. The Great Scottish Exodus* (London, 2003), is a thematic study of Scottish emigration in the 19th century, while *Emigration from Scotland Between the Wars* (Manchester, 1998, pbk 2009), by the same author, focuses on the key decade of the 1920s. In the absence of any published statistical study for the second half of the twentieth century, recourse has to be made to a variety of original sources, including the census and the reports of the Oversea Migration Board and the Office of National Statistics. N.H. Carrier and J.R. Jeffery, *External Migration. A Study of the Available Statistics* (London, 1953) remains the standard secondary source for the quantification of migration before 1950.

Eric Richards, *Britannia's Children. Emigration from England, Scotland, Wales and Ireland since 1600* (London and New York, 2004), offers a general scholarly overview of emigration from the British Isles across four centuries. More recently, migration has been a recurring theme in several publications in the Companion Series to the Oxford History of the British Empire. The British diaspora is the central subject of Marjory Harper and Stephen Constantine, *Migration and Empire* (Oxford, 2010) and Robert Bickers (ed.), *Settlers and Expatriates. Britons Over the Seas* (Oxford, 2010). Canadian and Australian perspectives on migration are included in Phillip A. Buckner (ed.), *Canada and the British Empire* (Oxford, 2008) and D.M. Schreuder and Stuart Ward (eds), *Australia's Empire* (Oxford, 2008), and it is one of the main themes in John M. MacKenzie and T.M. Devine (eds), *Scotland and the British Empire* (Oxford, 2011). Migration also features, *inter alia*, in Carl Bridge and Kent Fedorowich (eds), *The British World: Diaspora, Culture and Identity* – special issue of the *Journal of Imperial and Commonwealth History*, 31: 2 (2003); Andrew Thompson, *The Empire Strikes Back? The Impact of Imperialism on*

Britain from the Mid Nineteenth Century (Harlow, 2005); Andrew Thompson and Gary Magee, *Empire and Globalisation: Networks of People, Goods and Capital in the British World, c. 1850–1914* (Cambridge, 2010); and Andrew Thompson (ed.), *Britain's Experience of Empire in the Twentieth Century* (Oxford, 2012).

Migration-related publications in the Manchester University Press series, 'Studies in Imperialism' include Stephen Constantine (ed.), *Emigrants and Empire. British Settlement in the Dominions Between the Wars* (Manchester, 1990); Kent Fedorowich, *Unfit for Heroes: Reconstruction and Soldier Settlement in the Empire Between the Wars* (Manchester, 1994); Marjory Harper (ed.), *Emigrant Homecomings: The Return Movement of Emigrants, 1600–2000* (Manchester, 2005); John M. MacKenzie with Nigel R. Dalziel, *The Scots in South Africa. Ethnicity, Identity, Gender and Race, 1772–1914* (Manchester, 2007); and Angela McCarthy, *Personal Narratives of Irish and Scottish Migration, 1921–65: 'For Spirit and Adventure'* (Manchester 2007).

Popular publications on the Scots overseas include Arthur Herman, *How the Scots Invented the Modern World: The True Story of How Western Europe's Poorest Nation Created Our World and Everything In It* (New York, 2001); Billy Kay, *The Scottish World. A Journey into the Scottish Diaspora* (Edinburgh, 2006); Kenny MacAskill and Henry McLeish, *Global Scots. Voices from Afar* (Edinburgh, 2005); also by MacAskill and McLeish, *Wherever the Saltire Flies* (Edinburgh, 2006); and Ken McGoogan, *How the Scots Invented Canada* (Toronto, 2010).

A number of area-based studies deal with twentieth-century migration, either exclusively, or in the context of a broader chronological approach. The Highland perspective takes centre stage in James Hunter, *Scottish Exodus. Travels Among a Worldwide Clan* (Edinburgh, 2005), and Highland emigration is also the subject of his earlier book, *A Dance Called America: The Scottish Highlands, the United States and Canada* (Edinburgh, 1994). The Hebridean exodus of April 1923 is the theme of Jim Wilkie, *Metagama. A Journey from Lewis to the New World* (Edinburgh, 2001, originally published 1987).

Scots in England have been subjected to patchy treatment, with the focus being more on scholarly articles than on monographs. The exception is David Stenhouse, *On the Make. How the Scots took over London* (Edinburgh, 2006). General reflections on the Scots in London are also included in Justine Taylor, *A Cup of Kindness: The History of the Royal Scottish Corporation, a London Charity, 1603–2003* (East Linton, 2003).

The North American diaspora has been relatively well-served. In addition to Jenni Calder, *Scots in Canada* (Edinburgh, 2003), there is a stable of publications by Lucille Campey on 18th- and 19th-century Scottish settlements, including *The Scottish Pioneers of Upper Canada, 1784–1855: Glengarry and*

Beyond (Toronto, 2005) and *An Unstoppable Force: the Scottish Exodus to Canada* (Edinburgh, 2008). Among edited collections, we have Marjory Harper and Michael Vance (eds), *Myth, Migration and the Making of Memory. Scotia and Nova Scotia, c. 1700–1900* (Halifax and Edinburgh, 1999); Peter E. Rider and Heather McNabb (eds), *A Kingdom of the Mind. How the Scots helped make Canada* (Montreal, 2006) and Phillip A. Buckner and R. Douglas Francis (eds), *Canada and the British World: Culture, Migration and Identity* (Vancouver, 2006). The post-war era, from a British perspective, is addressed in Barry Broadfoot, *The Immigrant Years. From Britain and Europe to Canada 1945–1967* (Vancouver, 1986); and Freda Hawkins, *Critical Years in Immigration: Canada and Australia Compared* (Kingston, 1989). An overview of immigration policy is found in Ninette Kelley and Michael Trebilcock, *The Making of the Mosaic: A History of Canadian Immigration Policy* (Toronto and London, 2010).

On the other side of the border, Jenni Calder provides an overview in *Scots in the USA* (Edinburgh, 2006); and a more focused study in *Frontier Scots: the Scots Who Won the West* (Edinburgh, 2010), Ferenc Morton Szasz touches on the early 20th-century in *Scots in the North American West, 1790–1917* (Norman, Ok., 2000) while cultural issues are at the heart of Richard Blaustein, *The Thistle and the Brier: Historical Links and Cultural Parallels between Scotland and Appalachia* (Jefferson, NC, 2003) and Celeste Ray (ed.), *Transatlantic Scots* (Tuscaloosa, AL., 2005). Older works include Charlotte Erickson, *Invisible Immigrants. The Adaptation of English and Scottish Immigrants in Nineteenth-Century America* (Ithaca, NY, 1990, originally published 1972).

Immigration to Australia has been extensively investigated by Eric Richards, whose publications include *Destination Australia: Migration to Australia since 1901* (Sydney, NSW, 2008) and an edited collection with Jacqueline Templeton, *The Australian Immigrant in the Twentieth Century: Searching Neglected Sources* (Canberra, 1998). The Scottish contribution is highlighted in Richards *et al*, *That Land of Exiles: Scots in Australia* (Edinburgh, 1988) and in a republication of Malcolm Prentis, *The Scots in Australia* (Sydney, NSW, 2008, originally published 1983). Other studies of Australian immigration include James Jupp, *From White Australia to Woomera: The Story of Australian Immigration* (New York and Cambridge, 2002); Jupp, *The English in Australia* (Cambridge, 2004); Leigh S.K. Straw, *A Semblance of Scotland: Scottish Identity in Colonial Western Australia* (Glasgow, 2006); and A. James Hammerton and Alistair Thomson, *Ten Pound Poms. Australia's Invisible Migrants* (Manchester, 2005).

Scots in New Zealand have come under the spotlight in the last decade, most recently in Tanja Bueltmann, *Scottish Ethnicity and the Making of New Zealand Society, 1850–1930* (Edinburgh, 2011) and Angela McCarthy,

Scottishness and Irishness in New Zealand since 1840 (Manchester, 2011). Tom Brooking and Jennie Coleman (eds), *The Heather and the Fern: Scottish Migration and New Zealand Settlement* (Dunedin, 2003), offers nine essays from a conference that explored aspects of the 19th- and 20th-century Scottish migrations to New Zealand. The wider context is explored in Jock Phillips and Terry Hearn, *Settlers: New Zealand Immigrants from England, Ireland and Scotland, 1800–1945* (Auckland, 2008), while insights into immigration policy can be gleaned from John E. Martin, *Holding the Balance. A History of New Zealand's Department of Labour 1891–1995* (Christchurch, 1996).

Recent years have seen a handful of anthropological, sociological and cultural studies. These include Paul Basu, *Highland Homecomings: Genealogy and Heritage Tourism in the Scottish Diaspora* (London, 2007); Duncan Sim, *American Scots. The Scottish Diaspora and the USA* (Edinburgh, 2011); and Tanja Bueltmann, Andrew Hinson and Graeme Morton (eds), *Ties of Bluid, Kin and Countrie: Scottish Associational Culture in the Diaspora* (Guelph, 2009). Migrant networks are addressed in Angela McCarthy (ed.), *A Global Clan: Scottish Migrant Networks and Identities since the Eighteenth Century* (London, 2006). The personal testimonies which form the core of Chapter 6 are informed by general and specific scholarship in the field of oral history, including Robert Perks and Alistair Thomson (eds), *The Oral History Reader* (London, 2006, 2nd edition); Peter Morton Coan, *Ellis Island Interviews. In Their Own Words* (New York, 1997); and Megan Hutching, *Long Journey for Sevenpence: An Oral History of Assisted Immigration to New Zealand from the United Kingdom, 1947–1975* (Wellington, 1999), as well as Hammerton and Thomson, *Ten Pound Poms*.

The theme of the dysfunctional migrant is explored in Barbara Roberts, *Whence They Came: Deportation from Canada, 1900–1935* (Ottawa, 1988); Catharine Coleborne, *Madness in the Family: Insanity and Institutions in the Australasian Colonial World 1860–1914* (Basingstoke, 2010); and most recently in Angela McCarthy and Catharine Coleborne (eds), *Migration, Ethnicity and Mental Health: International Perspectives, 1840–2010* (New York, 2012). The equally controversial area of child migration has been addressed in recent years by a number of studies, including Stephen Constantine, 'The British Government, Child Welfare, and Child Migration to Australia after 1945', *Journal of Imperial and Commonwealth History*, 30 (2002), 99–132; and Marjorie Kohli, *The Golden Bridge: Young Immigrants to Canada, 1833–1939* (Toronto, 2003). The Scottish contribution to the phenomenon is discussed in Anna Magnusson, *The Quarriers story: A History of Quarriers* (Edinburgh, revised edition, 2006); and Marjory Harper, 'Halfway to Heaven or Hell on Earth? Canada's Scottish Child Immigrants', in Catherine Kerrigan (ed.), *The Immigrant Experience* (Guelph, 1992), 165–83.

Index

Luath Press Limited

committed to publishing well written books worth reading

LUATH PRESS takes its name from Robert Burns, whose little collie
Luath (*Gael.*, swift or nimble) tripped up Jean Armour at a wedding
and gave him the chance to speak to the woman who was to be his wife
and the abiding love of his life. Burns called one of the 'Twa Dogs'
Luath after Cuchullin's hunting dog in Ossian's *Fingal*.
Luath Press was established in 1981 in the heart
of Burns country, and is now based a few steps up
the road from Burns' first lodgings on
Edinburgh's Royal Mile. Luath offers you
distinctive writing with a hint of
unexpected pleasures.
Most bookshops in the UK, the US, Canada,
Australia, New Zealand and parts of Europe,
either carry our books in stock or can order them
for you. To order direct from us, please send
a £sterling cheque, postal order, international
money order or your credit card details (number,
address of cardholder and expiry date) to us at
the address below. Please add post and packing as
follows: UK – £1.00 per delivery address; overseas
surface mail – £2.50 per delivery address; overseas
airmail – £3.50 for the first book to each delivery address, plus £1.00
for each additional book by airmail to the same address. If your order is
a gift, we will happily enclose your card or message at no extra charge.

Luath Press Limited

543/2 Castlehill
The Royal Mile
Edinburgh EH1 2ND
Scotland
Telephone: +44 (0)131 225 4326 (24 hours)
Fax: +44 (0)131 225 4324
email: sales@luath. co.uk
Website: www. luath.co.uk